# THE SOUND OF
# THE ONE HAND

# THE SOUND OF THE ONE HAND

## 281 ZEN KOANS
## WITH ANSWERS

TRANSLATED, WITH A COMMENTARY BY

# YOEL HOFFMANN

FOREWORD BY ZEN MASTER HIRANO SŌJŌ

INTRODUCTION BY BEN-AMI SCHARFSTEIN

*Basic Books, Inc., Publishers*

NEW YORK

TO MY PARENTS

FRĀNZE AND AVRAHAM HOFFMANN

TO MY WIFE

VARDA

# CONTENTS

## PART FOUR

# THE SOUND OF
# THE ONE HAND

# FOREWORD

When the Japanese edition of this book, *Gendai Sōjizen Hyōron* ("A Critique of Present-day Pseudo-Zen"), was first published in 1916, it caused a great sensation. The reason for this lay in the fact that the koans and their answers had been secretly transmitted from master to pupil in the Rinzai sect since the origination of the koan-teaching system in Japan by Zen Master Hakuin (1685–1768). This publication of the "secrets" of Zen seems to have embarrassed many masters at that time. Furthermore, I have heard that the recent appearance of photocopies of this 1916 edition has caused alarm among Zen masters of today. Yet . . . if anyone finds himself troubled, he has only himself to blame—the book itself is not to blame. As for myself, I feel there is no reason whatsoever to be alarmed in any way.

The attempt to prevent such publications is not new in the history of Zen. For example, the widely known Zen classic, *Hekiganroku* ("The Green Grotto Record"), consists of one hundred koans selected by Zen Master Setchō (A.D. 980–1052), including his comments, and to which the comments of Zen Master Engo (1063–1135) were later added. Master Dai-e, Engo's disciple (1085–1163), was of the firm conviction that such a book should not be made public, and he burned it. In time, however, this book became a Zen classic; not only was it harmless to the koan teaching, on the contrary, it did much to aid the understanding of Zen.

More than fifty years have passed since the Japanese publication of *Gendai Sōjizen Hyōron*, which can now be said to deserve the status of a classic of Zen. Therefore those who would wish to prevent the contents of this book from being made public are misguided. Of course, in judging such matters, what is most important is the attitude of those reading the book. What is revealed in this publication is the approach of Zen masters of approximately two centuries ago to the Zen koans. It should by no means be assumed that those reading the book today will come to an "understanding" in a flash. However, I am convinced that this book, like the *Hekiganroku*, *Rinzairoku*, and other Zen classics, will have the effect of contributing to the attainment of a correct conception of Zen.

ZEN MASTER HIRANO SŌJŌ

# INTRODUCTION
# ZEN: THE TACTICS
# OF EMPTINESS

You have opened the pages of an odd, tension-filled book. If you already know Zen well enough, or if you are simply impatient, skip this introduction and go on immediately to the text. It is the text that should be read, for reasons that I shall try to make clear.

Now, at the beginning, I ask you to remember that the world you are entering is odd to almost everyone, even to those who have lived in it for a long time. It multiplies paradoxes; and yet its oddness, like the paradoxical oddness of a dream, verges on the familiar. Odd and familiar as a dream, Zen is meant, however, to occupy the daylight, by means of an irrational reversal of the quality of our lives. For Zen says that we are self-deceived, split, and unhappy. Its disciples are trained to arrive at least at equanimity. This aim is, no doubt, subject to practical limitations. Maybe it, too, is a dream of sorts; but, if you are open-minded, you may prefer to consider it tentatively before deciding whether or not to shrug it off. Even if Zen is not what it takes itself to be, it is an unusually interesting human and cultural phenomenon.

## Zen History

Let me begin with a word of Zen history. Indian Buddhism, spread abroad by missionaries, seems to have entered China during the first century A.D. Foreign by nature to the Chinese, it assumed the disguise of a native Chinese philosophy and religion, that of Taoism. This disguise was possible because, like Taoism, it cultivated a ritual and a technique of breathing, which was related to a technique of meditation, and because it was concerned with survival beyond the ordinary span of life. Missionaries continued to bring scriptures to China, but centuries passed before translations of these scriptures became genuinely intelligible, and before the Chinese were able to see Buddhism for what it was, a detailed proposal to teach mankind how to escape from life's inescapable sufferings by escaping from life itself.

When this message and its practical consequences became clear, traditionally minded Chinese protested. To them, the monks, who lived on charity, were no more than parasites. To them, the monks' celibacy and shift of allegiance from family and emperor to religious master and monastery were endangering the survival of society. Furthermore, they said, the monks, though supposedly indifferent to worldly things, were accumulating monastic wealth and power. It was also a particularly galling and un–Chinese insult that the monks were ready to be cremated at death and so to destroy their bodies, which the traditional Chinese regarded as gifts that their ancestors had put into their safekeeping.

On the whole, however, Buddhism prospered and became increasingly Chinese and increasingly assimilated into Chinese culture. I shall not attempt to say anything of the contribution of Buddhism to Chinese culture, much of which still lay in the future, or of its involvement in the politics of the imperial court, where its fortunes rose and fell. But in the middle of the ninth century, in an atmosphere of hostility to everything foreign, a great attack was leveled on Buddhism. Its monasteries were destroyed, its wealth confiscated, its icons melted down, its leaders scattered, and its monks and nuns forced to return to lay life.

The Buddhism that survived was predominantly of two kinds, Pure Land and Ch'an. Looked at in a somewhat unkind light, Pure Land Buddhism may be said to have succeeded because it demanded little and promised much, for which reason the common people turned to it enthusiastically. Pure Land Buddhism fostered the belief that the Buddha of Mercy would actively help to rescue everyone, regardless of who he was or what he had done. Its panacea, by which, it taught, anyone could attain salvation, was simple: repeat and repeat the name of a Buddha or the title of a Buddhist scripture. Ch'an Buddhism, which I shall from now on call Zen Buddhism, in deference to the Japanese origin and content of the present book, was also an adaptation to Chinese life, though of a very different kind. No one knows just why Zen survived the decline of the other forms of Buddhism, but a number of plausible reasons can be given. One reason may well have been geographical. Zen was strong in provincial centers that were remote from imperial influence and perhaps resistant to it. Zen was intuitive and down-to-earth, and therefore acceptable to the Chinese, who fostered these qualities. Zen was also optimistic, because it believed that nirvana, the state to which every Buddhist aspired, could be reached in a single lifetime, and not only as the result of a prolonged series of merit-accumulating lives. Finally, in spite of an express scriptural prohibition which forbade Buddhist monks to farm the land, because a farmer necessarily destroys plants and other living things, the Zen novitiates worked as farmers. Zen accepted the motto, "One day no work, one day no food." Zen diligence thus answered the accusation of parasitism and, in any case, helped to maintain the Zen community.

Zen might even be described as a kind of monastic humanism. Robust, earthy, and energetic, it reacted against the tendency of each of the competing sects to favor one particular scripture, and, in general, it opposed heavy reliance upon sacred texts. According to Zen tradition, men of lesser understanding might need the aid of words and scriptures, but Buddhism, in the highest sense, was wordless. The tradition said that when Buddha had turned a flower in his fingers, only his disciple, Kashyapa, had understood what was meant. Kashyapa, understanding, had smiled, so Buddha chose to transmit his enlightenment to him, wordlessly and directly. As a sign of the transmission, Buddha handed him his robe and begging bowl and initiated the formal act of transmission that has been preserved in Zen in various ways.

The tradition says that Zen Buddhism was brought from India to China by the monk, Bodhidharma. In the course of time, Zen Buddhism prospered, but it split into sects, each organized around some dominant master, with his own personality, conceptions, and methods. Many of these masters are named in the present text; but the one who most concerns us is Lin-chi, called Rinzai in Japanese. He was the originator of the sect whose attitude informs this collection of koans. I shall say of him now only that he was a magnetic, enigmatic, inventive man, perhaps, as he has been described, a sort of less reasoning Socrates.

Between Rinzai and Hakuin, the Zen master I should like to mention next, there lies a whole complex history. Zen was effectively transferred from China to Japan in the twelfth and thirteenth centuries. It encountered hostility in Japan, and, like the other Buddhist sects, it engaged in politics. Like the other sects, it, too, contributed much to both the aristocratic and popular culture of Japan.

Hakuin, a distant but attractive and energetic inheritor of Rinzai Zen, was born in 1686 and died in 1769. It was he and his pupils who devised the training method embodied in this book, and it was the tradition stemming from him that established, not only the kind and sequence of koans to be used in training, but also the "rightness" of the answers that are given here. Hakuin's personal experience had taught him that the Zen riddles, as the koans may be called, were the essential source of enlightenment. The rival sect, the Soto school of Zen, thought that extensive reliance upon koans might be an attempt to force enlightenment, and it therefore preferred enlightenment to come "silently," by itself. But Hakuin wanted active, unremitting questioning by means of koans. Again and again he insisted that "dead sitting and silent illumination" were destructive. To him, the ideal was the commingling of meditation with the activity of life, until the two became indistinguishable, whether in the life of the monk or of the layman. If, he said, "dead sitting and silent illumination" prevailed, so would its ideal of passivity, and then everyone would abandon his work, and the country would collapse. "Then the people, in their anger and resentment, would be sure to say that Zen was an evil and ill-omened thing."

Although a Buddhist who has achieved enlightenment ought not to hate anything or anyone, I suspect that Hakuin hated those whom he accused of destroying Buddhism. He particularly opposed the union of Pure Land with Zen. The tendency to unite them was old and quite in keeping with the Chinese desire to mitigate human friction by means of compromise. When the Chinese Zen master, Hui-hai, had been asked whether Confucianism, Taoism, and Buddhism were one doctrine or three, his answer had been that when employed by men of great understanding, they were the same. This tendency to harmonize became particularly strong in China during the sixteenth and seventeenth centuries. The famous Zen monk, Chun-hung (1535–1615), who is said to have revived Buddhism by synthesizing Pure Land and Zen, was deeply opposed to sectarianism. "Whoever clings to Ch'an and denigrates Pure Land," he said, "is denigrating his own Original Mind. He is denigrating the Buddha. He is denigrating his own Ch'an doctrine. He is simply not thinking."

This view carried the day in China, where Pure Land and Zen were freely joined. The tendency to harmonize was imported, like everything else Chinese, into Japanese Zen, but it was overcome there in time by the force of Hakuin's objection. The method adopted by Pure Land, of simply repeating a Buddha's name, was lazy, shallow, and ineffective, he said. It could not provoke the crisis of doubt that was necessary, he was sure, to provoke enlightenment. He therefore said that Chu-hung had "displayed an incredibly shallow understanding of Zen." It does seem as if Japanese Zen remained more determinedly pure and sectarian than its Chinese counterpart.

## Zen Discipline

It may already be clear from what I have said that Zen has had a strong element of individualism and even rebelliousness. This should not obscure the fact that Zen monks have lived under severe discipline. Their very skepticism of scriptures made their dependence upon their masters more complete. Dogen, the relatively conservative monk who established Soto Zen, retained his respect for scriptures, but insisted that "if a learned priest says that a toad or a worm is the Buddha, then one must abandon ordinary knowledge and believe that a toad or a worm is the Buddha." When asked why meditation was carried on only in the sitting position, he answered that monks had always meditated sitting down and that the matter should not be questioned any further.

This conservative outlook, which may not have been shared by his own Chinese masters, led him to expect absolute conformity to the rules of Zen, which were and which remain minute and strict. Hakuin also demanded strict obedience to the rules. These regulate the monk's sleeping, arising, washing, eating, evacuating, conversing, and, of course, praying and meditating. The differences that distinguish Soto from Rinzai Zen lend themselves easily to satire. Jonathan Swift could have made much of the little fact that monks in Soto Zen monasteries must sleep on their right sides, while those in Rinzai Zen monasteries must sleep on their backs.

An investigator, Holmes Welch, has gathered testimony from Chinese Zen monks on monastic life during the first half of the twentieth century. Much of their testimony is on the Chin

Shan monastery, which was situated on the Yangtze River, between Nanking and Shanghai. Its meditation hall was regarded as the foremost in all China. To make clear the nature and minuteness of the discipline at such a monastery, let me cite Welch's descriptions of the ceremonies on awakening, of the rather ceremonious evacuation that follows breakfast, and of the manner of meditation.

First, the ceremonies on awakening:

> The monks get up to the sound of four strokes on a small portable board. They have slept only five hours and the sun will not rise for two hours more. It is dark and cold. They have put on their full-sleeved gowns and over this their robes. The clang of the large bell has led into the booming of the large drum and by the time the drum has ceased, they are ready to march in procession to the great shrine hall. . . .
>
> In the great shrine hall all the monks of the monastery except the kitchen staff have gathered to recite morning devotions. Here too everyone has his place. . . . The center of the hall is occupied by hundreds of monks, standing row on row. In general, the higher their rank, the closer they stand to the Buddha image. . . . No one may leave without the permission of the proctor and he is a fierce disciplinarian.

We leave this scene even before the morning liturgy has begun and shift to something more profane, by non-Zen standards, that of the rules of the evacuation that follows breakfast:

> The manner of excretion is exactly prescribed. . . . Defecation is full of taboos. The code of rules of the Kao-min Ssu [i.e., Kao-min monastery] prescribes that the lid must be lifted silently and then the monk must "snap the fingers of his right hand three times toward the opening of the pit. This is to avoid having the excrement dirty the heads of the hungry ghosts, thus incurring their revengeful wrath. It is terribly important." Certain kinds of hungry ghosts are apparently attracted by the smell of faeces. After snapping his fingers and seating himself, the monk must sit up straight and keep his legs covered with the corners of his underclothes. "He must not look this way or that, talk with people nearby, lean against the partition, or scratch his private parts"—and he must be quick about it, because others are waiting. When he is finished, the code of rules prescribes that he go to the

water basin, dip in the middle two fingers of his right hand, wipe them on his left palm, and then run his hands quickly over the towel.

And now to the critical business of meditation:

Almost everyone sits in the order of rank. . . . In a well-run hall the monk should be able to forget his body and let it be guided like an automaton by the bell and board. He sits on the narrow bench, his eyes fixed on a point no further than the third and no nearer than the second row of tiles on the floor. He tries to keep his spine perfectly straight and to control his respiration. Talking is forbidden. The silence must be absolute. If a monk in the east makes a sound, the precentor goes over and beats him then and there with his incense board—and beats him hard. . . .

Those who are new at meditation usually sit cross-legged with only one foot up. Even then it may be so painful that they cannot sleep at night. Some lose courage and flee the monastery. According to one informant, "The pain is cumulative. It hurts until the sweat pours from your body. Some people cheat by uncrossing both legs under cover of their gowns, but eventually the precentor will catch them at it and give them a beating. The loss of face is one reason why so many run away." How many? "About 30 percent in the first week or two of each semester."

Old hands, of course, are untroubled by leg cramps and sit with both feet up. A few even learn to sleep in this posture and do not retire to the sleeping platform at night. But no one is allowed to sleep or even to doze during meditation. If they do, they are awakened by a meditation patrol, who stands facing the altar, holding an incense board horizontally before him in two hands. . . . At eight o'clock the hand-chime is struck. This signifies the end of the "morning meditation period."

And so on and, on.

## Zen Meditation and Enlightenment

The word "meditation" has already been used here many times, and it has become necessary, I think, to say a preliminary word on its nature and effects. In Rinzai Zen, with which we are here concerned, to meditate on a koan is to engage in an active process, like that we engage in when we try to solve a mathematical problem. As in mathematics, the solution is supposed to come suddenly. But Zen's belief in the suddenness of enlightenment has not been accepted by many of the other Buddhists. This difference in belief requires us to return for a moment to the history of Buddhism.

In seventh- and eighth-century China there was a long and finally bitter controversy between those of the Zen Buddhists who believed in gradual and those who believed in sudden enlightenment. The debate had begun in India. Indian Buddhists had usually assumed that the understanding of the truth was progressive. The training system that expressed this assumption was long and complicated, and there were, therefore, Buddhists who tried to simplify it. The most radical simplification was aimed at the instantaneous understanding of the truth. The mere exclamation, "Oh suffering!," it was said, could lead to instantaneous enlightenment. The justification for this belief was based not only upon appropriate scriptural passages but also on the idea that once we see illusion for what it is, the truth can be grasped all at once.

During the first few centuries of Buddhism, the two theses, that of slow, successive and that of unique, "in one time" enlightenment confronted one another. There was a venomous debate in eighth-century Tibet, in which the "sudden" method, represented by a Chinese master, was defeated by the "gradual" method, represented by the Indian master, Kamalashila.

The variant of this debate conducted in China itself also led to bitterness. The exponents of gradualism, known as the Northern school, were charged with attempting to steal Bodhidharma's robe, with mutilating the stele that recorded the transmission of enlightenment, and with cutting the head of the Sixth Patriarch from his mummified body. On the other side, the leader of the "sudden" or Southern school was charged with sedition.

Neither the Northern nor the Southern schools remained in existence very long, but in Zen Buddhism it was the sudden method that was victorious. It was accepted, as an old Buddhist master had put it, that "the fruit drops when it is ripe," or, in the kind of landscape metaphor that the Chinese understood, "When the mountain has been climbed the landscape of the goal appears all at once."

It seems that in China conciliation eventually settled this issue too. Holmes Welch, whom I have previously cited on the life of Zen monks in China, reports that none of the monks he questioned saw any contradiction between sudden and gradual enlightenment. "As they put it, the sudden enlightenment of the Sixth Patriarch [the founder of the "sudden" school] must have been the result of long training and self-cultivation in earlier lives." In other words, the few who reach sudden enlightenment must have been prepared by long, gradual efforts, extending over many lives.

Welch asked the Chinese monks why they were willing to put up with the austerities of the meditation hall, "leg cramps, mosquitoes, the exhaustion of meditation weeks, the confinement within the monastery, and, most of all, the inherent boredom of trying to think about the same thing for nine to fifteen hours a day." Most of his informants denied having been bored. The enigmatic question that had been posed was effective, they said. "A monk pursued it and concentrated all his energy upon it. He also learned to control his mind—to watch the stream of consciousness and, as soon as bad thoughts arose (greed, anger or stupidity), to dissolve them in the silent recitation of Buddha's name. Thus busied with learning, how could he get bored? Furthermore, his character was improved. Bad habits were weeded out. Through meditation even the most active person became peaceful and indifferent to the abuse of others."

But when Welch asked the abbot of Chin Shan about the possibility of boredom he got what he took to be a franker answer. "If you did not have the mental equipment to cope with the work," he said, "then the meditation hall was worse than prison. So every year there were monks who fled. On the other hand, if your mind was really on your work, then there was nothing boring about it. Those who were doing well with meditation could hardly wait to get started each day."

The question on whether or not any enlightenment was achieved was usually not answered. Welch says, "I have been largely unsuccessful in getting an answer to this question. For one thing, it has not pleased the venerable monks with whom I have raised it. To them it seems inappropriate and in bad taste. Other people's spiritual accomplishments were their personal affair and, baldly put, none of my business. If I wanted to find out about spiritual accomplishments, I had better have some of my own. This was not because such things were esoteric or mysterious, but because they were private, like a man's intimate relation with his wife."

Yet reward there must have been. Otherwise, asks Welch, why would so many of the monks have enrolled for a second and third year? He draws on the testimony of John Blofield, who sat relatively long in a Chinese meditation hall, and who reported that some of the monks found meditation an ordeal, while others profited greatly. Blofield recalled one of those who profited as saying:

> I don't know how many of us younger monks here really understand the Preceptor [instructor]. I find his lectures far from clear. Still, I have discovered for myself that if I just sit perfectly still, so still that I am conscious of the blood drumming in my ears and open my mind to—no, not to anything— just open my mind; though nothing happens the first time or the second, one day I begin to feel some response. My heart seems to be talking to me, revealing secrets of which I have never so much as dreamed. Afterwards I am left in a state of marvelous happiness. A Light shines within me and about me and they are One. . . . Then, sooner or later, from habit I do something which brings me against the current of the stream; the Light fades and I am as before, but for a while I am as lonely as when I first separated from my mother.

Zen literature itself has many reports of the experience of enlightenment; but while some of those queried by Welch brought up the experiences of the famous monks, others refused to be drawn into such evaluations. An old rector, that is, a high-ranking monk, told him that he had often seen cases of enlightenment. He could tell them, he said, from the way people answered questions during tutorials. However, "the abbot of Chin Shan took the opposite position. When I asked him whether he could detect enlightenment in the monks who came to him for tutorials, he replied: 'No, for I have not gotten paranormal powers. . . . Only with paranormal powers—telepathic powers—could I have known whether a disciple was enlightened or not.'"

## Zen Words

For whatever it is worth, my own attitude toward words is favorable. I think that the intellectual and other difficulties we run into are inherent in the situation or in ourselves, and not particularly in words as such. But there is an old, deeply rooted suspicion, most obvious in certain poets and in mystically inclined philosophers, that words are essentially inaccurate and unable to convey whatever matters to us most. This suspicion is expressed early in India in the Upanishads, in China in Lao-tzu and Chuang-tzu, and in Greece in Plato. Closer to Zen Buddhism, the Lankavatara Sutra says that true learning requires familiarity with meaning and not with words.

In Zen itself, as in other religions, scriptures were (and are) often recited without understanding. Reacting to this situation, a Zen master forbade people to recite sutras, that is scriptures, and explained, "Such people are like parrots mimicking human speech without understanding its meaning. . . . To comprehend meaning we should go beyond unsteady words; we should leap beyond writings. . . . That is why those seeking enlightenment forget all about wording after having arrived at the meaning." Then, alluding to some apt words in Chuang-tzu, the master said, "Awakening to reality, they throw away the doctrine just as a fisherman, having caught his fish, pays no more attention to his nets."

It appears to have been only a short step from an attack on the uncomprehending use of words and on the distance created between words and "meaning" to an attack on words as such, and therefore to a rejection of scriptures because they were composed of words. I doubt that this rejection was ever consistent and unequivocal, but some Zen masters, speaking with their customary earthy directness, heaped scorn on Zen scriptures, masters, and images. One of them warmed himself with a statue of Buddha he had set afire. Another said, starkly, that the Buddha was a barbarian turd and sainthood an empty name. Rinzai, using the same stark terminology, said, "Do not take the Buddha for the Ultimate. As I look at him, he is still like the hole in the privy." And Hakuin, echoing Rinzai, said, "All the scriptures are only paper good for wiping off shit." In an excess of enthusiasm, which, if taken seriously, would have ended his career, he said as well, "Studying Zen under a teacher is an empty delusion."

This attack on words may seem to you arbitrary or theatrical, by which I mean, consciously designed to shock. It may not have been difficult to enlist the latent resentment of monks against the scriptures they had so often parroted; but we, I assume, are not party to their resentment. What are we to think of the attack? I have already said that I like words and have no general fault to find with them. But they can be used without a sense of their nature and limitations. Philosophers, for example, may press them to artificial extremes, and almost anyone may sometimes be tempted to confuse a word or set of words with something it is not. There is, then, a basic truth in the Zen attack on words, at least in their more philosophical and abstractly coercive uses, and I should like to put this truth to you in my own way.

I am writing these words, on the inadequacy of words, in the circle of light cast by my lamp. This is a moment in my life much like many others, and yet, though I find it hard to say exactly how, it is unique. As I write, I repeat the words softly to myself. In spite of their generality, there is something absolutely individual in myself and in them as I am using them now.

The quality of absolute individuality is one that philosophers have considered and even invented names for. It is the inseparable "thisness," the *haecceitas*, of every object, according to the medieval European philosopher, Duns Scotus. The Indian philosophers known as the Vaisheshika call it *vishesha*. Buddhist philosophers express that which is unique, with no tinge of otherness, with the concept of *sva-lakshana*. But although suitable names have been invented for absolute individuality, no one, not even a philosopher, can live in a world all made up of unique particulars. If everything would be completely different from everything else, it would be impossible to learn from experience. Strictly speaking, such a world, consisting of nothing but unique particulars, cannot even be thought, because thinking, whatever else it may be, is also a generalizing and a relating. Is it a sophism, or is it the lack of a theory of levels of language that tempts us to say that absolute individuals have their individuality in common, as is demonstrated by the use for all of them of the same name, whether *haecceitas*, *vishesha*, or *sva-lakshana*. Does not every argument in their favor have to generalize about them and therefore imply that they are not merely individual particulars?

I think I know where the trouble lies, though I have no ambition to analyze it exactly. Concepts, that is, abstractions, are useful because they are isolating. We use proper names to name natural beings that are more or less complete in themselves; but we use abstractions to stand for characteristics that have no independent existence. The number system is a simple, persuasive example. We could hardly get along without numbers. Even animals need an ability equivalent to counting. We need and believe in numbers firmly enough to feel uncomfortable when someone suggests that their reality may be qualified. Yet, whatever in the end we care to think of numbers, it is true that nothing we perceive with our senses, not even the symbol for number, is simply "one" in itself, or "two." It is always one thing of some particular sort, or two things, and so on.

The difficulty arises when abstractions come to be regarded as if they were things or parts of things, or when it is supposed that reality is made up of "abstractions," or that reality must conform exactly to abstractions, be cut, so to speak, to exactly their pattern. Sometimes I think that the tendency, so evident in the history of thought, to see reality in this light, is only the philosopher's obsession with neatness, as if he could not bear to live in a world he had not swept clean, straightened up, and protected with antimacassars wherever an oily head or sweaty arm might lean. We know well enough that even the most useful abstractions cannot fit experience perfectly or exhaustively. The strict "either-or" of the logician is not always more adequate to experience than the paradoxical-sounding union of opposites of the mystic, or the mystic's refusal to commit himself to any clear final statement. I do not think that this is true because of any radical defect in the principle of contradiction, but because of the inadequate ways in which we choose or are impelled to use it. We often use it crudely in a world that remains beyond even our subtlest analysis.

What I am saying suggests the unease felt by many philosophers at the uncomprehending use of abstractions. Wittgenstein was particularly uneasy at the use of abstractions of the philosophical kind. Speaking in his name, his disciple Renford Bambrough insists that the normal "yes-no" or "either-or" standard of reasoning may not work well in philosophy. That is, it may happen that a certain statement or proposition, *p*, and its contradictory, *not-p*, may both be misleading. We may then try to say what we need without either making the crucial-seeming statement or contradicting it. "Wittgenstein preaches this method and he often practices it. When he 'assembles reminders for a particular purpose,' when he abjures explanations and allows what used to be called 'aseptic' description to take its place, he is doing his best to escape from the standard philosophical forms of words precisely because he has noticed that they are incurably misleading, that to deny what is expressed by one of them is as misleading as to assert what is expressed by it."

Chuang-tzu makes much the same point, though more radically. He knows, as we do, that analytic thought must, by its very nature, apply definite names, concepts, and values to our experience. All these are necessarily subjective, because they are derived from particular and limited points of view, and all are necessarily too definite, because they are inadequate to the fluidity, to the ebb and flow of nature. All these are therefore necessarily distorting. They lead us, he says, to become entangled in contradictions. We should learn to relax our conceptual definiteness and our incessant distinguishing between one thing and another. Things merge no less than they separate. Consider, for example, fixity and change, or, in words with a more human connotation, living and dying. Everything that exists is changing and so vanishing, and so to live is in a sense to die; and dying is a process that, as such, takes place, that is, exists, and so to die is in a sense to persist or live. Opposites are in a sense the same, "the admissible is simultaneously the inadmissible," and every definite thing, every "it," as the translator puts Chuang-tzu's word, is also the same as that which is other than itself. "What is 'it,'" says Chuang-tzu, "is also 'other,' what is 'other' is also 'it.' . . . Are there really It and Other? Or really no It and Other?"

The question can have no answer. "Therefore," says Chuang-tzu, "the glitter of glib debate is despised by the sage. The contrived 'that's it' he does not use, but finds things in their places as usual. It is this that I call 'throwing things open to the light.'"

Chuang-tzu does his best to stretch the medium of words to what he thinks it can or cannot quite express. He appears to agree that unambiguously unique or particular things are impossible, and that words, which signify that things are unambiguously definite, are always problematic. He uses words and recognizes their use; he sees their imperfections; he asks about them but gives no dogmatic answer. He takes the middle, indefinite path. He says, "Words are not just wind. Words have something to say. But if what they have to say is not fixed, then do they really say something? Or do they say nothing? People suppose that words are different from the peeps of baby birds, but is there any difference or isn't there?"

Can such a view be put without Chuang-tzu's impish paradoxicality? Perhaps. Perhaps it is put more clearly by the Indian philosophers of the Jain sect, when they insist that all ordinary descriptions of reality, because they must be made from a limited standpoint, should be prefixed, "in a sense" or "somehow." It is a mistake, they say, to describe the whole of reality by means of a single predicate, such as "unchanging" or "changing." Reality is neither the Vedantist's permanence nor the Buddhist's impermanence, but change *in* permanence and permanence *in* change. To drive this argument home, they tell the now famous parable of the blind men trying to describe an elephant. One of the blind men said that an elephant was ear-shaped, another that it was trunk-shaped, a third that it was tail-shaped, and so on. But reality has ears, a trunk, a tail, and very much else, and it is not just one of them and maybe not even exactly all of them either separately or together.

The Taoists and the Jains are both saying that abstractions, like mass-produced clothing, cannot fit all natures perfectly, and certainly not nature as such, in the absolute. Like many Indian philosophers and like the neo-Platonists, they try to get below the surface of things and find inexpressible reality there. Inexpressible it must be if it is unique, either in the sense of a unique whole or that of a whole made of unique parts. It must then be inexpressible because uniqueness evades the generality of abstract words. Both radical monists and radical pluralists ought to be silent. But silence, like speech, has its shortcomings. As a Zen master said, "Both speech and silence transgress."

The disciple of Wittgenstein that I have quoted ascribes to his teacher an approximation of this last Zen moral. He says, plausibly enough, that Wittgenstein maintains that there is something *impossible* about words in their philosophical use:

> A characteristically philosophical form of words is always capable both of expressing something true and of expressing something false, and when such a form of words is used the speaker may mean by it only what is true or only what is false or *both* what is true *and* what is false in what the expression is naturally capable of expressing. Correspondingly, someone who denies an assertion made with such an expression may intend to deny the false content of the assertion, or the true content, or both. (This paragraph is itself a most misleading philosophical remark.)

Chuang-tzu, who takes a similar position, says:

> Treat as 'it' even what is not, treat as 'so' even what is not. . . . Therefore behind dividing there is something undivided, behind disputation there is something not argued out. 'What?' you ask. The sage keeps it in his breast.

I know that these words on the inadequacy of words are unclear. Let me try, then, to explain, because I have no ambition to rival Zen or other riddles with any of my own making.

If what I am saying makes no sense to you, I am not really speaking, certainly not to you. But suppose the contrary. Here we are, you and I. We are invisible to one another. We are at different times. We do not know one another at all. Each of us comes from a different place and is going somewhere else, every day and all his life, and has different thoughts and fantasies filling his mind. And yet, as I am writing and you are reading these words, they enter the consciousness of each of us, and as long as they remain at the center of my consciousness and yours, you and I are thinking the same thoughts. In this sense we are internally one.

I will be more radical. I am not simply writing to you, and you are not simply reading me. I am you and you are I because we are simultaneously having the same thoughts—simultaneously, not at the same clock time, but at the intended simultaneity of writer and reader. I could go further still and say that at the moment that we share the same thoughts I am not speaking to you, because, if I am the same as you, I cannot speak to you—speaking to someone else implies that he is different from me. It is of course true that we speak to ourselves, and true that, when we do so, we divide ourselves into two; but in this condition the words sinking into the consciousness of the listener, who is also the speaker, unite the two.

Because I am talking about difference and oneness, let me suggest an impossible experiment in counting. If we could now take off our hands, feet, and bodies, how many consciousnesses would there be left? If, all containing the same thoughts, they would all be the same, why not say "one"? Or if "one" seems too definite and arithmetical a number for a situation so hard to count, why not say, with the Taoists and Zen Buddhists, "neither one nor many"? Listen to Chuang-tzu again as he states such a paradox (in a necessarily interpretive translation):

The universe and I exist together, and all things and I are one. Since all things are one, what room is there for speech? But since I have already said that all things are one, how can speech not exist?

Difference and sameness, manyness and unity, illusion and reality. Do these really constitute a problem or are they, paired or single, merely the nature of the world, which we should accept as it obviously is, without surprise? Read the Zen paradoxes in this book and the reactions to them, and see if an answer insinuates itself into your mind. The English philosopher John Wisdom said, Wittgenstein-like, "I have said that philosophers' questions and theories are really verbal. But if you like we will not say this or we will also say the contradictory." It may be helpful to set koans and Wisdoms in some framework if we recall the opinion of a strange, mystical genius, the mathematician Luitzen Brouwer. "The language of introspective wisdom," he wrote, "appears disorderly, illogical, because it can never proceed by systems of entities which have been imprinted on life, but can only accompany their rupture and in this way perhaps aid the unfolding of the wisdom that causes the rupture."

## Zen Koans

*Koan*, or, in Chinese, *kung-an*, means "public case." I am not sure whether the relevant connotation of the word is "record of a public discussion" or "precedent for public use." Koans appear to have developed out of Zen conversations and out of stories describing the masters' intuitive wisdom. The old Zen masters were resourceful educators, and they must have vied with one another in the invention of verbal and physical techniques to arouse their students to the elusive truth. It was inevitable that the words of the revered old masters, the "old cases," should be collected, systematized to a degree, and provided when necessary with answers, clarifications, and atmospherically fitting verses. Zen tradition came to see the koans as exemplifications of the transcendent principle, received silently from the Buddha himself, and, as such, beyond logic, beyond transmission in writing, and beyond measure by reason. To use one of the grander expressions of Zen rhetoric, the koan is "a divine mirror that reflects the original face of both the sacred and the secular."

It has been said, with what degree of truth I do not know, that the early Zen masters of China put things more simply, less enigmatically, and that some of them were even prepared to accept philosophically logical answers. On the whole, however, the koans were designed to break down ordinary rationality. Rationality or intellectuality was regarded as a defense against the truth. Intellectually plausible answers were therefore taken to be "dead words," and only non-rational, apparently irrelevant ones to be "living words." The disciple, given a koan to see through, was encouraged to put his whole strength into the singleminded search for its solution, to be "like a thirsty rat seeking for water, like a child thinking of its mother." The disciple was to carry the problem with him everywhere, until suddenly, if he were successful, the solution came, or, as the Zen phrase went, "the ball of doubt was shattered." This vivid expression had been lifted out of an old Zen poem, whose author had written:

> Everywhere I went I met with words,
> But I couldn't understand them.
> The ball of doubt within my heart
> Was as big as a wicker basket.

However, as the poem recounts, the doubt was shattered by an opportune blow delivered by the Zen master:

> The Master, from his mat of felt,
> Rose up like a dragon,
> And, baring his right arm,
> Struck my chest a single blow.
> My ball of doubt, fright-shattered,
> Fell to the ground with a crash!

Hakuin himself always emphasized that the koan could lead to enlightenment only through such enormous effort that the Great Doubt, as he called it, would be aroused. The shattering of the Great Doubt was enlightenment and the welling up of a flood of exaltation. The koan that gives this book its title was devised by him as the most effective possible way of evoking the Great Doubt and leading to the first stage of enlightenment. "If you take up one koan," he said, "and investigate it unceasingly, your mind will die and your will will be destroyed. It is as though a vast, empty abyss lay before you, with no place to set your hands and feet. You face death and your bosom feels as though it were fire. Then suddenly you are one with the koan, and body and mind are cast off. . . . This is known as seeking into one's nature. You must push forward relentlessly and with the help of this complete concentration you will penetrate without fail to the basic source of your own nature."

As the poem on the shattering of the ball of doubt intimates, and as this whole book shows, the Zen master used what might be called, somewhat pretentiously, psychophysical methods. Rinzai, with a dialectical verve that belies his anti–intellectualism, carried on the practice of therapeutic hitting that he had learned from his teacher. He administered his blows selectively. "Many students," he said, "are not free from the entanglement of objective things. I treat them right on the spot. If their trouble is due to grasping hands, I strike them there. If their trouble comes from their mouths, it is there I strike. So far I have not found anyone who can be set free by himself. That is because all have been entangled in the useless mechanics of their old masters. As for me, I do not have a single method to give to everyone, but what I can do is relieve the troubles and set them free."

Rinzai was famous, not only for his hitting, but also for his effective shouting of *Katsu!*, which, like the precisely timed interpretation of a psychoanalyst, was meant to catalyze insight. *Katsu!*, like blows, was used discriminatingly by Rinzai, who has therefore been said to have constituted a semantic system of the cry. It is only one of a group of now conventionalized cries used to respond to koans. The Zen cries, and, sometimes, Zen blows, may be used in a kind of dialectical duel, in which each contestant tries to transfix his partner on the sword of enlightenment.

Other techniques were resorted to, as ingenuity or experience suggested. These techniques included the giving of an irrelevant response, the repetition of the question as the answer to the same question, and the use of a disconcerting negation or series of negations. Nose twisting, we learn, was also available to the enterprising master.

Like any educational technique, that of koan Zen has sometimes, in its own terms, succeeded and sometimes failed. At its extreme, Zen technique suggests a strain of masochism or sadism. The first is suggested by the story of Bodhidharma's would–be disciple, who proved his sincerity and earned his discipleship by cutting off his arm. The second, sadism, is more than hinted at by the famous koan, which can be read in the following pages, in which the master, Nansen, makes his point by cutting a cat into halves, a deed that would have horrified the many generations of Buddhists who believed in the utmost mercy for every living thing.

It should perhaps be said here that, although Hakuin was a benign and public-spirited man, there was something military and even militant in his attitudes, as his language often betrays. He told a disciple to *raise* his mental lance, *destroy* the enemy to enlightenment, *march against* the black demon of sleep, and *attack* the concepts of active and passive and right and wrong. It should perhaps also be said that Zen Buddhism was prominent in the education of the Japanese warriors. It taught them a single-minded, at once alert and relaxed use of weapons. As this swordsman's ideology and training was put in the fifteenth century, "The essence of swordsmanship consists in giving yourself up altogether to the business of striking down the opponent." Zen also trained warriors to lose their fear of death. Hakuin commended his koan training for the production of courageous soldiers. Zen Buddhism was evidently a double-edged sword, good for the conquest of both enlightenment and territory.

Something more must be said of the possibly unfavorable effects of koan training. Zen monasteries, like all such places of refuge from the world, have always had their share of the outcast, the unfortunate, and the unstable. It is natural that psychotic breakdowns occur among them. But the method itself of koan meditation is said to be capable of inducing depressions and hallucinations, that is, a specific "Zen sickness." Hakuin recalls predecessors attacked by it and gives a moving description of his own suffering and his recovery, made with the help of an old monk.

The victims or apparent victims of Zen training also appear in the account of the lives of twentieth-century Zen monks in China:

> One hears of monks who found it impossible to make any mental breakthrough either because they were "stupid" or because they could not stop thinking about their parents, wife, children, and the other things they had left behind. At first they would be unable to keep their minds on anything. Then they would begin to have hallucinations and "talk nonsense." At this point they were usually locked in a room and a Chinese doctor called to examine them. Some re-

covered; some died. According to one informant, fatalities were most common during meditation weeks and the bodies were not buried immediately. It was felt that their death must be retribution for sins committed in former lives, so they were wrapped in quilts and left to be disposed of when the meditation weeks were over.

## Zen Dada

The fantastic humor of Zen Buddhism is derived not from India but from China, specifically from Taoism, and, more specifically, from that wild and subtle philosopher (or group of philosophers) called Chuang-tzu. He enjoyed dissolving clever debates into long, clever metaphors and humorous fantasies. When Hui-tzu told him that his words were big and useless, just like Hui's own big, gnarled tree, no good for lumber or anything else, Chuang-tzu answered:

> Now you have this big tree and you're distressed because it's useless. Why don't you plant it in Not-Even-Anything Village, or the field of Broad-and-Boundless, relax and do nothing by its side, or lie down for a free and easy sleep under it? Axes will not shorten its life, nothing can ever harm it. If there's no use for it, how can it come to grief or pain?

Such philosophical Taoism resisted duties and artificiality and fostered a not unmystical "naturalness." Its adherents believed in floating along with nature in general and their own natures in particular. Infected with this naturalness, there were Chinese poets and painters who indulged and even paraded their idiosyncrasies. They came to regard themselves as the men of "wind and stream," who lived each one in accord with himself. They tried, like the yet non-existent Zen Buddhists, to respond to things but not to be ensnared by them. The more intellectual among them conducted terse and maybe precious "pure conversations."

It is amusing to see how Taoistic behavior was converted, sometimes with minimal change, into Zen behavior. Take for example the story of a Taoist, Huan Yi, famous for his skill with the flute. Another Taoist worthy heard that he was traveling nearby and sent a messenger to ask him to come and play for him.

So Huan Yi "descended from his chariot, sat on a chair, and played the flute three times. After that, he ascended his chariot and went away. The two men did not exchange even a single word."

In its Zen transmutation this becomes the story of the Zen master, Kakua, an early pioneer of Zen in Japan. When he returned from China, the emperor asked him to tell him everything he had learned of this new sect. Kakua produced a flute, blew a note on it, bowed politely, and walked out.

We are also told of a Chinese Zen master who answered questions by rolling the wooden balls he played with, and another who did his meditation perched, like a bird, in a tree. More ominously, we hear that the Zen monasteries of China "ended by turning into madhouses." We hear, too, that in the sixteenth century, a period of social disorganization in China, there were Zen-inspired Confucians with "a truly remarkable ability to bring a person to sudden enlightenment by means of clever dialogue." They formed a "realization" school, whose members included a "mad" group. The "madmen" despised rules and attacked the conventions that, they said, kept men imprisoned. One of them went so far as to proclaim freedom of speech and equality of the sexes. It is said that such Confucians and followers of Zen "gave birth to the heresy of mad and irresponsible actions" and deliberately flouted the moral code.

There is something in this anti-establishmentarianism, stubborn whimsicality, and creative disorder that recalls the spirit of Dadaism. I am referring to the less bitter, more benign and creative Dadaists, such as Schwitters and Arp. Let me make some comparisons to persuade you of what I have just said. You will discover in the present book that Master Mumon pondered for six years on the koan on Mu. Then he suddenly achieved enlightenment and composed the following poem:

> Mu! Mu! Mu! Mu! Mu!
> Mu! Mu! Mu! Mu! Mu!
> Mu! Mu! Mu! Mu! Mu!
> Mu! Mu! Mu! Mu! Mu!

It may be only my own stubbornness that leads me to insist, as I do, that, granted the cultural differences involved, this repeated Mu! is a Dadaist poem, reveling in its own literal meaninglessness and irony.

The same variant of the same koan may also be answered by

the recitation of the first twenty letters of the alphabet. The letters of the alphabet, in or out of their fixed order, are the substance of more than one Dadaist poem, for example, Schwitters' "Register [elementary]," beginning

$$Z$$
$$A \quad R \quad P$$
$$A \quad B \quad C$$

and ending, as the alphabet dictates,

$$Z$$
$$Z$$
$$Z$$

Further comparisons are easy. It is easy to recall the "Ursonata" of Schwitters, composed of meaningless sounds, his "Poem 25," made up completely of numbers, and his "Composed Picture Poem," which looks like a more complicated and mechanical version of the circles, signifying "emptiness," or the quasi-symbolic square-triangle-circle that Zen artists used to paint. The purely typographical poems and pictures, called, in our times, "concrete poetry" or "concrete art," also come to mind.

The comparison between Zen and Dada extends to the explicit ideas of Dadaists and Surrealists. Arp, for example, believed that we should not create by imposing artificial forms upon nature, but by submitting to chance, which "embraces all other laws and is as unfathomable to us as the depths from which all life arises." Only by submission to the law of chance, he said, can one attain perfect life, the perfection and order of which are the perfection and order of nature itself.

In the vein of Zen "suchness," the ninth-century Zen master Ch'an-sha Ching-ts'en (Chosha Keijin, in Japanese) once said to his monks:

> The entire universe is your eye; the entire universe is your own luminance; the entire universe is within your own luminance. In the entire universe there is no one who is not your own self.

Kurt Schwitters, somewhat likewise, and for somewhat similar reasons, though in the vein of European pantheism, wrote:

> I am the hand.
> The hand is the man.

The man is the hand.
The earth is the world.
We men are great.
Never do men overbear over.
I am the hand.
Never do hands overbear over.

## Zen Hands

The technique of the Zen koan is, obviously, to tempt the learner into logic, into the giving, that is, of a rational response. He must be taught to resist the temptation. His response must reflect reality unqualified, unanalyzed, unrationalized. The Zen response is therefore often by act rather than by word. Consider three examples.

The first example is the following dialogue:

> MONK: Where is the reality in appearance?
> MASTER: Wherever there is appearance, there is reality.
> MONK: How does it manifest itself?
> The master lifted his saucer.

The second example, from the koan on the one finger, ends in typical Zen hyperbole:

> Whenever Master Gutei was asked a question, he would simply raise one finger.
> ANSWER: The pupil raises one finger.
> MASTER: What if I cut this finger off?
> ANSWER: Even if you cut it, it cannot be cut. From the top of the thirty-third heaven down to the deepest layer of earth, it is the one finger.

The third and last example is from the koan on the sound of the one hand:

> MASTER: In clapping both hands a sound is heard. What is the sound of the one hand?
> ANSWER: The pupil faces his master, takes a correct posture, and, without a word, thrusts one hand forward.

This demonstrative, wordless form of argument is not totally foreign to Western thought. When Boswell told Samuel Johnson that the philosopher, Berkeley, had argued that matter did not exist, Johnson made a famous response. In Boswell's words:

> After we came out of the church, we stood talking for some time together of Bishop Berkeley's ingenious sophistry to prove the non-existence of matter, and that everything in the universe is merely ideal. I observed that though we are satisfied his doctrine is not true, it is impossible to refute it. I shall never forget the alacrity with which Johnson answered, striking his foot with mighty force against a large stone, till he rebounded from it, "I refute it *thus!*"

Boswell adds, "To me it is inconceivable how Berkeley can be answered by pure reasoning." But this is precisely why, by Zen standards, Johnson is right. To answer Berkeley's reasoning with reasoning would be a mistake, a trap, Zen would say. Johnson is not engaged in the philosopher's usual epistemological analysis, and, indeed, most philosophers regard his response as irrelevant. After all, you can't really kick an argument. But by Zen and Johnsonian standards, the kick, though technically irrelevant, is relevant in fact. That is to say, Berkeley has not only an abstract argument, but a goal. He wants to get rid of the belief in matter and, by doing so, to cause a change in attitude toward the world. Johnson commonsensically denies Berkeley's right to tamper with his natural reaction to objects or, for that matter, with his religious views. In Johnson's world, stones are not, as Berkeley would have them, immaterial messages being spoken immaterially to an immaterial Johnson by an immaterial God. Berkeley, or the stone that represented him, had the kick coming to him, or to it.

But not only philosophically unsophisticated men have come on this kind of demonstrative argument. It was used, not very many years ago, by the English philosopher G. E. Moore. His purpose was to refute Kant, who held that the only possible proof for the existence of external things was the one that he, Kant, had given. Moore's response was:

> I can now give a large number of different proofs, each of which is a perfectly rigorous proof. . . . I can prove now, for instance, that two human hands exist. How? By holding up my two hands, and saying, as I make a certain gesture with the right hand, "Here is one hand," and by adding, as I make a certain gesture with the left, "and here is another." And if, by doing this, I have proved *ipso facto* the existence of external

things, you will see that I can also do it now in numbers of other ways: there is no need to multiply examples.

But did I prove just now that two human hands were then in existence? I want to insist that I did; that the proof I gave was a perfectly rigorous one; and that it is perhaps impossible to give a better or more rigorous proof of anything whatever.

Contemporary philosophers may or may not be satisfied with Moore's proof. Zen Buddhists would surely approve it, though they might sadly note that the tradition of English philosophizing made it necessary for Moore to accompany the motion of his hands with explanatory words. Even the few he used would be too many for the pure Zen taste.

## Zen and Other Riddles and the Reasons for Riddling

If we look at the koans historically, it is not difficult to see how they were evolved and how they came into vogue as a training method. But I should like to try to understand, independently of the Zen tradition, what their usefulness might have been.

What are riddles and enigmas good for, apart from amusement? They have been created everywhere, I suppose, and seem to be a natural accompaniment of the pleasure humans take in exercising their intelligence. Black Africa, for example, abounds in them. Riddles have been used there as an instrument of traditional education and as a challenge to verbal contests. African riddles may have symbolic meanings known only to initiates. My rather offhand explanation of the interest in riddles in Africa and elsewhere is this: riddles pose difficulties that, when solved, give much of the satisfaction of having solved real, that is, really disturbing difficulties of which the riddles are the invented simulacra. When solved, they also give the feeling of an ability to solve mysteries and penetrate secret intentions. To solve a riddle is to gain or regain confidence in oneself.

If, however, we choose Africa for the comparison, we find that Zen koans resemble African riddles less than they do African dilemma tales, tales that end with difficult alternative conclusions. Some such tales are provided with a "correct" answer, but, in any case, they provoke lively discussion.

Let me give an example of an African dilemma tale, "The

Leftover Eye." It begins with the situation of four blind persons, a man, his wife, his mother, and his wife's mother, all living together on an impossibly poor farm. To improve their lot, they leave the farm. On the road, the man stumbles over something. This something turns out to be seven eyes. He immediately gives two eyes to his wife and two to himself. Of the remaining three eyes, he gives one to his mother and one to his wife's mother. He now has a single eye left in his hand. To whom should he give it, to his mother or his wife's mother. "If," says the tale, "he gives the eye to his mother he will forever be ashamed before his wife and her mother. If he gives it to his wife's mother, he will fear the angry and disappointed heart of his own mother. A mother, know you, is not something to be played with."

The dilemma is rubbed in a bit more, and then the narrator ends with the question, "If this thing would come to you, which would you choose?"

The African imagination shown in this tale resembles that of Zen in that both seize on imaginative dilemmas in order to force apparently impossible solutions.

Before I comment further on dilemmas, I should like to contrast a pair, one of them African, the other Zen.

According to the African dilemma tale, "a man's helpless mother was fed by his wife. One day she bit the wife's hand and would not let go. Not knowing what to do, the man asked the judge, and the judge asked the people. The young people said, 'Break the old lady's jaw.' The old people said, 'Cut off the young woman's hand.' The judge was unable to decide. What would you do?"

The Zen dilemma is one of the koans of this book. "Let us suppose," it begins, "that a man climbs up a tree." It continues, rather implausibly, "He grips the branches with his teeth, his hands do not hold onto the tree, and his feet do not touch the ground. A monk below asks him about the meaning of our founder's coming from the West [i.e., about the essential meaning of Buddhism]. If he does not answer, he will be avoiding the monk's question [and demonstrating cruelty, which is forbidden to a Buddhist]. But if he opens his mouth and utters a word, he will fall to death. Under such circumstances, what would the man do?"

Here, in this book, the sensible comment is made that it is plausible to assume that the man would, anyway, soon fall.

"Answering or not is not his problem. He needs not philosophy but someone kind and courageous enough to help him down."

How do the two dilemmas compare? They have at least their drastic alternatives and black humor in common, and they are equally difficult to answer persuasively. An African will normally weigh alternatives and choose the one that seems best to him, or he will think of a clever strategem to solve the dilemma. The Zen monk, in contrast, will try to cut through the difficulty, as if it were the proverbial Gordian knot. Both African and Japanese dilemmas provoke an attempt to apply traditional rules or modes of vision to perplexing particular cases. The dilemma is, then, an exercise in the maintenance of a traditional set of values, and, further, an exercise in self-revelation, for the individual who attempts to solve a dilemma must decide how he would interpret these values. The dilemma also shows all those who join in the attempt to solve it what they have in common.

To speak of the Zen koan alone, it does appear to have both an individual and a social usefulness. This becomes clear if the context of monastic life is recalled. Riddle-solving, under the personal direction of a teacher, provides an important degree of autonomy given within a highly regulated life; for every monk knows that the effort is engaged in for his own sake, at his own pace, and must, if it is to be successfully concluded, end in an internal victory achieved by himself.

If we remember, too, that many of the monks are orphans or others cast adrift or troubled by life, we see that the koan training, if sincerely practiced, represents their attempt to fulfil themselves by means of a viable integration of mind and body, or intellect and emotion. The monks have a vague but sufficiently orienting background of explicit philosophy, they find a truth for the simple-minded and another, higher one for the more demanding or insightful, and they learn that they must always preserve an intimate communion between thought and action. Briefly, koan training is a formal method of giving the monk his personal value and satisfaction, and it is, no less, the method of linking him tightly to master and monastery, the master guiding and the monastery disciplining him, and together making his personal accomplishment possible.

This said, it should also be remembered that Zen Buddhism was a training ground for poets, artists, and warriors. I cannot think of anything much better than koan meditation to drive home the lesson, so well learned in traditional China and Japan, that the aim of the poet, artist, or warrior is creative intuition, and that this is achieved by the attentive fusing of discipline, intelligence, and emotion.

This granted, the possible usefulness of koan meditation to the individual can be stated. As I have said, it unites the externally imposed discipline of the monastic community with his self-interest. His meditation is conducted under the rule of the master, who acts the role of a super-parent. The strain of meditation may trigger a psychosis, but, generally speaking, meditation makes use of the monk's inward sense of omnipotence and his mystical tendencies in order to stimulate him to feel an essential identity between himself, his community, and the universe. His meditation merges solitariness and sociability, limitation and infinity.

When I say this, I am reminded of a friend who could not remain at peace with himself unless he heard a concert of classical music every week. It seemed to me that the music first aroused his emotions, as, in its initial development, it ranged from soft to loud and low to high. His emotions were then carried along by the music and accentuated and made to clash, for classical music, before it ends, enters into a war with itself. Finally, music and emotion having become one, both came as one to a classic, harmonious resolution.

The very strain, it seems to me, of koan meditation is not unlike the self-imposed strain of a creative mathematician, writer, or artist. Such a person deliberately sets himself difficult problems, and deliberately renews them once they have been solved, in order, so to speak, to compose or harmonize or solve himself by his internalization of the difficulty that he is composing, harmonizing, or solving. He is using his effort, ostensibly directed at something external, so that, by ordering the external object, he can order himself internally. The result of such a self-conquest can be an access of pleasure, optimism, and self-confidence. It can bring on the ecstatic states of which Hakuin speaks with great emotion. These states can feel good, better, or superlative. The process, by which one rises from doubt or ambivalence to pleasure or more, suggests what psychotherapists have often said, that, to be healed, one must first bring to the surface difficulties that have been suppressed and, because suppressed, have brought on neurotic suffering. One must, they have said, summon up trouble in order to get rid of it. Zen meditation is at least a form of psychotherapy, and, as such, its most obvious aim is psychophysical wholeness.

## Zen Ordinariness

Zen teaches vigilant carelessness and detached involvement. In a more high-sounding phrase, it teaches transcendental ordinariness. In a simpler, more sympathetic phrase, it teaches nothing but ordinariness itself.

Long before Zen came into existence, when, in India, mysticism had flourished and had been attacked by philosophical opponents and unmystical realities, there had been Buddhist philosophers who arrived at a subtle solution of the problem. What problem? The one that has been stated in these pages in various forms. One form is that of impermanence and permanence, which, when put in the light of human concerns, becomes the problem of death and survival, which, put in another form, is the problem of relative and absolute. The philosophers I am speaking of put this problem in terms of "emptiness," which is to say that they regarded everything as devoid of substance and, in the final analysis, as inconceivable. The philosophers of emptiness, having despaired of the philosophers' prolonged debate, regarded the debate as essentially insoluble—Kant, in Europe, said the same. It is true, these Buddhists said, that there is no immutable substance, nothing, at least nothing that can be put into words or logic, that underlies the eternal flux. Nothing either positive or negative can be said to characterize reality. Reality, they said, is not dual, for there is no essential difference between subject and object, impure and pure, or relative and absolute; but neither is reality single. It is neither individual nor non-individual, neither one nor many. It is, instead, "empty."

It should be obvious that this was the conclusion adopted by the Zen Buddhists; except that they had usually grown to dislike the too explicit philosophizing by which it had been maintained. They also adopted the "empty" Buddhist conclusion that there was and could be no difference between the ordinary world, the round of birth and death, as the Buddhists saw it, and the superlative goal of Buddhism, nirvana. In Buddhist terminology, they concluded that *samsara* is identical with nirvana. Common sense reality, therefore, cannot be denied, because it is identical with superlative reality. The moral is that we ought to learn to experience the "suchness" or "thisness" of the common sense world.

All, then, that we can do, and all that enlightenment can teach, is the paradox of the enlightened acceptance of the world as it is. Be empty, the Zen masters advised, or, in other words, be intuitively ordinary. When a monk said to a Zen master, "Your disciple is sick all over. Please cure me," the master answered, "I will not cure you." When the monk asked, "Why don't you cure me?," the master's answer was, "So that you neither live nor die." And when another monk asked another master where silence, that is, emptiness, would finally be expressed, the master's answer was, "Last night at midnight I lost three pennies by my bed." His meaning was, "Get your attention back where it belongs, on ordinary life."

Ordinariness is not difficult unless one makes it particularly elusive. When an early Chinese Zen master, thinking of the difficulties of achieving enlightenment, allowed the words "Difficult, difficult, difficult" to escape him, his wife, who, at the moment, was wiser than he, answered, "Easy, easy, easy, just like touching your feet to the ground when you get out of bed." Her response, however, seemed too explicit to another Zen master, who added the characteristic formula, "Neither difficult nor easy."

It was ordinariness that led Rinzai to say to his disciples, with a touch of exasperation, that they had come from everywhere to search for deliverance from the world; but if delivered from the world, where, he asked, could they go? The advice he gave was to be ordinary. "Just carry on an ordinary task," he said, "without attachments," meaning, without blind, enslaving desire. "Shit and piss, wear your clothes, eat your meals. When you're tired, lie down. The fool will laugh at you, but the wise man will understand."

But the most charming expression of ordinariness, to my mind, is the invitation to have a cup of tea. Look at the contrast between poetic transcendence and courteous ordinariness, which is the invitation to have a cup of tea, in the following koan and the insightful response to it:

> The disciple Hokoji visited Master Baso and asked, "Who is he that transcends existence?" Baso said, "When you have

swallowed the waters of the West River in one gulp, I shall answer you." In an instant Hokoji realized the answer and said the poem which goes: "People from all over come and meet together; each one seeks to learn the way of non-doing. This is the place where Buddhas are born. I, having been chosen for holding the heart of nothingness, can now go back."

Answer: "I'll have a cup of tea," the pupil says, taking a cup of tea.

To Zen, tea, like ordinariness, cures everything.

## Zen Terminable and Interminable

In one of his later essays Freud asked whether a psychoanalysis could ever be terminated. He said that it was evident that analysis could never attain absolute psychic normality, or that, if something like such normality appeared to have been attained, it was probably because the person in question had been spared from too searching a fate. The analysts themselves, said Freud, could not quite reach the standards of normality that they set for their patients. At this point, he added endearingly, "It almost looks as if analysis were the third of those 'impossible' professions in which one can be quite sure of unsatisfying results. The other two, much older-established, are the bringing up of children and the government of nations." I wonder if the profession of Zen master should be added to Freud's list.

Freud went on to say that every analyst ought to reenter analysis at intervals because his task, like the patient's, is in fact interminable. But he continued, as common sense dictates, that in practice analyses do come to an end.

Compare Hakuin's view. Hakuin, when speaking of enlightenment, told of a famous Chinese master who had experienced eighteen "great awakenings" and an uncountable number of smaller ones. Hakuin himself experienced great awakenings at least six or seven times, each awakening superseding in insight those that had preceded. Hakuin believed, as a result, that once the student attained the initial awakening, he had to go on with the study of his koans, arranged to become progressively more difficult.

Perhaps Zen, like psychoanalysis, should be regarded as an

ideally interminable education. I doubt if any Zen master has said so explicitly because, if he has, he might seem to be reverting from belief in sudden enlightenment to belief in gradual enlightenment. Yet there must be something interminable in Zen meditation, for what master could accept his condition of ordinariness and yet claim never to lapse from enlightenment? Zen is, as it claims to be, the condition of ordinary men and is embodied in ordinary institutions. But ordinariness is an ambiguous state, and the goal may be lost sight of. Institutionalization, for instance, has dangers that can never be escaped for long, by Zen or anything.

I say this because, before I end, I want to pay tribute to the Zen master whose introduction opens this book. Without his help, the translation of these koans and answers would necessarily have been less authentic, and their traditional intent could only have been guessed at. Surely the tendency, so clear in this book, to institutionalize the questions and, above all, the answers works against the Zen demand that we should remain spontaneous and open. The fear that the publication of the secret answers might weaken the whole system of Zen education is a comment on the dilution that the Zen ideal has suffered. By its own best standards, it should be reformed. That is why the help given by Master Hirano Sōjō demonstrates that respect for the truth is everywhere the same.

BEN-AMI SCHARFSTEIN

# TRANSLATOR'S NOTE

This book contains all the koans which the Zen novice has to answer during the long course of his training for qualification as a Zen master, together with their traditional answers. My decision to bring the translation of this book before the general public was not easily made, and I am well aware that there will be Zen masters and Zen disciples in Japan and elsewhere who may regard such a publication with discomfort. One can hardly expect the teachers and disciples of a religious sect to welcome the publication of the "secrets" of their sect.

Since the publication of this book in 1916 and its republication in 1917, there has been no new edition. In Kyoto, only a photocopy of it is sold in a shop that specializes in Buddhist literature. To the best of my knowledge, this book cannot be found in libraries, nor does it appear in bibliographies on Buddhism or Zen. I have been told by the shop owner in Kyoto that almost all the buyers of the book are Zen novices. A certain Japanese Zen master told me that he had tried to compose his own koans in order to prevent his novices from relying on the answers in the book. He admitted, however, that he found it extremely difficult and was, in the end, forced to rely on the traditional koan teaching as presented in this book.

Though the teaching of Zen was introduced into Japan as early as the seventh century, it was not until the beginning of the eighteenth century that the koans were first systematized into the traditional method of teaching presented here. It was the Japanese Zen Master Hakuin (1686–1769) who first selected the koans in this book from among those recorded in Chinese sources. (There are close to two thousand recorded koans altogether.) It was he who also determined the order of their presentation to novices and composed many of the traditional answers. Hakuin created many koans of his own, the most famous of them being the koan on "the sound of the one hand." This system was further developed by Hakuin's disciples, Inzan Ien (1751–1814) and Takujū Kosen (1760–1833), into the teaching method which has prevailed in Japan until the present day. In the course of time, Hakuin's teaching came to be interpreted by a number of different schools, each using the method to give different answers to some of the koans. But these differences are, for the most part, nonessential.

Most scholars of Zen believe that "the koans that Hakuin created are still transmitted only by word of mouth to the student in the master's room."[1] But it is in fact the custom in Zen monasteries that the novice compiles his own notes on the various koans and their answers, exactly as transmitted to him by his master. When the novice, after ten or more years of practice, is qualified as a Zen master, his master goes over the notes and corrects and approves them. The pupil then vows to keep the notes a secret and, when he himself becomes a master, to transmit them only to his own disciples. Taking into account the traditional loyalty of the Japanese to their teachers and masters, it is no wonder that scholars of Zen in Japan and the West were led to believe that there existed no written records of the koans and their answers. The present book must have created a scandalous sensation when first published nearly sixty years ago. Why so few Japanese scholars and, it seems, not even a single Western scholar knew about this publication remains a mystery.[2] Ruth F. Sasaki writes, "Neither Hakuin nor his disciples compiled any collection of koans, at least none that were ever published.[3] It seems that the silence of Japanese scholars and students concerning the existence of this publication was, in effect, a clever method of dealing with the scandal, much more effective than the destruction of the book.

The lack of sources for the answers to the koans has created a serious handicap for researchers on Zen. In Japan, very few Zen masters work on the translation of the koans into modern Japanese; but even those who do, being bound by their vow to reveal the answers only in "dokusan" (the private meeting between novice and master), are extremely reluctant to refer even to the "meaning" of koans, not to speak of their answers. Thus scholars who are

[1] I. Miura and R.F. Sasaki, *The Zen Koan* (Kyoto: First Zen Institute of America, 1965), p. 28.
[2] After these words were written, I found a reference to the book in P.B. Yampolsky, *The Zen Master Hakuin* (New York: Columbia University Press, 1971), p. 13n.
[3] Miura and Sasaki, *The Zen Koan*, p. 28.

forced to rely on no more than the Chinese version of the koan have to speculate on the meaning of phrases and expressions which could be clarified if they knew the "official" answer to the koan, or at least the way the koan was presented and commented upon by the Zen master in private meetings.

Zen research in the West suffers from the same handicap. Because none of the translators knew the answers to the koans, they had to rely upon their own intuitions as to their meanings or on the mood or usage of the particular koan in the context of Zen teaching. As a result, many of the translations, though linguistically possible, have often missed the essential point of a koan. I suspect that even D.T. Suzuki, who introduced Zen to the West a few decades ago, did not know the answers to the koans. His presentation of the doctrine of Zen, its history, and its affinity with other Buddhist schools of thought is scholarly and reliable. However, Zen masters generally agree that his comments on koans are impressionistic and in many cases excessively "Western." When Zen began to attract the attention of intellectuals outside Japan, many Westerners took to writing on Zen. Some of these writers, endowed with poetic sensitivity, have given insight into the meaning of some koans. However, comments such as theirs cannot generally convey the rooted attitudes of Zen tradition.

My decision, then, to translate and publish this book was above all motivated by my firm conviction that it would introduce to the Western world the clearest, most detailed, and most correct picture of Zen. In trying to make the translation as clear as possible to the Western reader, I have refrained whenever possible from using terms that would not be understood by a reader with a limited knowledge of Buddhism. Where Buddhist terms were unavoidable, I provided their explanation either in the text itself or in notes. The notes I have added to the koans deal mainly with the philosophical background and the psychological relations between the persons who appear in the koan in question. The notes to the answers are designed, above all, to explain the reasons for the pupil's specific response.

For those interested in further research into the koans, I have provided a list of the Chinese sources to the koans of Part Three. As for the discourse on the two koans of Part One, a great part of the koans of Part Two, and the answers to the koans of Part Three, there is, to the best of my knowledge, no source other than the Japanese edition of this book.

# The Japanese Edition and Its Author

The translation presented here includes the main part of the Japanese edition. It includes, that is, the complete body of "Hakuin-Zen"—two hundred and eighty-one koans and their answers according to the traditional order of the koan teaching system. The Japanese edition also includes some one hundred additional koans which are used only rarely in Zen teaching; the Zen monastic law; and a doctrine concerning the five stages of enlightenment related in its structure to an ancient Chinese divination system. None of these is included in the present book.

The Japanese edition was entitled *Gendai Sōjizen Hyōron*. *Gendai* means "modern" or "present-day"; *sōji* means "resemblance" or "similarity"; and *hyōron* means "critique." The title as a whole may be translated "A Critique of Present-Day Pseudo-Zen." The author of the book wrote under a pseudonym to "protect" himself, as he says, and to avoid "unnecessary" quarrels. The pseudonym chosen by him was "Hauhōō." The character of "ha" means "break" or "destroy"; "u" means "existent"; "hō," "law" or "order"; and "ō," "king." The name as a whole may be translated as "The Arch-Destroyer of the Existent Order." It is not clear at what age the author published his book, but he could not possibly have been young, for the material he revealed on the various "schools" of Zen indicated that he had completed the whole course of training for the position of a Zen master at least once, and had repeated parts of the course under several masters before he published these "secret" notes. The author considered himself a "reformer" of Japanese Buddhism in general, and of the Rinzai Zen sect in particular. As his pseudonym suggests, his "reform" was meant to be primarily destructive.

The author considered contemporary Zen masters (those of the end of the Meiji and the beginning of the Taishō era) and most of their followers to be fakes, and he declared himself determined to reveal their "true face." He added that it was useless to look for enlightenment among the Zen masters for they were nothing but "envoys of the devil clad in a monk's robe." He declared that his real masters were the Chinese Zen masters of the past, such as Rinzai, Chūhō, Bassui, and Takusui. In this way, he was suggesting that he accepted the Chinese koans as "Zen teaching" but rejected both the Japanese koans and the answers to the Chinese koans composed by Hakuin and his disciples. In his attacks on masters and novices of his time, the author avoided revealing their real names. He justified this restraint by his desire to prevent sensationalism, but it is clear he wished to hide his own identity.

The author declared that his aim in revealing the secrets of Zen was to destroy the position of the "masters" of his time. From now on, he said, anyone who read this book would know no less that the Zen masters—that is, he would be able to speak and act "Zen." Therefore, *anyone* could become a Zen master. The author also presented his own viewpoint on questions of Buddhist doctrine: generally speaking, he believed that the essence of Buddhist teaching is "deliverance from the cycle of life and death" and "insight into one's true nature." He thought that the koan system of "Hakuin-Zen," as revealed in this book and as employed by Zen masters, did not satisfactorily describe the essence of Buddhism.

From the author's approach to religion, his style, and the mood of his writing, it is quite obvious that whatever the state of institutionalized Zen in his time may have been, he was by his nature not suited for the world of Zen. He must have been the uncompromising, puritanical kind of reformer. He apparently could not find much in common with his masters and fellow novices, and seemed to have moved from one master to another in search for a "real" master. Disappointed and bitter, he finally gave it all up and devoted himself to an all-out attack on what he calls "pseudo-Zen."

There is, however, much truth in the author's criticism that some of the koans and quite a few of the answers are stereotyped and artificial. Many of the answers also seem to be missing the point of the koan. It seems fair to assume that the worst part of the traditional system of "Hakuin-Zen" was not composed by Master Hakuin himself but by some of his less-gifted disciples. It can only be hoped that the Zen masters of our time have enough insight to distinguish between what is old and good, and what is simply old.

I am deeply grateful to Zen Master Hirano Sōjō, who unsparingly gave his time, went over the Japanese edition with me, and offered invaluable suggestions as to the meaning of the koans. This book could not have been completed without his generous help.

I acknowledge my indebtedness to Mr. Leung Hau Yeong, Mr. Iwamoto Mitsuyoshi, and Miss Carol Chinaka for their help in preparing the translation. Especially deep thanks are due to Carol for her devoted work.

Had I not been blessed throughout the years with the guidance of a true teacher and thinker, I could never have written this work. I owe more than can be expressed in words to Professor Ben-Ami Scharfstein.

YOEL HOFFMANN

# PART ONE

# THE KOAN ON THE SOUND
# OF THE ONE HAND
# AND THE KOAN ON MU

# THE KOAN ON THE SOUND
# OF THE ONE HAND
# AND THE KOAN ON MU

## I

## The Way of the Inzan School

A.   *The Koan on the Sound of the One Hand*

In clapping both hands a sound is heard; what is the sound of the one hand?

### ANSWER

The pupil faces his master, takes a correct posture, and without a word, thrusts one hand forward.

## DISCOURSE

1                        MASTER

If you've heard the sound of the one hand, prove it.

### ANSWER

Without a word, the pupil thrusts one hand forward.

2                        MASTER

It's said that if one hears the sound of the one hand, one becomes a Buddha [i.e., becomes enlightened]. Well then, how will you do it?

### ANSWER

Without a word, the pupil thrusts one hand forward.

3                    MASTER
After you've become ashes, how will you hear it?


                     ANSWER
Without a word, the pupil thrusts one hand forward.


4                    MASTER
What if the one hand is cut by the Suimo Sword?


                     ANSWER
"It can't be."
*Or:*
"If it can, let me see you do it." So saying, the pupil extends his
hand forward.
*Or:*
Without a word, the pupil thrusts one hand forward.


5                    MASTER
Why can't it cut the one hand?


                     ANSWER
"Because the one hand pervades the universe."


6                    MASTER
Then show me something that contains the universe.


                     ANSWER
Without a word, the pupil thrusts one hand forward.


7                    MASTER
The before-birth-one-hand, what is it like?


                     ANSWER
Without a word, the pupil thrusts one hand forward.


8                    MASTER
The Mt.-Fuji-summit-one-hand, what is it like?


                     ANSWER
The pupil, shading his eyes with one hand, takes the pose of
looking down from the summit of Mt. Fuji and says, "What a

splendid view!" naming several places to be seen from Mt. Fuji—or others would name places visible from where they happen to be.

9                                   MASTER
Attach a quote to the-Mt.-Fuji-summit-one-hand.


                                    ANSWER
*(Quote)*
            Floating clouds connected the sea and the
                    mountain,
            And white flat plains spread into the states of
                    Sei and Jo.


10                                  MASTER
Did you hear the sound of the one hand from the back or from the front?


                                    ANSWER
Extending one hand, the pupil repeatedly says, "Whether it's from the front or from the back, you can hear it as you please." *Or:*
"From the back it's caw! caw! [the sound of a crow]. From the front it's chirp, chirp [the sound of a sparrow]."


11                                  MASTER
Now that you've heard the sound of the one hand, what are you going to do?


                                    ANSWER
"I'll pull weeds, scrub the floor, and if you're tired, give you a massage."


12                                  MASTER
If it's that convenient a thing, let me hear it too!


                                    ANSWER
Without a word, the pupil slaps his master's face.


13                                  MASTER
The one hand—how far will it reach?

The pupil places his hand on the floor and says, "This is how far it goes."

14                          MASTER
The before-the-fifteenth-day-one-hand, the after-the-fifteenth-day-one-hand, the fifteenth-day-one-hand, what's it like?

ANSWER
The pupil extends his right hand and says, "This is the before-the-fifteenth-day-one-hand." Extending his left hand he says, "This is the after-the-fifteenth-day-one-hand." Bringing his hands together he says, "This is the fifteenth-day-one-hand."

15                          MASTER
The sublime-sound-of-the-one-hand, what is it like?

ANSWER
The pupil immediately imitates the sound he happens to hear when sitting in front of his master. That is, if it happens to be raining outside, he imitates the sound of rain, "Pitter-patter"; if at that moment a bird happens to call, he says, "Caw! Caw!" imitating the bird's call.

16                          MASTER
The soundless-voice-of-the-one-hand, what is it like?

ANSWER
Without a word, the pupil abruptly stands up, then sits down again, bowing in front of his master.

17                          MASTER
The true-[mental]-sphere-of-the-one-hand, what's it like?

ANSWER
"I take it to be as fleeting as a dream or phantom, or as something like an illusory flower. That's how I think of it."

18                          MASTER
The source-of-the-one-hand, what is it?

ANSWER

"On the plain there is not the slightest breeze that stirs the smallest grain of sand."
(*Quote*)

> All communication with places north of the
> White Wolf River is disconnected,
> And south to the Red Phoenix City,
> autumn nights have grown so long.

*Or:*

"It is from the place where there is not even one rabbit's hair that I have struck the sound of the one hand."
(*Quote*)

> The wind blows and clears the sky of all
> floating clouds,
> And the moon rises above those green hills
> like a piece of round white jade.

*Or:*

> Arriving at the river, the territories of the
> state of Go seem to come to an end,
> Yet on the other bank, the mountains of the
> state of Etsu look so far away.

## B.   *The Koan on Mu*

A monk asked Master Jōshū, "Does a dog have Buddha-nature?" Jōshū said, "Mu" [i.e., "no," "non-existence," or "no-thing"].

ANSWER

Sitting erect in front of his master, the pupil yells, "Mu——!" with all his might.

### DISCOURSE

1                               MASTER

Well then, bring forth the proof of this "mu."

ANSWER

Sitting erect in front of his master, the pupil yells, "Mu——!" with all his might.

2                               MASTER

If so, in what way will you become a Buddha [i.e., be enlightened]?

(51)

ANSWER

Sitting erect in front of his master, the pupil yells, "Mu——!"
with all his might.


3                       MASTER

Well then, this "mu"—after you've become ashes, how do you
see it?

ANSWER

Sitting erect in front of his master, the pupil yells, "Mu——!"
with all his might.


4                       MASTER

Jōshū, on another occasion, when asked whether a dog has
Buddha-nature or not, responded in the affirmative [i.e., "yes"
or "there is"]. What do you think of that?

ANSWER

"Even if Jōshū says there is Buddha-nature in a dog, I'll simply
yell 'Mu—— !' with all my might."


5                       MASTER

If I say that a dog does not have Buddha-nature because of his
karma [non-enlightened state], how about that?

ANSWER

The pupil yells, "Mu—— !" with all his might.


6                       MASTER

When Jōshū was asked why he responded in the affirmative, he
answered, "Knowing yet trespassing." How about that?

ANSWER

Sitting erect in front of his master, the pupil yells, "Mu—— !"
with all his might.


7                       MASTER

Master Mumon recited "mu" twenty times. You do it in one
breath.

ANSWER

The host and I do not know one another.

(*Quote*)

> I sit here for a moment because of the trees
>    and spring.
> Please do not worry yourself wantonly about
>    buying wine.
> Money will be there in your pocket all right.

[The above Chinese quote is composed of twenty characters. It is in the sum of characters that the Master's question is answered. Therefore, any quote consisting of twenty characters or syllables, or even, as some monks respond, the plain recitation of the first twenty letters of the alphabet will do.]

8                              MASTER

The essence of "mu"—what's it like?

                               ANSWER

Without a word, the pupil places both hands on his chest and stands up.

9                              MASTER

The working of "mu"—what's it like?

                               ANSWER

The pupil stands up and, swinging his arms back and forth, walks five or six steps saying, "When it's necessary to go, go." Sitting down again he says, "When it's necessary to sit, sit."

10                             MASTER

Explain the difference between the "mu" state and the ignorance [or karma] state.

                               ANSWER

The pupil describes the course one takes four to eight miles to and from his place of meditation. For example, if he meditates in Ueno [a place in Tokyo] he may say, "From here [Ueno] I went out to Hirokoji Street, got on a streetcar which passed the stops of Sudachō, Kyōbashi, Nihonbashi, Shinbashi, and got off at Shinagawa. After completing my business, I again got on the streetcar at Shinagawa and returned the same way."

11                             MASTER

Attach a quote to that.

*(Quote)*

> It has just gone away with the fragrant
>    grasses,
> Yet returns again chasing after the falling
>    flowers.

*Or:*

> I entered the East Gate living quarters in the
>    morning,
> And went up to the Kayō Bridge in the
>    evening.


12                          MASTER

The source of "mu"—what's it like?


ANSWER

"From    there-is-not-the-slightest-breeze-that-stirs-the-smallest-grain-of-sand-vast-plain, the sky, the earth, mountains, rivers all come into view."

*Or:*

"There is no sky, no earth, nor mountains nor rivers, no trees, no plants. There is nothing—neither I nor any other. Even these, my words, are no-thing ['mu']."


# II

# The Way of the Takujū School

A.    *The Koan on the Sound of the One Hand*

> There is no sound to the one hand—
> Come hear this soundless voice.


ANSWER

In some cases the response is identical to that of the Inzan School: the pupil faces his master, takes a correct posture, and without a word thrusts one hand forward.

   However, with certain Zen masters, the pupil may also reply

using words similar to the following: "The sky is the one hand, the earth is the one hand; man, woman, you, me are the one hand; grass, trees, cows, horses are the one hand; everything, all things are the one hand."

## DISCOURSE

1                                    MASTER
If you've heard the soundless voice of the one hand, prove it.

2                                    MASTER
If you've heard the sound of the one hand, can you be absolutely delivered from life and death, or can't you?

ANSWER
To questions (1) and (2) the pupil, without a word, thrusts one hand forward.

3                                    MASTER
What if the one hand is cut by the Suimo Sword?

ANSWER
"Try it—no matter how hard one tries, it couldn't be cut. The sword's no match for the one hand."

4                                    MASTER
The essence of the one hand—in what way does it exist?

ANSWER
"It pervades all—extending from the top of Mt. Shumi [a legendary mountain signifying the top of the universe] down to the bottom of the lowest layer of hell."

5                                    MASTER
What is the shape of the one hand?

ANSWER
The pupil places both hands on his chest and stands up.

6                                    MASTER
What if the one hand is burnt?

ANSWER

"Even if you burn it, it won't be burnt."


7                            MASTER

What is the-Mt.-Fuji-summit-one-hand like?


ANSWER

(Identical with that of the Inzan School)

Shading his eyes with one hand, the pupil takes the pose of looking down from the summit of Mt. Fuji and says, "What a splendid view!," naming several places to be seen from Mt. Fuji—or others would name places visible from where they happen to be. (*Quote*)

> Arriving at the river, the territories of the
> state of Go seem to come to an end,
> Yet on the other bank, many are the hills
> in the state of Etsu.


8                            MASTER

Now that you've heard the sound of the one hand, of what use is it?


ANSWER

"Get up in the morning, wash your face, read your prayer, take your bowl to the dining room, eat your rice porridge, perform your evening duties. . . . " In this way, the pupil enumerates the daily routine.
*Or:*
"Light the charcoal brazier, boil water in the kettle, rub the ink stick, light the incense."


9                            MASTER

Grind the one hand into powder and swallow it.


ANSWER

"Red pepper is powder and is to be eaten; noodles made from powder one eats."


10                           MASTER

Did you hear the one hand in Kyoto or did you hear it in Harima [a district in the Hyogo Prefecture]?

"In Kyoto, at Gion, Maruyama, Kinkakuji [places in Kyoto].
In Harima at Suma, Maiko, and Awashi [places in Harima]."

11            MASTER
The lifting of the one hand—say something about it.

ANSWER

"Any garbage for pickup? Beans, bean curd for sale!" So saying,
the pupil imitates the ways of traveling peddlers.

12            MASTER
Burn the one hand, gather the ashes into a fist and bring it here.

ANSWER

"You think one can do such a stupid thing?!" With that the
pupil slaps the face of his master.

13            MASTER
If you've heard the sound of the one hand, let me hear it too.

ANSWER

Again the pupil slaps the face of his master.

14            MASTER
The source-of-the-one-hand, what's it like?

ANSWER

"Don't be stupid—there's no such thing! Nyaaa!" [He makes a
face]. With that the pupil stands up as if to leave.

15            MASTER
Did you hear the one hand from the back or from the front?

ANSWER

"From the back as well as from the front. During the first fifteen
days of the month, I heard it from the front; the latter fifteen days,
from the back."
Or:
"On the road in front, a man, a cart go by; at the back road, the
sparrow calls chirp, chirp, the crow calls caw!"

16                          MASTER
The-Zen-monk-one-hand, what's it like?


ANSWER
"To eat meat, to take a wife is absolutely forbidden."


17                          MASTER
When every possible effort is made, every means exhausted, the
absolute, decisive one hand—how is it?


ANSWER
Concentrating all his energy, his eyes sharp as though burning
with anger, the pupil thrusts one hand forward.


18                          MASTER
Encompassing the whole of the one-hand koan, recite a quotation.


ANSWER
*(Quote)*

> The white plain is desolate under the
>     autumn sky,
> But someone is coming east on horseback.
> Do you know who he is?


## B.   *The Koan on Mu*

A monk asked Master Jōshū, "Does a dog have Buddha-nature?"
Jōshū said, "Mu" [i.e., "no," "non-existence," or "no-thing"].


ANSWER
Sitting erect in front of his master, the pupil yells, "Mu——!"
with all his might.
This answer is identical with that of the Inzan School.


## *DISCOURSE*
I                           MASTER
When you don't say "mu," what do you say?


ANSWER
The pupil yells, "U——!" [opposite of "mu," meaning "is" or
"existence"].

(58)

2                 MASTER

Distinguish between "mu" and "u."

ANSWER

The pupil separately yells, "Mu——!" "U——!"

3                 MASTER

How far away is "mu" from "u"?

ANSWER

From where he sits in the room, the pupil points to objects [for instance, the threshold or door] and says, "From here to the threshold is so-and-so-many feet; up to that door it's so-and-so-many feet."

4                 MASTER

The whole of "mu," how far does it reach?

ANSWER

The pupil stands up and with one hand pointing towards the sky says, "It extends from the summit of Mt. Shumi" [the top of the universe]. Then, stamping his foot once, he points to the ground with the other hand continuing, "And down to the bottom of the lowest layer in hell."

5                 MASTER

Hand "mu" over to me.

ANSWER

The pupil takes whatever object is on hand and hands it over to his master.

6                 MASTER

Let me see you use "mu" with ease.

ANSWER

"Jakenpo," the pupil says, with his hands making the forms of scissors–stone–paper [a Japanese children's game].
*Or:*
"One, two, three, four . . . " bending his fingers, the pupil counts to ten.

7                           MASTER
Cut "mu" into dice form and bring it to me.


                            ANSWER
"Please have some yakkodōfu" [bean curd cut in cubes and served
with soy sauce], the pupil says and makes a gesture of offering it
to his master.


8                           MASTER
Put "mu" through a strainer and bring me the strained "mu."


                            ANSWER
The pupil says, "Please have some wheat flour" and makes a
gesture of offering it to his master.


9                           MASTER
Tell me how tall "mu" is.


                            ANSWER
The pupil gives his own height.


10                          MASTER
What form of figure does "mu" take?


                            ANSWER
The pupil places both hands on his chest and stands up.


11                          MASTER
What does "mu" look like from the back?


                            ANSWER
With both hands still on his chest, the pupil turns around and
turns his back to his master.


12                          MASTER
The measurements for "mu," about how many inches is it?


                            ANSWER
"The cuff length is such–and–such inches, the full length is such–
and–such inches." Thus the pupil enumerates the measurements of
the gown which he is wearing.

**13**  **MASTER**

Make the "mu" walk seven steps in a circle.

**ANSWER**

The pupil walks one circle around the room.


**14**  **MASTER**

The "mu" of this fan (which I am holding now)—first know it well, then let me see you use it.

**ANSWER**

The pupil takes the fan which the master extended to him and examining it carefully, appreciates it saying, "What a beautiful fan this is! The frame is made of bamboo, the calligraphy in front is so-and-so, the design in the back is so-and-so, etc." Then without further ado he casually fans himself.


**15**  **MASTER**

Say the "mu" clearly enough that even a child can understand and then put it into practice.

**ANSWER**

The pupil says, "Yoshi, yoshi," as if nursing a child.


**16**  **MASTER**

Now that you've seen "mu," what will you do?

**ANSWER**

"Get up in the morning, wash my face, clean up, eat . . . ." Thus the pupil enumerates the daily routine.
*Or:*
In accordance with the tradition of other Zen masters, the following may also be said: "Being the master of the house, being the servant; being a welder, a carpenter, a plasterer; being a fish peddler, etc." Thus the pupil enumerates and imitates the various occupations of people.


**17**  **MASTER**

If you've seen "mu," fill the "mu-mind" [or the "mindless-mind"] in a bottomless bowl and bring it here.

The pupil spreads out his arms and recites, "A bottomless bowl";
next, using both hands as if forming some concrete object, he
recites, "Mu-mind." On top of that, as if raising a huge bowl
high into the air, he recites, "Fill it and bring it."

18                        MASTER
In an unhampered and free manner, distinguish "mu" and use it.

ANSWER
The pupil imitates the behavior and actions of various occupations
such as a carpenter, a plasterer, a fencing teacher.
*Or:*
The pupil says, "Use 'mu' in an unhampered and free manner"
and answers, "Getting up, sitting down, lying, walking . . ."
accompanying his words with gestures.

19                        MASTER
In the selling of common, everyday articles, distinguish "u"
["is," "being"] from "mu" ["no," "no-thing"].

ANSWER
"One yard of this cloth costs so-and-so, half a yard will be so-
and-so."
*(Quote)*

> The same tree bathed by the spring wind has
>     two different states:
> The southern branches facing warmth, the
>     northern ones facing cold.

*Popular Saying*
The sprawling clusters of calabash originate in one stem.

20                        MASTER
Capture "mu" and show it forth.

ANSWER
The pupil takes hold of any object lying about him and extends
it toward his master.

21                        MASTER
*(Quote)*
Master Daie said, "Jōshū said 'mu' like this." (How about that?)

ANSWER

The pupil energetically yells "Mu——!"

22                                       MASTER
(Quote)
The ancients said, "What if the monk had never asked about Buddha-nature and Jōshū had never answered 'mu'?" (How about that?)

ANSWER

The pupil energetically yells "Mu——!"

23                                       MASTER
(Quote)
The song on "mu," written by Zen master Ryōfu, says:
>     "Jōshū's dog has no Buddha-nature,
>     Ten thousand green mountains are hidden in
>         an ancient mirror,
>     The one-footed Persian goes into China,
>     And the eight-armed Nata carries out
>         administrative orders."

How about this?

ANSWER

a. The pupil says loudly, "Jōshū's dog has no Buddha-nature" and then yells, "Mu——!"
b. While surveying his surroundings, the pupil recites, "Ten thousand green mountains are hidden in an ancient mirror." With that he drops his head and steadily stares at his chest.
c. The pupil imitates a weary traveler coming from far away, walking with a cane and sighing, "Ahh, it hurts, it hurts."
Or:
Limping, he walks around the room. "You bloody bastard! How dare you not obey my command!" With that the pupil hits his master's back.
Or:
First the pupil says, "Mu." Then, making a fist, he punches the base of his master's skull. In this case, the master says, "Explain!" and the pupil answers, "This is called the-hit-on-the-base-of-the-skull."

24                                       MASTER
The eight "mu's" of Master Chūhō. (What about that?)

"When eating a meal, 'mu'; when drinking tea, 'mu'; when sleeping, 'mu'; when getting up, 'mu' . . . ." The pupil continues enumerating eight actions, reciting "mu" after each one.

*Or:*

"When eating a meal, when drinking tea, when sleeping, when getting up, when walking, when sitting, when cold, when warm, when farting, when shitting, when a bird cries, when a dog barks— mu, mu, mu," and on and on the pupil continues until his master says, "That's enough!"

25                                                    MASTER

The twenty "mu's" of Master Mumon—recite in a quote.


ANSWER

*(Quote)*

> My heart is like the autumn moon and the
> blue lake clear and bright,
> Nothing affords a comparison, how can you
> make me explain?

[This quote is composed of twenty characters. Any quote consisting of twenty characters or syllables may be recited.]

26                                                    MASTER

In a way that even a child can understand, recite it (the twenty "mu's" of Master Mumon).


ANSWER

"A B, C, D, E, F, G, H, I, J, K, L, M, N, O, P, Q, R, S, T."


27                                                    MASTER

What is the distinction between "u" and "mu"?


ANSWER

"Well, if you're 'u,' then I'm 'mu.'"


28                                                    MASTER

What's the distance between "u" and "mu"?


ANSWER

"If the threshold is 'u,' then the pillar is 'mu'; if the ceiling is 'u,' then the floor is 'mu.'"

29                     **MASTER**

It is said that in Zen we do not rely upon words for enlightenment, nor do we instruct the way through the written letter. Well, without the use of letters—ultimately, HOW IS IT?!

**ANSWER**

"The threshold lies flat."

30                     **MASTER**

Well then, using letters, ultimately, HOW IS IT?!

**ANSWER**

"The pillar stands erect."

31                     **MASTER**

Rush into this leather bag.

**ANSWER**

"Each and every god, Buddha, Dharma, Confucius, Mencius are all in this stomach." So saying, the pupil pats his belly.

32                     **MASTER**

The source of "mu"—what's it like?

**ANSWER**

"Don't be stupid! There's no such thing! Why don't you go wash your face," he snickers. "Nyaa!" [Any gesture of ridicule.] With that the pupil stands up and leaves, slamming the door shut. (*Quote*)

> The cold nocturnal hours came to an end
>     while I was listening to the rain,
> I opened the door and found that fallen
>     leaves were plentiful.

*Or:*

> The bottom of the sea can finally be seen
>     when it dries,
> But a man's heart can never be known even
>     till he dies.

*Or:*

> Clouds stood still after the rain, and the day
>     had just begun to dawn.

The few peaks looked picturesque with their
green height and massiveness.


33                                    MASTER
The "mu" of karma [non-enlightened state of mind]—go and see
what it's like.

                                   ANSWER
With a grave, heavy voice, the pupil recites, "Karma, karma . . . ."


34                                    MASTER
Let's see you say it [i.e., "karma"] in simpler words.

                                   ANSWER
"How hateful; how charming, I don't want to lose it; I wish it
were mine. . . . "


35                                    MASTER
Separate non-enlightenment [karma] into two.

                                   ANSWER
"U." "Mu."


36                                    MASTER
Master Jōshū (on another occasion, when asked whether a dog
has Buddha-nature or not) said, "U ['is,' 'being']." How about
that?
                                   ANSWER
"U."


37                                    MASTER
Let me see you say "u" in simpler words.

                                   ANSWER
"Thinking of that which is not a man, as man; of that which is not
a woman, as woman; of that which is not a mountain, river, or
flower, as mountain, river, flower—this is 'u.'"


38                                    MASTER
Now, there's the state of consciousness of one's deeds [or of one's
karma—such as realizing something is wrong yet still doing
it]. What do you think of that?

"Standing on the border of life and death with complete freedom;
facing heaven and hell and all forms of life with a playful mind,
stable, unshakable. This being so, should I become a cat or a dog,
it wouldn't make the slightest difference—I couldn't care less."
*Or:*
[The pupil says something like] "Cold is white, snow is black."


39                                    MASTER
Taking the whole of [the koan on] "mu," say a quote.


                              ANSWER
*(Quote)*
          The clouds obscured the three thousand miles
                of the Kenkaku mountain range,
          And water separated the twelve peaks
                of the Kutō gorge.


40                                    MASTER
Show me proof that you have understood [the koan on] "mu."


                              ANSWER
The pupil yells, "Mu——!" with all his might.


41                                    MASTER
If you've understood "mu," can you be absolutely delivered
from life and death?


                              ANSWER
The pupil yells, "Mu——!" with all his might.


42                                    MASTER
Burning "mu," it becomes ashes; bury it, it becomes earth—
what do you think of that?


                              ANSWER
The pupil yells, "Mu——!" with all his might.

# PART TWO

# MISCELLANEOUS KOANS

# MISCELLANEOUS KOANS

1                                    MASTER

The original face—the face before you were brought into this world by your mother and father—what is it?

ANSWER

Placing both hands on his chest, the pupil stands up.

2                                    MASTER
*(Quote)*
It is questioned, "What is the body of truth [Dharma-body]?" It is answered, "A metal ship floating on water." (What of it?)

ANSWER

Placing both hands on his chest, the pupil stands up.

3                                    MASTER
*(Quote)*
When someone asks you in a dream about the purpose of our founder coming from the west, how will you answer? If you can't answer this, then the truth of Buddhism will have no effect on you.

ANSWER

The pupil snores, "Zzz . . . zzz," imitating one soundly asleep. *Or:*
With certain masters, should the pupil respond as above, they immediately demand, "You think this answers it?" If the pupil answers, the master fails him. If, without a word, the pupil continues the pretense of sleeping soundly, the master passes him.

MASTER

Give a popular [Japanese] saying for that.

*(Quote)*

> In this world, there is nothing more carefree
> than sleep,
> But the dumb folk of this floating world
> get up and work.

MASTER

Give a [Chinese] quote for that.

ANSWER

*(Quote)*

> I slept so soundly that I did not know the
> mountain rain had stopped.
> Waking up, I felt the whole house airy
> and cool.

4                              MASTER

A man walks straight. How will you walk straight through the forty-nine curves of the narrow mountain road?

ANSWER

Twisting and turning, the pupil winds about the room as if walking a narrow mountain road.

5                              MASTER

It is said, "To pick up a stone from the bottom of the deep Ise Sea without even wetting your sleeve." How do you understand this?

ANSWER

The pupil pretends to jump into the ocean and bring up a big stone.

6                              MASTER

What is this stone called?

ANSWER

The pupil gives his own name.

7                              MASTER

About how heavy is this stone?

The pupil gives his own weight.

8            MASTER

On the sea, a Chinese junk with its sails full is racing in the wind. Stop it!

ANSWER

Standing up, opening his arms wide, and freeing his kimono sleeves, the pupil imitates a sailboat racing on the sea.

9            MASTER

There's a rowboat—stop it.

ANSWER

Getting up and imitating the creaking of oars, the pupil pretends to row a boat.

10            MASTER

There's a quarrel going on across the river—stop it.

ANSWER

"What the hell is that bastard muttering about?! You bloody fool! I'll kick your sides in and slam this damn bottle into your guts!" So saying, the pupil grabs his master by the neck and with his face raging with anger, he pretends to fling his fist at his master.

11            MASTER

Stop the sound (or echo) of the bell.

ANSWER

"Gonggg——." The pupil imitates the lingering, resonant sound of the bell.

12            MASTER

What'll you do if four different sounds come at once?

ANSWER

"Boom, boom [sound of a drum]; strum, strum [sound of a

stringed instrument]; jingle, jingle [sound of a bell]; tweet, tweet [sound of a whistle]."
*Or:*
"Boom, strum, jingle, tweet," the pupil combines the sounds.


13                                MASTER
Extinguish the light that lies a thousand miles away.


                                 ANSWER
"The lamp is lit in the other room but with no one there, it's dangerous and a waste of fuel so I'll go and blow it out . . . whoosh!" So saying, the pupil pretends to blow out a lamp.
*Or:*
With the tips of his fingers, the pupil makes the form of a rising flame. Then, saying "Whoosh," he blows it out.


14                                MASTER
From the second drawer of the medicine case draw out Mt. Tate [the highest mountain in the Hokuriku district].


                                 ANSWER
"Master, if your stomach hurts let me give you some mankintan [an old-fashioned restorative medicine]."


                                   OR
                                MASTER
From the first drawer of the medicine case draw out Mt. Fuji; from the second drawer, Mt. Haku [in the Ishikawa prefecture]; from the third drawer, Mt. So-and-so.


                                 ANSWER
"Let me give you some seishintan, seikaigan, hōtan [names of old-fashioned Oriental medicines]."


15                                MASTER
Without using your hands, make me stand.


                                 ANSWER
The pupil stands up and walks two or three steps.

**(74)**

OR

MASTER

Without using your hands, make this old monk [i.e., me] get up.

ANSWER

"Ahhh." With a heavy sigh, the pupil imitates an old man getting up.

16                    MASTER

Walk Mt. Fuji in three steps.

ANSWER

The pupil stands up and takes three steps.

17                    MASTER

Make the Tōji [a temple in Kyoto] Pagoda stand in a teapot.

ANSWER

The pupil stands erect.

18                    MASTER

In the middle of a duck egg, grind the tea mill.

ANSWER

The pupil walks in a circle around the room.

19                    MASTER

What's the age of Monju [a legendary Buddha representing wisdom]?

ANSWER

"This year it's so-and-so (giving his own age), the exact age of Amida [the Buddha of the Western Paradise sect]."

MASTER

How old is Amida Buddha?

ANSWER

"As old as I am."

20                    MASTER

Say the Five Moral Principles and the Five Cardinal Virtues [of Confucianism] in one breath.

ANSWER

"It's a nice day today!"

21                              MASTER
How high is the sky?

ANSWER

Pointing toward the ceiling, the pupil says, "From here it's seven feet."

22                              MASTER
Let me see you enter this stick [referring to the flat rod used by Zen masters when hitting novices].

ANSWER

The pupil hides the stick in his bosom.

23                              MASTER
Rush into this pillar!

ANSWER

The pupil rams his whole body against the pillar.
*Popular Saying*
Leave me but it's not the end; I'll stick a five-inch nail into a straw doll and curse you to hell.

24                              MASTER
Let me see you take out the Tennoji [a temple in Ōsaka] Pagoda from a teapot.

ANSWER

"If Your Reverence is thirsty, let me offer you some tea."

25                              MASTER
Why do birds shit on Buddha's head?

ANSWER

"What the hell! Some damned bird shit on my head!" Saying this, the pupil makes the pretense of shaking it off his head.

26               MASTER
*(Quote)*
The wooden cock crows, midnight.


ANSWER

"Cock-a-doodle-doo" [the pupil crows like a rooster].


27               MASTER
*(Quote)*
The straw dog barks, daybreak.


ANSWER

"Bow-wow" [the pupil barks like a dog].


28               MASTER
*(Quote)*
Drink up all the water of the Seikō River [a river in China]
in one gulp.


ANSWER

The pupil pretends to swallow the five continents in one gulp.


29               MASTER
*(Quote)*
The peonies of the city of Rakuyō [a Chinese city] have just
come to blossom.


ANSWER

"The peonies growing in the garden have indeed blossomed
beautifully."


30               MASTER
*(Quote)*
I arrived at the Western Heaven [India] in the morning, and even-
ing saw me returning to the Eastern Earth [China].


ANSWER

While repeating the above quote, the pupil walks around the room.

31                 MASTER
*(Quote)*

Hit a piece of wood and you hear no sound. Knock the empty air and there comes a noise.


ANSWER

While saying, "Hit a piece of wood and you hear no sound," the pupil hits the floor. Continuing, "Knock the empty air and there comes a noise," he strikes the air.
*Or:*
In either case the pupil hits the floor.


32                 MASTER
*(Quote)*

Hold the spade empty-handedly.


ANSWER

The pupil pretends to take a spade and dig the earth.


33                 MASTER
*(Quote)*

Ride a buffalo while walking.


ANSWER

Rolling up his trousers, the pupil pretends to cross the river.
*Or:*
Getting on all fours, the pupil pretends to be a buffalo.
*Or:*
Jumping on his master's back the pupil says, "Giddy-up!" slapping the master's rear end.


34                 MASTER
*(Quote)*

A man walked past on a bridge.


ANSWER

Crossing his arms and saying, "Clack, clack" [sound of wooden sandals], the pupil assumes the pose of walking across a stone bridge.

**35**    MASTER
*(Quote)*
The bridge flows on while the water does not.

ANSWER
Placing both hands on the floor, the pupil bends his body into a bridge. Then, rolling over, he pretends to be a running river.
*Or:*
Taking his kimono sleeve and fluttering it in the air, he makes the form of waves.

**36**    MASTER
There's a story about the lady-in-waiting Kasuga who saved a spirit [from this world of suffering] by filling a teacup with water. Then, taking her hair ornaments, she laid them, one after another, on the rim of the cup. Now you, a Zen monk, how would you save it?

ANSWER
The pupil makes a terrifying face (imitating a revengeful spirit) saying, "I'll have my revenge! I'll have my revenge!"

OR
MASTER
(Simply saying)
Let me see you save a spirit.

ANSWER
Imitating a spirit pleading for salvation, the pupil brings together both hands begging, "Please! Save me!"

**37**    MASTER
Bind up space with a thick rope and bring it here.

ANSWER
The pupil takes any object within reach, pretends to tie it up, and hands it over.

**38**    MASTER
Make space into a vegetable salad and bring it here.

"This soup is made of turnip leaves. Please have some," the pupil says as he pretends to offer it to his master.

39                MASTER

Make space into powder and bring it here.

ANSWER

The pupil pretends to offer to his master buckwheat flour or any other type of food made from flour.

40                MASTER

Is Shōki the Devil-Queller a god [of Shinto] or a Buddha?

ANSWER

"Any dummy who asks such a question must be out of his mind!"

41                MASTER

In the Chinese character "dai" of the word Daijingu [Ise shrine] there is a dot. The striking of this dot [in brushwriting] is considered to be a secret mystery of Shinto. Well then, in the case of Buddhism, where [in what character] will you strike such a dot?

ANSWER

Standing up, the pupil points one finger to the sky, the other finger to the earth, and recites, "Between heaven and earth there is nothing nobler than I."

42                MASTER

In the painting of Buddha's entrance into nirvana, where is the inexpressible subtlety?

ANSWER

"If you, my master, were to pass away at this moment, alas! whom will I turn to as my teacher?" So saying, the pupil pretends to be dejected.

43                MASTER

The state of nirvana—what's it like?

ANSWER

Facing his head to the north and lying on his side, the pupil recreates the reclining state of Buddha entering nirvana [as depicted in the famous paintings].

MASTER

But the *real* state of nirvana—what's it like?

ANSWER

As above; however when the master places his hand over the pupil's mouth to see if he is breathing, the pupil must hold his breath for a while.

44 MASTER

In Tōfukuji [a temple in Kyoto], why is there a cat in the picture of Buddha entering nirvana?

ANSWER

"Why isn't there a mouse?"
*Or:*
"Why don't you have a wife?"

45 MASTER

From what direction does Amaterasu [the Sun Goddess of Shinto] proceed?

ANSWER

*(Quote)*
> There are no two suns in the universe,
>  And there is only one man between heaven
>   and earth.

46 MASTER

When the world was created, in what way did Kunitokutachi [a Shinto god—the founder of Japan] appear?

ANSWER

Placing both hands on his chest, the pupil stands up.

47 MASTER

Next, give birth to a mountain [as Kunitokutachi did].

ANSWER

Palms facing, hands tense and slightly spread apart, the pupil stands up and says, "This is one mountain."

48                          MASTER
Now give birth to a land.


                            ANSWER
Prostrating himself on the floor, the pupil says, "This is land so-and-so of great Japan," naming a part of Japan.


49                          MASTER
Recently I made a statue of Buddha. Where do you think it should be placed?


                            ANSWER
"Please have a cushion." So saying, the pupil pretends to welcome a guest.


50                          MASTER
It is said that when Master Kyō-ō left his mountain monastery, he received fire as a parting gift. How should it be taken?


                            ANSWER
"Please put it in here." So saying, the pupil opens wide his kimono sleeve [usually used to carry small objects].


51                          MASTER
The tea ladle which passes through the heat and cold of hell has no mind and therefore suffers not. This "has no mind and therefore suffers not" needs to be restated. How would you do it?


                            ANSWER
"If there's no mind, gobo-gobo [imitating the gurgling sound of boiling water]."


52                          MASTER
Where will you go after death?


                            ANSWER
"Excuse me for a minute, I have to go to the toilet."


53                          MASTER
(Quote)
On top of Mt. Godai the clouds are steaming rice.

"In the kitchen, they are cooking the noon rice."

54     MASTER
*(Quote)*
In front of the old Buddhist temple, a dog urinates towards the sky.

ANSWER
"A dog has pissed on the telephone pole."

55     MASTER
*(Quote)*
To try hammers on top of a ten-foot pole.

ANSWER
"They're cooking potatoes and turnips in the kitchen."

56     MASTER
*(Quote)*
Three monkeys tossed coins at night.

ANSWER
"On the road in front, the children are tossing coins and playing gambling games."

57     MASTER
*(Quote)*
The cow in the state of Kai eats the rice plants, but it is the stomach of the horse in the state of Eki that gets swollen.

ANSWER
"If only you eat, that's enough for me. It doesn't matter if I don't."

58     MASTER
*(Quote)*
Chōkō drank wine and Rikō got drunk.

ANSWER
"If only you eat, that's enough for me. It doesn't matter if I don't."

*(Quote)*
Last night the clay cows fought their way into the sea, and nothing has been heard about them till this hour of the night.

ANSWER

"Isn't that Seijuro over there? That sure looks like his umbrella."

60                                      MASTER
Master Suiō said to Master Tōrei, "Lately, wherever you go everybody is impudently saying, 'I've heard the sound of the one hand! I've heard the sound of the one hand!' But all these people, just what sound do they think they have heard?!" Now you monk, taking the place of Master Tōrei, how would you answer? Hurry up—say it! say it!

ANSWER

"Hmmph! Such troublesome things you talk about! Your mouth ought to be clamped shut with a horse bit." So saying, the pupil clamps his master's mouth with his hand.

61                                      MASTER
How many hairs do I have in my nose?

ANSWER

The pupil points his finger at the master's nose and counts, "One, two, three. . . . "

62                                      MASTER
The other day there were these two young monks cleaning up. One of them picked up a piece of broken tile, placed it on a rock, turned to the other, and said, "Say something!" The other monk remained silent. If it were you, what would you have said?

ANSWER

"What do you think you're saying?!" With that the pupil raises his foot and kicks his master's knee.

63                                      MASTER
The light's blown out—where did it go? The darkness is back in the room as before.

"The maid's washing clothes at the side of the well. The servant is pissing in the field."
*Or:*
The pupil may use one or several of the following answers [in response to the second half of the master's koan]:
"Let's dig up the burdock root from the back field."
"I'll ram my head into that pole."
"I slipped on a watermelon rind."
"To pull the cow out from the back shed."

64                    MASTER
Put the Great Buddha of Nara [a huge statue] on your back and bring it here.

ANSWER
While saying, "Well, I'll pack it on my back; I'm packing it," the pupil pretends to pack his master on his back.

65                    MASTER
The light of the night soil bucket [container of excreta], what is it? Say it quick! Say it!

ANSWER
"Ugh, it stinks! It stinks!" the pupil says, holding his nose.
*(Quote)*
The stupid and the wise send out light one after another.

66                    MASTER
There is a golden chime attached to the lion's neck—who can grab it?

ANSWER
"Excuse me," the pupil says, removing the upper covering of his master's gown.

67                    MASTER
All the Buddhas of past, present, and future—what do they now preach?

ANSWER
"Chirp, chirp [the sound of a sparrow]; caw, caw [the sound of a crow]; meow, meow [the cry of a cat]; bow-wow [the bark of a dog]."

68            MASTER

The main pillar of the house—what does it preach?

ANSWER

"The Zen master wakes up early in the morning and takes care
of his pupils. In an ordinary house, the father, from early morning,
raises his voice and looks after his family's affairs."

69            MASTER

Try entering this incense burner.

ANSWER

Discreetly, the pupil takes the incense with his fingers, thanks his
master and pretends to burn it.

70            MASTER

From where were you born and to where will you return?

ANSWER

"I just came from the temple hall and I'll return there again."

71            MASTER

It is said that big waters and small waters all return to the eastern
sea. The waters of the Sumida River [in Tokyo]—where will
they flow back to?

ANSWER

The pupil opens the front of his kimono and pretends to urinate.

72            MASTER

Take a bone from the body of the living Dharma [Bodhidharma—
the founder of Zen Buddhism].

ANSWER

The pupil pretends to take out ear wax from his ear and hands it
over to his master.

73            MASTER

If you're a Zen monk, try and say it with your mouth closed.

ANSWER

"Whether it can be said or not—you try it first." So saying, the
pupil covers his master's mouth.

74                         MASTER

There is the famous stone bridge of Mt. Tendai [in China, noted as a center of Buddhism]. Where would you start working on it?

ANSWER

The pupil takes his master's hand, stands up, and while saying, "Heave ho! Heave ho!" [the cry of encouragement workers use to keep time as they pull in unison], he drags his master.
*Popular Saying*
Once you've played with a geisha at Seki [a place in Japan], your wife looks like an old badger from over the hills.

75                         MASTER

In building the wooden gate of Asakusa Temple [in Tokyo], where does the ax first fall?

ANSWER

The pupil stands up saying, "Chop! Chop!" as he pretends to use an ax.

76                         MASTER

In the room a monster lies spread out on the floor, sleeping. If you were told, "There are some important documents on the shelf in that room, just go and get them for me," what would you do?

ANSWER

"Please forgive me," the pupil says, opening the door. "I'm terribly sorry to disturb your sleep and very much obliged to you, but please excuse me awhile," as he goes over to the shelf and takes the documents. Returning to the door he says, "Thank you most kindly. Have a good sleep."
*Or:*
The pupil may simply say, "Excuse me" as he pretends to walk around the pillow.

77                         MASTER

This fan—did it fall down from heaven or spring up from earth?

ANSWER

"I bought it at the shop of Haibara in Nihonbashi in Tokyo for twenty-five yen."

78          MASTER
How many hairs in the back of your head?


ANSWER
The pupil stands in back of his master and counts, "One hair, two hairs, three hairs. . . . "

79                    MASTER
What is the color of wind?


ANSWER
Taking his kimono, the pupil describes it, saying, "The front is black cotton cloth, the inside is lined in the color of rust."
*Popular Saying*
The young girl in the spring field picking herbs; the wind from the valley blowing her kimono hem.
*(Quote)*

> The pink cheeks and green brows of the ladies
>     complemented the round clouds of the
>     State of So.
> With peach blossoms blooming, someone in
>     a pomegranate dress was riding on horse-
>     back.

*Or:*

> The birds seemed whiter because of the green
>     river,
> And the flowers looked as if they were ready
>     to burst into flame in the verdant hills.

80                    MASTER
Where does rain come from?


ANSWER
Taking the sleeve of his robe and shaking it in the air, the pupil says, "Zaa——zaa——" [the sound of heavy rain], imitating the fall of rain.
*Or:*
Using his ten fingers, the pupil flutters them over his master's head in the form of falling rain.
*(Quote)*

> Clouds were patrolling along the waistline of
>     the hills,

> Thunder and a downpour are certain
> > tomorrow.

*Or:*

> The southern mountain became cloudy,
> And the northern mountain got rain.

*Or:*

"Pitter-patter," the pupil imitates the sound of rain.

*Or:*

With certain masters, the pupil may answer: "From the meditation hall, I came to the bell of summons [used to announce the entrance of the pupil into the master's room]; from there I entered into the consultation room. Hereafter I'll pass the summons bell and return immediately to the meditation hall."

81                              MASTER

*(Quote)*

You cannot do it this way, you cannot do it the other way. This or that are all impossible.

ANSWER

Extending both hands in one direction the pupil says, "Wonder what it's like over there." Extending both hands in the other direction, he says, "Wonder what it's like over here." Then placing both hands on his lap, "Whew!" he heaves a sigh, relaxing. In this way, the pupil takes the rhythmic stances [of a Japanese dance].

82                              MASTER

Deliver [enlighten] this ink stick.

ANSWER

The pupil pretends to rub the ink stick on an ink stone.

83                              MASTER

That flower in the garden in front—is it alive or dead?

ANSWER

Staring at the garden the pupil says, "It has indeed blossomed beautifully."

84                              MASTER

In this whole wide world—how many raindrops fall?

Looking outdoors the pupil counts, "One drop, two drops, three drops. . . . "

85                          MASTER

Well, the tree in the garden in front—how many leaves are there?

ANSWER

Looking outdoors the pupil counts, "One leaf, two leaves, three leaves. . . . "

86                          MASTER

Well then, how many stars in heaven?

ANSWER

Looking upwards the pupil counts, "One, two, three stars, four. . . . "
*Or:*
"Aren't there five or six; or is it twelve or thirteen?" the pupil says nonchalantly.

87                          MASTER

All living things are flesh and bones. Why is a turtle flesh and bones?

ANSWER

Drawing in his hands and feet, the pupil imitates a turtle stretching its neck, withdrawing its neck.

88                          MASTER

Go in and out of this wine flask.

ANSWER

As if holding a wine flask, the pupil says, "Master, let me pour you a glass."

89                          MASTER

Among the eight dragon gods, which is the one that makes the rain fall?

ANSWER

The pupil pretends to urinate in front of his master.

MASTER

Show me the tree that does not move in a strong wind.


ANSWER

The pupil stands up and waves his hands in the air. Saying, "Ooooo——" [the sound of wind blowing], he sways to and fro like a tree.


91                    MASTER

Stamp [as Sumo wrestlers do] on bean curd.


ANSWER

The pupil stands up, and saying, "At the wrestling arena," stamps his foot.


92                    MASTER

The woman coming from over there, is she the older sister or is she the younger sister?


ANSWER

The pupil imitates a woman walking.


93                    MASTER

Try and pass through a smoking pipe.


ANSWER

Lying straight on his side and twisting only his neck into the form of a pipe bowl, the pupil takes the pose of a smoking pipe.


94                    MASTER

The ashes of the cigarette smoked the day before yesterday— bring them here.


ANSWER

Making his body round, the pupil takes the pose of cigarette ashes.


95                    MASTER

You're put behind a stone gate which is bolted from the outside. How are you going to get out?

"Hey! Somebody let me out of here!," the pupil says, making the pretense of shaking the gate.

96                                     MASTER

The essence of the wind and the working of the wind—what's it like?

ANSWER

Extending both hands in front and gently waving them, the pupil says, "Ooooo, ooooo," imitating a passing breeze. [This is for "essence".] Next, "Up to now it's been south wind; it seems as though it's changing into east wind." So saying, the pupil points out the direction of the wind. [This is for "working."]

97                                     MASTER

It is said that Master Ummon [864–949] was reborn into Master Daitō [1282–1337]. During the several hundred years in between, what in the world was he doing?

ANSWER

The pupil briefly enumerates his personal history from childhood to the present.

98                                     MASTER

Say this room in one phrase!

ANSWER

"Ultimately, ku" ["void"], the pupil solemnly declares.

99                                     MASTER

Bring forth Mt. Fuji tied up with a lamp wick.

ANSWER

"Even this tattered rag will do as a head cover . . . it's time to go." So saying, the pupil moves to leave, heading toward the door. *Or:*
"Can you do such a thing? If that's possible, let me see *you* do it."

100                                    MASTER

Through the left sleeve, survey the eight hundred and eight towns of Edo [Tokyo].

Peering into his sleeve, the pupil says, "I can see the string of the loincloth; under the armpit, lice are scurrying around."

101                                    MASTER
Without taking the cover from the lunch box, say what's inside.


ANSWER
The pupil pretends to take the cover from the lunch box and says, "Ah, rice cakes! Thank you very much!"


102                                    MASTER
Look at the back of your head.


ANSWER
Facing his master the pupil says, "Master, would you turn around and I'll look at it for you?"


103                                    MASTER
(Quote)
When he and I die, where shall we meet?


ANSWER
Imitating a chance meeting with an acquaintance on the street, the pupil says, "My, it's been such a long time! How are you?"


104                                    MASTER
(Quote)
Turn the heavenly switch, and spin the earthly axis.


ANSWER
The pupil turns a somersault in front of his master.


105                                    MASTER
(Quote)

> I sauntered along and the murmer of the
>     brook was crushed beneath my feet.
> The traces of the birds I recognized in a
>     panoramic view.

As against, "I sauntered along and the murmer of the brook was crushed beneath my feet."

ANSWER

Rolling the hem of his kimono to his waist, the pupil pretends to cross a stream.

*Or:*

Folding his arms across his chest and saying, "Trickle, trickle [murmer of a brook]" the pupil pretends to slowly walk along a brook.

As against, "*The traces of the birds I recognized in a panoramic view.*"

ANSWER

The pupil imitates a flying sparrow that comes to pick up crumbs.

*Or:*

Emitting, "Coo, coo" [a bird call], the pupil imitates a bird in flight.

106                             MASTER

*(Quote)*

"The realm-of-no-thought" [enlightenment] is for what kind of people?

ANSWER

"In the Zen world—the distinguished Dokuon, Keichū, Kaion, Gasan [Zen monks of the Meiji era] have passed away. How truly sorrowful this is. In the secular world—Ito, Inoue, Katsura, Nogi [statesmen of the Meiji era] have died. What a pity."

107                             MASTER

In the universe there are greatly enlightened ones. How do they reveal themselves?

ANSWER

"See how the many are gathered for the sake of practice [in search of enlightenment]. There is some affinity to it."

*(Quote)*

Fire goes where it is dry,
And water flows to where it is damp.

108                             MASTER

*(Quote)*

People who endeavor to know the truth do not really know it only

because they, having once in their studies come across the miraculous power of Buddha, and heard about the origin of life and
death countless eons ago, call the unenlightened self the true self.
What is the ultimate truth really like?

ANSWER

"In looking for that, you achieve nothing."

109                 MASTER

The great sky is a drum and Mt. Shumi its drumstick. Who can
hit it?

ANSWER

"You can't hit a broken drum, can you?"

110                 MASTER

The Emperor Shukusō asked his Zen teacher, Etchū, "My
teacher, what sort of wisdom have you acquired?" Master Etchū
replied, "Your Majesty, do you see the piece of white cloud in
the sky?" The emperor said, "Yes, I see it." The master said,
"Is it being pinned up by a nail or is it dangling in midair?"

ANSWER

Looking down saying, "Fuuu, fuuu——," the pupil imitates a
floating cloud.

111                 MASTER

(Quote—Monk Daiji and His Mind-Reading Power)

There came the monk Daiji from the west to the capital. He said
he possessed the unusual power of mind reading. Emperor Daisō
ordered that his teacher Etchū should test the monk. The moment
the monk met the master, he bowed and stepped aside to the right.
The master said, "Have you got the power of mind reading?"
"To some extent," said the monk in reply. "Tell me where I am at
this moment," the master said. "You, the teacher of a nation, how
can you go to the West River to see the boat race?" "Tell me
where I am at this moment," the master said again. "You, the
teacher of a nation, how can you stay on the Tenshin Bridge and
watch monkeys performing tricks?" "Tell me where I am at this
moment," the master said a third time. After quite awhile the
monk still could not find the master's whereabouts. The master

scolded, "You fox! Where is your mind-reading ability?" The monk gave no answer. The master then said to the emperor, "Your Majesty, please do not be taken in by foreigners!"
WHERE DID THE MASTER GO?

ANSWER

With a fierce expression, the pupil exclaims, "What a despicable wretch!"
[In reference to the above answer the book comments, "Namely, being found out twice by Daiji, his whole being is consumed with hate."]

112                                    MASTER
(Quote)
If Jōshū drew out the blade of his sword, its light dazzling like cold, biting frost, and you were just about to inquire further concerning its meaning, you would be broken into two halves.

ANSWER

Pretending to draw out a sword, poised to attack, the pupil waves it, saying, "Pika, pika, chika, chika [referring to the glitter and shine of the sword]."

113                                    MASTER
Monju [a legendary Buddha representing wisdom] rides a lion. Fugen [a legendary Buddha of meditation and practice] rides a giant elephant. I wonder, what does [the historical] Buddha ride?

ANSWER

"Let's lay out a cushion."
Or:
"On a worn cushion I'm sitting, immovable."

114                                    MASTER
Make the teapot walk [around the room, as done during the reading of sutras].

ANSWER

The pupil folds his arms across his chest and walks a circle around the room as done during the reading of sutras.

115                    MASTER

*(Quote)*
How can you enter the realm of Buddha without leaving the realm of the devils?


                       ANSWER

"When in the living quarters, I converse with the guests. When returning to the meditation hall, I sit in meditation."


116                    MASTER

*(Quote)*
How to answer the calls from different directions with one body.


                       ANSWER

"Becoming densu [the monk in charge of reading the sutras], becoming tenzō [the monk in charge of cooking], becoming fuzui [the monk in charge of household affairs]."


117                    MASTER
When the light has appeared, where does the darkness go?


                       ANSWER

"When it becomes light, the lantern is put into the closet and the mattress is folded away onto the shelf."


118                    MASTER

*(Quote)*
All Buddhas of past, present, and future do not know that there is. Yet the raccoons and the white oxen know that there is.


                       ANSWER

"The sparrow—chirp, chirp; the crow—caw, caw; the dog— bow-wow; the cat—meow."


119                    MASTER

*(Quote)*
> The clouds lay on the summit in a can't-be-
>         more-leisurely manner,
> While the water hurries down the stream
>         with excessive fervor.

*As against, "The clouds lay on the summit in a can't-be-more-leisurely manner."*

### ANSWER

Saying, "Beer, sake, wine, tobacco, matches, rice balls," the pupil pretends to move about in a flurry.

*As against, "While the water hurries down the stream with excessive fervor."*

### ANSWER

Shouting, "Japan won! Russia lost!" [referring to the Russo—Japanese War], the pupil dances around the room.


120                              MASTER
*(Quote)*

To girdle a hundred thousand kan [1 kan = 8.25 pounds] around one's waist, and fly down to the city of Yōshū riding a crane.


### ANSWER

"I've come from such-and-such a place carrying all these bags and I'm so exhausted. Ahh, my back hurts! My back hurts!" So saying, the pupil pounds his own back.


121                              MASTER
*(Quote)*

Master Shishi said, "[In a fight] is it best to aim at a man's head, or is it best to aim at his waist, or is aiming at his feet best? The moment you hesitate [like that] your life is done for."


### ANSWER

The pupil takes a wrestling pose in front of his master.


122                              MASTER
*(Quote)*

A gentleman who loves money will get it through the proper channels.

### ANSWER

"Anything given, I'll take."


123                              MASTER
*(Quote)*

Morning—face to face with people. Evening—mingling with folks in a friendly way.

### ANSWER

"It's not just morning and evening; right now, aren't we sitting facing each other?"

124                              MASTER

*(Quote)*

Passion is the highest wisdom.

### ANSWER

"How hateful . . . how lovely . . ." the pupil says solemnly.

*Popular Saying*

When I think of you the bright sun clouds up, the clear moon turns dark.

125                              MASTER

*(Quote)*

The one who is good at shooting does not hit the center of the target.

### ANSWER

The pupil pretends to fix an arrow on the bow and upon shooting it [says] "Oh."

126                              MASTER

*(Quote)*

When suddenly caught from behind by a powerful giant ghost and thrown into a dazzling pit of fire, is there a way of escape?

### ANSWER

The pupil pretends to have fallen into a fire. He screams, "Hot! Hot! Hot!" as he writhes in pain.

127                              MASTER

*(Quote)*

Is the teaching of our founder and the teaching of the later masters the same or different? The ancients had said, "When cold, chickens go up the tree while ducks go to the water." Show the meaning of this in a quote.

### ANSWER

*(Quote)*

A cow drinks water and it becomes milk,
A snake drinks water and it becomes poison.

*Or:*

> Blow and you can extinguish a fire.
> Blow and you can make a fire.

*Or:*

> When you breathe out, the air is hot.
> When you breathe in, the air is cold.


128                                    MASTER
*(Quote)*

If a man wants to know throughly about all the Buddhas of the
past, the present, and the future, he should understand that the
realm of existence is but the creation of mind.
*As against, "Past, present, and future."*

ANSWER

"Yesterday, today, tomorrow."
*Or:*
"Just before, now, soon after."
*As against, "All the Buddhas."*

ANSWER

The pupil replies, "Mr. A, Mr. B, Master, me . . . " thus enumerating names of people nearby.
*As against, "All existence is but the creation of mind."*

ANSWER

"The bean curd man makes bean curd, the carpenter builds a
house."


129                                    MASTER
*(Quote)*

The Kongōkyō [the Diamond Sutra] says, "This being is shared
by all and there is no such thing as the high and low in it." Well
then, how come Mt. Shu is high and Mt. An is low?


ANSWER

"Mt. Fuji is high, Mt. Kamakura is low."


130                                    MASTER
*(Quote)*

The same scripture says, "Even though it is not a world, it is
called a world."

"To the west as far as Tansui City in Taiwan, to the east as far as the Kurile Islands in Saghalien" [the frontiers of old Japan].

131                    MASTER
(Quote)
The same scripture says, "The miraculous eye [that sees the smallest particle] and absolute wisdom [that knows every existence] all originate in this scripture." But how about the scripture [itself]?

ANSWER
The pupil slaps his master's face once.

132                    MASTER
(Quote)
The same scripture says, "If a man sees me [i.e., Buddha] in a physical object, or searches for me through sound, then this man has walked astray; he will not see the Truth."

ANSWER
With single-hearted concentration, the pupil in a loud voice recites a passage from the Hannyashin Sutra or from the Daihiju Sutra.
Or:
Reciting, "He-will-not-see-the-Truth," the pupil says, "I see into each and every."

133                    MASTER
(Quote)
The same scripture says, "It is impossible to have a past mind, it is impossible to have a present mind, neither can you have a future mind." With which mind do you eat?

ANSWER
"Old woman, I'm hungry. How much are these rice cakes? I'll have three or four."
Or:
"Up till now, I've only looked at the sutra and meditated. Now I am being taught in the master's room. Afterward, I'll go back and pull weeds."

*(Quote)*
The same scripture says, "That [true] mind comes into being when the mind does not dwell on any thought."

#### ANSWER
*(As father)*
"You lazybones! Get out of here!"
*(As mother)*
"Who are you saying get out to? Isn't it our dear son?"
*Popular Saying*
Upon seeing dumplings, "How cute"; upon seeing flowers, "How cute."
*Or:*
"Meditation, consultation, pulling weeds, cleaning, heating the bath. . . . " The pupil enumerates the daily routine, adding, "Not even a minute of rest."

135         MASTER
*(Quote)*
The breeze blows over the dark pine trees. The closer you come, the better the rustling of the leaves sounds.

#### ANSWER
With his right hand on his ear the pupil says, "Shhuu, shhuu" [the sound of wind in the trees], as he pretends to be listening to the breeze in the pine trees.

#### MASTER
[Additional quote added here by Master Hakuin] Listening close, just what do you hear?

#### ANSWER
"Oh that. It's a secret, so come close." Saying this, the pupil pretends to whisper some confidential talk into his master's ear.

# PART THREE

# THE ONE HUNDRED FORTY-FOUR KOANS

# THE ONE HUNDRED
# FORTY-FOUR KOANS

## 1. The Man up the Tree

Zen Master Kyōgen said, "Let us suppose that a man climbs up a tree. He grips the branches with his teeth, his hands do not hold onto the tree, and his feet do not touch the ground. A monk below asks him about the meaning of our founder coming from the west. If he does not answer, he will be avoiding the monk's question. But if he opens his mouth and utters a word, he will fall to his death. Under such circumstances, what should the man do?" A certain monk by the name of Kotō said, "Once the man is up the tree, no question should be raised. The man should ask the monk if the latter has anything to say to him before he goes up the tree." On hearing this, Kyōgen laughed out loud.

Later, Master Setchō commented, "It is easy to say it up on the tree. To say it under the tree is difficult. So I shall climb the tree myself. Come, ask me a question!"
*As against, "On the tree."*

### ANSWER
The pupil stands up and takes the pose of hanging down from a tree.

With certain masters, there are pupils who may stick a finger in the mouth; utter, "Uh . . . uh"; and, shaking the body slightly, give the pretense of one trying to answer but unable to.
*As against, "Under the tree."*

### ANSWER
The pupil pretends to fall from a tree. Landing on his bottom, he says, "Ouch! That hurt!"

## 2. The Man in the Well

Master Shōkū was asked by a monk, "What is the meaning of our founder coming from the west?" The master said, "It is like getting a man out of a thousand-foot-deep well without using one single inch of rope. This answers your enquiry." The monk said, "The monk Ō of the district of Konan recently became famous and that too has become the subject of people's gossip." Upon this Shōkū summoned the young monk Jaku and said, "Drag out the corpse."

Master Kyōzan (who heard about this dialogue) asked Master Tangen, "How can you get the man in the well out?" Tangen said, "You stupid fool! Who is in the well?" Kyōzan said nothing. Again, he later asked Master Isan, "How can you get the man in the well out?" Isan called out, "Kyōzan!" Kyōzan answered the call and Isan said, "He is out of the well already!"

Kyōzan always used to tell the story described above to the people, saying, "I got the principle from Tangen and learned the use from Isan."

ANSWER

Pretending to have fallen into a well, the pupil struggles in anguish, gasping for air.

*Or:*

Pretending to have fallen into a well, the pupil struggles in anguish, gasping for air. Then, as if choking and coughing up water, he says, "Oh, it was cold! It was cold! I thought I was inside the well, but it was right here in the master's room, wasn't it? Oh! How rude of me! Please forgive me!"

*Or:*

Pretending to have fallen to the bottom of a well, the pupil grabs onto the walls. Looking up, he says in a low voice, "Please help me. Please help me," as if pleading for sympathy.

## 3. Why a Monk's Garment?

Master Ummon said, "The world is so wide, why at the chime of the bell do you choose to put on a monk's garment?"

ANSWER

As if hearing the summons bell, the pupil pretends to put on his gown and go out to join the monks walking around the hall.

> When the king summons, one has to go
> > at once without waiting for a vehicle.
> When one's father calls, one has to answer
> > "Yes" without hesitation.

*Or:*

> The red headgeared night watchman
> > announced the morning hour.
> The king's wardrobe keeper had just carried
> > in a robe with green cloud patterns.

*Popular Saying*
At the clapping of hands, bring in the tea. When the clapping sounds again, fetch the ashtray.

## 4. The World a Grain of Rice

Master Seppō said, "The whole world, when gathered with the fingers, is no bigger than a grain of rice. Throw it before us, it will be impossible to find. Strike the drum for summons—let us all come together and look for it."

### ANSWER

The pupil, as if present in a high place, pretends to survey many peaks at a glance.

*(Quote)*

> The states of Go and So extend toward
> > the southeast.
> Heaven and earth, day and night, are all
> > floating on the water.

*Or:*

"To the west as far as Taiwan, to the east as far as the Kurile Islands in Saghalien." Thus the pupil demonstrates the phrase from the Kongōkyō [the Diamond Sutra] which says, "The world is non-world; upon this it is named world."

## 5. The Three Gates of Master Ōryū

Master Ōryū asked Master Ryūkei, "Everyone has got an origin, where is your origin?" Ryūkei answered, "I had eaten some gruel this morning and now I feel hungry again." "How is my hand when compared with the hand of Buddha?" Ōryū asked. "Playing biwa [a musical instrument] under the moon," Ryūkei answered. "How are my feet when compared with those of a mule?" he asked. Ryūkei answered, "A heron standing in the snow, not of the same color."

Ōryū always asked students these three questions, and none could reach the correct meaning. Monks the world over called them "the three gates." Even if someone returned to answer, the master never said yes or no. He just sat there erect and shut his eyes and none could guess what he meant. After a while, someone would ask the master again for the reason. Ōryū said, "For he who has passed the gate will wave his arms and go straight on without caring for the gatekeeper. If you ask the gatekeeper for permission, it shows that you have not yet passed the gate." *As against, "Where is your origin?"*

ANSWER

The pupil asks, "Where is the place that you are?" To this the master answers, "It's useless to ask for the place where I am."
*Or:*
The pupil says, "Yes, I was born in so-and-so prefecture, in so-and-so district, in so-and-so village," thus giving his own birthplace.
*Or:*
The pupil says, "Your reverence is where your reverence is, I am where I am."
*(Quote)*
Where do you live? I live in Ōtō [a district in China].
*Or:*

> A bird cried of cold on a dry branch,
> And wild monkeys whined amidst empty
> mountains.

*Or:*

> Once again I crossed the Sōken River for
> no apparent reason,
> And I wished Henshū were my native place.

*As against, "How is my hand when compared with that of Buddha?"*

ANSWER

Stretching his leg out, the pupil asks, "Why is a leg called a leg?"
*(Quote)*
To play biwa under the moon.
*Or:*
To change hands and hit the chest.

*As against, "How are my feet when compared with those of a mule?"*
ANSWER
Thrusting his hand in front, the pupil asks, "Why is a hand called a hand?"
*(Quote)*
To imprint the green moss with the sole of a clog.
*Or:*
To walk to and fro.

## 6. *Where Do the Snowflakes Fall?*

The time came when the layman Hōkoji bade farewell to Master Yakusan. Yakusan sent ten of his pupils to accompany Hōkoji to the front gate. Hōkoji pointed to the clouds in the sky and said, "All these lovely snowflakes do not fall on any particular place." At that time a monk by the name of Zen said, "Where do they fall then?" Hōkoji slapped him. Zen said, "Hōkoji, you should not treat me that roughly!" Hōkoji said, "How can you call yourself a Zen monk when the god of justice didn't place you as one!" Zen retorted, "What about you, Hōkoji?" Hōkoji gave him another slap and said, "You see, but you are just like the blind. You speak, yet you are no different from the dumb."

Later, Master Setchō commented, "I would have just hit him with a snowball when he first raised such a question!"

The pupil gives the image of snow gently falling to the ground.
*(Quote)*
> The mountain dwellers are rich with a
> thousand trees of silver,
> And the fishermen are elegant with their
> straw raincoats covered with pearls.

MASTER
[Certain masters may ask] The "particular place" of "All these lovely snowflakes do not fall on any particular place"—what does it mean?
ANSWER
The pupil slaps his master's face.
MASTER
This "I would have just hit him with a snowball when he first raised such a question!"—what does it mean?

ANSWER

The pupil slaps his master's face.

MASTER

"To hit with a ball of snow, to hit with a ball of snow"—what of it?

ANSWER

The pupil slaps his master's face.

## 7. *Round Are the Lotus Leaves*

> Round are the lotus leaves, round like a mirror.
> Pointed are the water chestnuts, pointed like a
> drill.
> The wind blows and willow flowers roll like
> hairy balls.
> The rain beats and plum blossoms flutter like
> butterflies.

MASTER

"Round are the lotus leaves, round like a mirror"—from the standpoint of self-centeredness, what's it like?

ANSWER

Stroking his head, the pupil says, "It's round like this."

MASTER

How is it like from the other-centered point of view?

ANSWER

"Gonbē and Hachibē and Ohachi and also Osan [common Japanese names of the working class], covered from head to toe with mud, are working."
(Quote)

> Everything in the southern and northern
> villages is soaked in rain.
> The newly married woman is serving her
> mother-in-law food,
> While her father-in-law is feeding the son.

"Pointed are the water chestnuts, pointed like a drill"—from the standpoint of self-centeredness, what's it like?

ANSWER

"Sharper than a drill," the pupil says, violently spreading out his crossed arms.

MASTER

How is it like from the other-centered point of view?

ANSWER

"The merchant poring over his abacus is fighting for every single penny."

MASTER

"The wind blows and willow flowers roll like hairy balls. The rain beats and plum blossoms flutter like butterflies"—how about this?

ANSWER

Mimicking the striking sound of the master's stick and the chime of bells, the pupil imitates the various happenings in the meditation hall.

OR

(According to another school)

*As against, "Round are the lotus leaves, round like a mirror. Pointed are the water chestnuts, pointed like a drill."*

ANSWER

"With an iron pot to boil water, with a lamp to light a flame, with a set of drawers to store goods away, with an incense burner to burn incense."

*(Quote)*

> The monkey retreats to the back of the green
>     mountain, carrying its offspring.
> The bird flies down the blue cliff, holding
>     flowers in its beak.

*Or:*

> Blow at the stove of burning charcoal
>     below the pot and it will be
>     extinguished.
> Roar, the forest of swords and the mountain
>     of knives will crumble and fall.

MASTER

"The wind blows and willow flowers roll like hairy balls. The rain beats and plum blossoms flutter like butterflies"—how about this?

ANSWER

"When the rain falls, the plum blossoms will scatter. When the wind blows, the willow flowers will scatter."
*(Quote)*
When cold, chickens go up the tree while ducks go to the water.
*Or:*

> Stand on top of a high peak without getting
> your head damp with dew.
> Walk at the bottom of a deep sea without
> getting your feet wet.

*Or:*

> To jump over the four big continents in one
> leap,
> And to bring down Mt. Shumi in one blow.

OR

(According to another school)
*As against, "Round are the lotus leaves."*
ANSWER

From his sitting position, the pupil folds his body and rolls around in a circle.
*As against, "Water chestnuts."*
ANSWER

The pupil pretends to float on the water as water chestnuts do.
*As against, "Willow flowers" and "butterflies."*
ANSWER

For both, the pupil uses his body to imitate their appearance.
*As against the master's, "Distinguish the four phrases of the koan in accordance with the four classes"* [*warrior, farmer, artisan, merchant*].
ANSWER

The pupil compares the lotus leaves with the appearance of a farmer wearing a rain hat; water chestnuts he compares with the strict ranking of warriors; the hairy balls he compares with merchandise; and the fluttering plum blossoms he compares with artisans.

(112)

## 8. *The Sound of Rain*

Master Kyōshō asked a monk, "What is the noise outside?" The monk said, "The sound of rain." Kyōshō said, "The people are in a topsy-turvy condition, they have blinded themselves in the pursuit of material pleasure." The monk said, "How about you, Your Reverend?" Kyōshō said, "I can almost understand myself perfectly." The monk said, "What does understanding oneself perfectly mean?" Kyōshō said, "To be enlightened is easy. To put it into words is difficult."

ANSWER

"Bisha, bisha." The pupil imitates the sound of rain.

## 9. *The Three Questions of Master Tosō*

Master Tosō set up three questions to examine students. He said:
1. "One clears the weeds of idiocy and is enlightened by Buddha's teaching so that one can see one's nature. Now where is human nature?"
2. "After you have learned of your true nature, then you can escape from the cycle of life and death. But when you're on the brink of death, how will you escape?"
3. "If you have left the cycle of life and death, you will know where to go. But when the four elements [that form a physical body] are separated, where will you go?"

*As against, "Now where is human nature?"*

ANSWER

The pupil looks around, giving the pretense of one searching. At this point, the master adds, "Everything is filled with it. It is not that it does not exist, only it cannot be seen by the eye." *(Quote)*

> I only know that I am in the middle of this
> mountain,
> But the clouds are so thick that I cannot
> figure out where exactly I am.

*Or:*

> The lotus leaves trembled though it was
> windless.
> Definitely there were fish moving about
> underneath.

*Or:*

> When the forest is dense, the cries of the
> monkeys become loud.
> When the water is clear, the reflection of
> the wild geese becomes sharp.

*Popular Saying*

Every year it blooms—the mountain cherry blossoms of Yoshino [near Nara]. Come, let's split the tree apart. From where the flowers bloom?

*Or:*

> The voice is heard but the figure unseen,
> You, hiding in lush fields—the grasshopper.

*As against, "On the brink of death."*

ANSWER

The pupil gives the pretense of one in agony—grappling his arms in the air, kicking his legs, twisting, turning, writhing in pain.

*(Quote)*

> Poisoned arrows stuck in the breast.
> Like the falcon seizing the dove.

*Or:*

At the lion's roar, the fox's brain is shattered.

*As against, "When the four elements are separated, where will you go?"*

ANSWER

Lying on his back, the pupil takes the pose of a corpse.

MASTER

*(Quote)*

What happens when there are not enough places to go?

ANSWER

The pupil retains the above pose of a corpse.

*(Quote)*

A monumental stone lay broken across an ancient path.

*Or:*

The monumental stone dedicated to Shin-u [a legendary figure] at the summit of Peak Shunrō.

*Or:*

Nothing but a slab of stone is left standing eternally on Mt. Enzan.

*Or:*

[With certain masters, in response to "Where will you go?"]:

It has just gone away with the fragrant
    grasses,
Yet returns again chasing falling flowers.

## 10.   *The Sentence of Being and the Sentence of Nothing*

Master Ran-an said, "The sentence of being ['u'] and the
sentence of nothing ['mu'] are just like a wisteria vine twining
around a tree." Master Sozan heard of this and said, "I have
something to say to that old man." So at the end of that summer,
he went to the province of Bin to see Ran-an. When Sozan came
to him, Ran-an was plastering a wall. Sozan asked, "'The sentence of being and the sentence of nothing are just like a wisteria
vine twining around a tree,' are those Your Reverend's words?"
Ran-an said, "Yes." Sozan said, "If suddenly the tree falls and the
wisteria vine withers, where will those sentences go?" Ran-an put
down his plaster tray and laughed aloud. Then he went back to his
living quarters. Sozan said, "But I have sold my sheets and come
here from a place three thousand miles away especially for this matter! Why won't Your Reverend speak to me?" Ran-an called his
servant, "Bring some money and give it to this small priest."
Then he turned to Sozan and said, "Someday a single-eyed man
will explain to you."

Later, Sozan went to Master Meishō and told the above story.
Meishō said, "Ran-an is a straight man from head to toe, only he
has not encountered someone who knows him." Sozan said,
"If suddenly the tree falls and the wisteria vine withers, where will
those sentences go?" Meishō said, "This will make Ran-an
laugh anew." Right at that moment, enlightenment dawned on
Sozan and he said, "In fact, there was a knife in Ran-an's laughter."

In a later period, Master Dai-e [when still a novice] joined
Master Engo. Engo gave him the post of a servant. Every day
Dai-e sent to Engo's room, accompanying the officials [who
came to visit Engo]. Engo would say nothing except that the
sentence of being and the sentence of nothing are just like a
wisteria vine twining around a tree. Whenever Dai-e opened his
mouth to say something, Engo would say, "No, not like this."
In this manner almost half a year passed. One day while Dai-e
was eating with the official Jōhyōshi, he held the chopsticks in
his hands and forgot about the rice. Engo looked at Dai-e, turned
to Jōhyōshi and said, "This fellow is practicing the zen of the

box tree [from which chopsticks are made]. . . . " And to Dai-e he said, "You have fallen into a pit and will have to stay there awhile." A moment later Dai-e turned to Engo and said, "I have heard that Your Reverend had asked Master Hōen [Engo's teacher] about the sentence of being and the sentence of nothing before. I wonder if you remember the answer." Engo only laughed. Dai-e said, "If I ask this question in front of gods and men, will there be no one who knows?!" Engo said, "Once I asked Hōen, 'What if the sentence of being and the sentence of nothing are like a wisteria vine twining around a tree?' Hōen answered, 'It is no use to make a sketch of it.' I asked again, 'What if suddenly the tree falls and the wisteria vine withers?' Hōen said, 'They come in succession.'" [Or, 'They go together.'] When Dai-e heard the story he called out, "I've got it!" Engo said, "I am afraid you don't thoroughly understand this koan." Dai-e said, "Will Your Reverend raise questions to test me?" So Engo asked him questions and Dai-e replied with no hesitation. Engo said, "So today you know I have not cheated you. . . . "

MASTER

Ran-an said, "The sentence of being and the sentence of nothing are like a wisteria vine twining around a tree." Using your own insight, how do you understand the sentence of being and the sentence of nothing?

ANSWER

"In the middle of the field, a sole pine tree."
(Quote)

> A lonely pine flourishes on top of the winter mountain.

Or:

> The single pine stood high on top of the mountain.

Or:

> The pine tree will still be green for a thousand years.

11.  Subject, Object

When the head monks of the two [meditation] halls came to see Master Rinzai, they shouted ["Katsu!"] at each other at the same time. A monk asked Rinzai, "At the instant these two head monks shouted at each other, were there subject ['host'] and object ['guest']?" The master said, "The role of 'host' and 'guest' are clearly distinct." And he added, "If you people want to understand my sentence concerning 'host' and 'guest,' go to the hall where the two head monks are and ask them."

ANSWER

"The pillar stands and the threshold lies; the mountain is high, the river low."
*(Quote)*
A mountain is a mountain, a stream a stream.
*Or:*
The willow is green and the flowers are red.
*Or:*
Straight is the pine and crooked is the briar.

OR
(According to another school)
ANSWER

The master is seated on the high seat, listening to the pupil who has come in for discussion. The pupil kneels on the floor, bowing his head.
*(Quote)*

> There is a three-foot-long sword at the head
>     of the bed,
> And in the vase there is a branch of plum
>     blossoms.

OR
(According to another school)
ANSWER

Alternately pointing his finger at his master and himself, the pupil says, "Guest and host are in this way clearly distinguished."

## 12. The Unrankable Being

Master Rinzai said in his lecture, "In your physical bodies of flesh, there is an unrankable being who often goes in and out of the doors of your faces. For those who have not yet proven the truth, see it! See it!" At that moment a monk came out and asked, "What is it [the unrankable being]?" The master came down from his seat, grabbed the monk, and said, "Say it! Say it!" Just as the monk was about to speak, the master pushed him away and said, "What dry dung is the unrankable being!" Then he returned to his room.

ANSWER

The pupil places one hand on his forehead, shading his eyes. [Taking the pose of "See it! See it!"]
(*Quote*)

> It may be that she has got a well-developed
> body,
> That she looks elegant naturally without
> putting on pink powder.

*Or:*

> On the contrary, she disliked cosmetics
> for they smeared her face.
> With brows lightly drawn, she went up
> to the emperor.

*Or:*

> He leaned his back on cold rocks, his face
> shining like a full moon
> Of which everyone on earth could see but
> one side.

OR

(According to another school)

MASTER

"See it! See it!"—what's it mean?

ANSWER

The pupil pretends to fall down in surprise.

MASTER

[The master comes down from his seat, grabs the pupil and says] "Say it! Say it!"

ANSWER

"I earnestly ask your pardon."

MASTER

The difference between "unrankable" and "not-unrankable"— say it quick! Say it quick!

"I earnestly beg your forgiveness."


## 13. *A Flower in Bloom*

A monk asked Master Ummon, "What is the pure body of truth?" Ummon said, "A flower in bloom." The monk asked, "At such a time, what is it like?" Ummon said, "A lion of golden fur."
As against, *"A flower in bloom."*

ANSWER

The pupil places both hands on his chest, stands up and says, "This shit hole."
As against, *"A lion of golden fur."*

ANSWER

The pupil pretends to shit in front of his master.
*(Quote)*
A refreshing wind moving inside torn clothes.
*Or:*

> There is a dead deer in the wilderness.
> I wrap it with beautiful flowers.

*Or:*
A flower vase holding waste matter.


OR
(According to another school)
MASTER

"A flower in bloom"—what's it mean?


ANSWER

"Maggots in the shit hole, pus of leprosy, scab over a boil."
*(Quote)*
To add rubbish on top of a pile of garbage.


MASTER

"A lion of golden fur"—what's it mean?


ANSWER

The pupil imitates a lion's roar.

## 14. *Will IT Be Destroyed?*

A monk asked Master Daizui, "When the fire of destruction blazes, the whole universe will be destroyed. I wonder if *IT* will be destroyed too?" Daizui said, "Yes, destroyed." The monk said, "Then shall we go with it?" Daizui said, "Yes, go with it!"

#### MASTER
Daizui said "destroyed"—what's it mean?

#### ANSWER
Saying, "Bari, bari, bari, bari," the pupil flickers his hands, giving the image of a blazing fire spreading in all directions.

#### MASTER
Daizui said, "Yes, go with it!"—what's it mean?

#### ANSWER
Saying, "Dotsu, dotsu, dotsu," the pupil moves his hands, giving the image of a streaming fire.

## 15. *Where Will ONE Return To?*

A monk asked Master Jōshū, "All existences return to *ONE*, but where will *ONE* itself return to?" Jōshū said, "When I was in the district of Sei, I made a cotton dress. It weighed seven jin" [1 jin = 14 ounces].

#### MASTER
"All existences return to *ONE*"—what's it mean?

#### ANSWER
The pupil slaps his knee, "Ah!" [i.e., "I see!"].
*Or:*
With his finger, the pupil writes the number one on the floor.

#### MASTER
"Where will the *ONE* return to?"—what's it mean?

#### ANSWER
"The *ONE* returns to the many."

*Or:*

[With certain masters]: "The *ONE* returns to the two, to the three, to the four, five, six, seven, eight, nine, ten, hundred, thousand, ten thousand, million, billion."

*(Quote)*

> There are plums at the end of the branch.
> Seven is the number of the fruit.

*Or:*

> The seven palaces crumbled because of the
> revolt started by one single man.

*Popular Saying*

In Mt. Hakone there is the man riding in the sedan chair. There is the one who pulls the sedan chair. And there is the one who makes the straw sandals of the one pulling the sedan chair.


## 16. *There Is No Such Thing as Holy*

Emperor Butei of the Ryō dynasty asked Daruma [Bodhidharma—founder of Zen Buddhism], "What is the highest of holy truth?" Daruma said, "There is no such thing as holy." The emperor said, "Who is it that answers me?" Daruma said, "I do not know." The emperor said nothing further. Daruma thus crossed the River Yōsukō and went into the state of Gi. The emperor later asked the same question of the Zen disciple Shikō and Shikō replied, "Does Your Majesty know this person by now?" The emperor said, "No, I do not know him." Shikō said, "This person is the incarnation of the Buddha of Mercy [Kannon] and he spreads the teaching of Buddha." The emperor felt regret and sent a mission to invite Daruma back. But Shikō said, "Even if the whole nation goes to carry him, he will not come back; to say nothing of Your Majesty's sending a mission to get him."


MASTER

"There is no such thing as holy"—what's it mean?


ANSWER

Folding his arms across his chest, the pupil stands up.

*Or:*

"Gonbe, Hachi, and San [common names], covered with mud, are working."

*(Quote)*
> Everything in the southern and northern
> villages is soaked in rain.
> The newly married woman is serving her
> mother-in-law food,
> While her father-in-law is feeding the son.

MASTER

[Daruma's] "I do not know"—what's it mean?

ANSWER

"If Daruma says he doesn't know, how should I know?"

MASTER

Why don't you know?

ANSWER

"Buddha as well as Amida don't know."
*(Quote)*
(Referring to "I do not know"):
> The light of the sun and moon cannot
> reach it,
> Neither can heaven nor earth completely
> cover it.

*Or:*
> The noise of talking woodcutters can never
> be heard in a deep mountain valley,
> While hunters can be found passing under
> shadowy cliffs.


17. *Words*

Master Jōshū said, "To reach the way of Zen is not difficult. The only setback is that of choice. The moment you use words, it is a matter of either choice or understanding. I am not in the realm of understanding. But you, are you not still thinking highly of it?" Then a monk asked, "Since you are not in the realm of understanding, what is there that you say should not be thought highly of?" Jōshū answered, "I do not know it myself." The monk said, "You say you do not know, but why then did you

say you are not in the realm of understanding?" Jōshū said, "It is only because you asked that I answered. Now go away."
*As against, "Reach the way."*

### ANSWER

The pupil folds his arms, stands up and says, "Reach the way."
*As against, "Not difficult."*

### ANSWER

"The mountain is high, the river low, the pillar stands, the threshold lies."
*As against, "The only setback is choice."*

### ANSWER

"What a pity! I want! How hateful! Lovable! Good! Bad!"

### MASTER

[Some masters may pose.] In "reach the way" and "not difficult," is it true that whichever way you see it there is no choice?

### ANSWER

"Everything is provided for in 'reach the way.'"
*(Quote)*

> I only love to read the new calendar
> published by the observatory,
> And am reluctant to glance over the dry
> prose sent by Kantaishi [a poet].

### MASTER

"I am not in the realm of understanding"—what's it mean?

### ANSWER

"I will never forget your favor to me for the rest of my life."

### MASTER

"Words reach from edge to edge" [from a quote attached to this koan by Master Setchō]—how about it?

### ANSWER

"Shut up!" the pupil says and slaps his master's face.
*(Quote)*
ONE has many varieties, but *TWO* has got none.

### OR
### ANSWER

"In one hand, five fingers. Five fingers make one hand."

## 18. *The Four Ways of Master Rinzai*

Master Rinzai said, "Sometimes you take away the man without taking the land; sometimes you take away the land without taking the man; sometimes you take away both the land and the man; and sometimes you take away neither the land nor the man."

MASTER

Using your hand as "land," your body as "man," demonstrate the four ways.
*As against, "Take away the man without taking the land."*

ANSWER

The pupil stretches out his hand and covers his master's face.
*(Quote)*

> When the music ended, no one was to be
> seen;
> Only the peaks along the river looked so
> green.

*Or:*

> The bright moon comes and is gone again by
> itself,
> There are no more people leaning against the
> jade railings.

*As against, "Take away the land without taking the man."*

ANSWER

Hiding a hand behind his back, the pupil edges his body forward a bit.
*(Quote)*

> There cannot be two suns in the universe,
> And there is only one man between heaven
> and earth.

*Or:*

> King Kō shouted angrily till his voice broke,
> And the thousand soldiers were nullified.

*As against, "Take away both the land and the man."*

ANSWER

The pupil quickly runs and hides behind the door.
*(Quote)*

> The universe is still void of the sun and moon
> of Shin Dynasty,
> And the Kan Dynasty emperor and his subjects
> are nowhere to be seen in the land . . .

*As against, "Take away neither the land nor the man."*

The pupil folds his arms across his chest and stands up.
*(Quote)*

> When evening falls in picturesque spots on the
> > river,
> Fishermen wearing straw raincoats are on
> > their way homeward bound.

*Or:*

> Wild geese flew over the city wall against a
> > night sky sparingly dotted with faint
> > stars.
> A long drawn note of the flute arose and
> > someone was leaning on the balcony.

OR
(According to another school)

*As against, "Take away the man without taking the land."*

ANSWER

"Ceiling, door, floor, charcoal brazier, stick"; the pupil thus enumerates the things within the room. Namely, these are things which take away the subject.
*(Quote)*

> The moon of the frosty night had climbed
> > right above my head.
> It would follow its natural course and fall
> > under the stream in front.

*As against, "Take away the land without taking the man."*

ANSWER

"In the whole world there is only me; I alone am the ruler of the universe."
*(Quote)*

Between sky and earth, I alone fill the universe.
*Or:*

> The four seas are under the enlightened rule
> > of the emperor.
> Who dares to invade our boundaries from
> > south, west, or north?

*As against, "Take away both the land and the man."*

ANSWER

'On the Tōkaidō Highway there's not a single man; on old Mt.

Kiso there's not a single cat; in old Tokyo there's not a single man; in Asakusa Park [in Tokyo] there's not a single man."
*(Quote)*

> The states of Shin and So failed for·excessive
> wealth.
> Fun-iku the warrior failed for courage.

*Or:*

Break into the city of Saishūjō and kill off Gogensai the rebel.
*As against, "Take away neither the land nor the man."*

ANSWER

"Host [subject], guest [object], things—where they are as they are."
*(Quote)*
The emperor has no greed, the people are all virtuous.
*Or:*

> There were five or six adults, six or seven
> children.
> We bathed in the river, sang to the dance
> music played when people prayed for
> rain,
> And then went home reciting poems.

*Or:*

> Young men from wealthy and noble families
> gathered under sweet-smelling trees.
> Delightful songs and dances were performed
> among falling petals.

## 19. *The Three Sentences of Master Rinzai*

When Master Rinzai came up to the lecture hall a monk asked him, "What is the first sentence?" Rinzai said, "When the seal is removed, the red ink comes into view. Even though the script has not been read yet, the role of host [subject] and guest [object] is already decided."

The monk asked, "What is the second sentence?" Rinzai said, "How can reckless questions be permitted for such a wonderful thought? And why should the working be inferior to the ideal?" The monk asked, "What is the third sentence?" Rinzai said, "Look at the puppet show on stage. The pulling is done by people within."

The first sentence—what of it?

ANSWER

"A, B, C, D, E, F, G."

MASTER

The second sentence—what of it?

ANSWER

"H, I, J, K, L, M, N."

MASTER

The third sentence—what of it?

ANSWER

"O, P, Q, R, S, T, U."

OR

ANSWER

"Today's a nice day [for the first sentence]!"
"Won't you have some tea [for the second sentence]?"
"Well, goodbye [for the third sentence]!"


20.  *Before and After*

A monk asked Master Chimon, "What is the lotus flower before it appears above water?" Chimon said, "It is a lotus flower." The monk said, "What is it after it has appeared above water?" Chimon said, "It is a lotus leaf."

MASTER

"Before it appears above water"—in place of Chimon, on your own, answer the question.

ANSWER

"An earthenware mortar."

MASTER

"After it has appeared above water"—what of it?

ANSWER

"A rice cake."

## 21.  *To Beat the Drum*

Master Kasan quoted, "To study is 'mon' [the character meaning "hear"]. To cut off study is 'rin' [the character meaning "near"]. Above these two there is 'shin'" [the character meaning "true"].

A monk asked, "What is 'shin' like?" Kasan answered, "To be able to beat the drum." The same monk asked again, "The essence of 'shin,' what is it like?" Kasan answered, "To be able to beat the drum." The monk asked once more, "I won't ask about the-mind-as-it-is-being-Buddha, but the-no-mind-no-Buddha, how about that?" Kasan answered, "To be able to beat the drum." The monk asked again, "If a person who is earnestly and wholeheartedly seeking for the truth comes to you, how will you treat him?" Kasan answered, "To be able be beat the drum."

ANSWER

"Boom, boom, boom, boom" [the sound of a drum].
*(Quote)*

> Gall is bitter to the root,
> Melon is sweet clear through.

## 22.  *No Great Masters?*

Master Ōbaku said, "You are all leftover eaters! If you walk around the world and search for truth in such a manner, what achievement can you expect? Do you know that there are no more Zen masters in China?" Then a monk stepped out and said, "Aren't there those who walk around earnestly instructing the masses? What of them?" Ōbaku said, "I did not say there is no Zen anymore, only that there are no great masters."

*As against, "Do you know that there are no more Zen masters in China?"*

ANSWER

"I alone am the ruler of the universe."
*(Quote)*

> King Kō shouted angrily till his voice broke,
> And the thousand soldiers were nullified.

*As against, "I did not say there is no Zen anymore, only that there are no great masters!"*

ANSWER

"You're right, you're right; I was wrong."

> A man of [the state of] So lit the fire,
> And everything turned into ashes.

OR

(According to another school)

*As against, "All of you are leftover eaters!"*

ANSWER

"This wretched leftover eater of a monk!"

*As against, "What achievement can you expect?"*

ANSWER

"If you dilly-dally you won't make headway, you know!"

*As against, "Do you know that there are no more Zen masters in China?"*

ANSWER

"In the great empire of China, with more than four hundred prefectures, there is not even one worthy to be called a man. This is really a lamentable state of affairs!"

(Quote)

> To surrender is to be left in the hands of
>     barbarians for the rest of my life.
> To fight, and I end up exposing my bones in
>     the desert waste.

*As against, "I did not say there is no Zen anymore, only that there are no great masters!"*

ANSWER

"What? If it weren't for your great compassion, master, where would I be today?"

## 23. *Where Did Nansen Go after His Death?*

Sanshō made monk Shū ask Master Chōsa the following question, "Where did Master Nansen go after his death?" Chōsa answered, "When Master Sekitō was a young priest he met Master Enō." Shū said, "I didn't ask anything about Sekitō's young priesthood. I asked, 'Where did Nansen go after his death?'" Chōsa said, "Go and ask Nansen!" Shū said, "Although Your Reverend possesses a thousand-foot-high pine tree that can stand severe cold, you have not got a small stalagmite." Chōsa was silent. Then Shū said, "I thank you for answering me." Chōsa remained silent. Shū went back and reported the above to Sanshō. Sanshō said, "If it is so, Chōsa must be somewhat greater than

Master Rinzai. But I shall go and see for myself tomorrow."
The next day he went and said, "I have the pleasure of hearing
about your answer concerning Nansen's whereabouts after death.
It can be fairly termed as unprecedented and will be unique in the
years to come. It really is something rarely heard of." Chōsa was
still silent.

As against, *"When Master Sekitō was a young priest he met Master
Enō."*

### ANSWER

"Monk So-and-so went out to buy bean curd."
As against, *"I didn't ask anything about Sekitō's young priesthood.
I asked, 'Where did Nansen go after his death?'"*

### ANSWER

"There's a guest coming today so I'll prepare dinner."
As against, *"The master was still silent."*

### ANSWER

The pupil just remains silent.
*Or:*
"Shut up!"
*(Quote)*

> I am now on the northern bank of River I,
>     under a tree below the spring heaven,
> While you somewhere east of Yōsukō River
>     may be staring at the clouds of twilight at
>     this moment.

*Or:*

> Spring is fading away in the city of Buryō.
> Trees behind tall buildings are getting green
>     and shady.

*Or:*

> The color of autumn trees on the plain,
> And the sound of an evening bell from the
>     foot of the sandy hill.

*Or:*

> As years go by my strength is leaving me.
> When people come to see me I am reluctant
>     to get down from my seat.

*Or:*

> A stream flows down by a path in the cold
>     mountain air.
> Enshrouded in thick clouds, a big temple bell
>     sounded.

*As against, "Go and ask Nansen!"*
### ANSWER
Looking all around, the pupil says, "I wonder where he's gone at this time?"
*(Quote)*

> The bundle of willow twigs scattered apart,
> Was blown with the wind on white jade
>     railings.

*Or:*

> When, alas, my luck failed me, I began to
>     meditate deep and long;
> I thought I saw my emperor in a dream, but
>     on awakening I was not too sure.

*Or:*

> On a night when cold frost falls,
> The moon as it is glides into the valley in
>     front.

*Popular Saying*
Isn't that Seijuro over there? That sure looks like his umbrella.

### OR
### (According to another school)
*As against, "Where did Nansen go after his death?"*
### ANSWER
"Excuse me a while—I'm going to the front gate to buy some straw sandals."

### MASTER
Forget about the sandals awhile—"Where did Nansen go after his death?"

### ANSWER
"Excuse me—I'm going to buy some paper."
*(Quote)*

> At night I departed from Seikei and headed
>     for Sankyō,
> I thought about you, but couldn't find you,
>     so I went down to Yushū.

*Popular Saying*
Ichidōmaru, in search of his father, went up Mt. Kōya.
*Or:*
Wonder where the sparrow's nest is.

*As against, "When Master Sekitō was a young priest he met Master Enō."*

ANSWER

Pretending to humor a baby, the pupil says, "Buru, buru, buru," clicking his tongue.

*As against, "Go and ask Nansen!"*

ANSWER

"Be it a bean cake or flower—how cute, how cute!"

*As against, "The master was still silent."*

ANSWER

The pupil just remains silent.

*Popular Saying*

The Sea of Genkai [near Kyūshū], which even birds cannot fly over, how shall we cross it?

*(Quote)*

> The surface of the water like a mirror,
> The mountain like a painting no bird flies
>   across.


## 24.  One, Two, Three

As the monk in charge of building Master Sozan's monument had finished his task, he came and reported it to Sozan, who asked, "How much will you give the constructor?" The monk said, "Everything is up to Your Reverend to decide." The master said, "Which is the best thing to do—give the constructor three mon [a monetary unit], or give him two mon, or just give him one mon? If you cannot answer me, I shall build the monument myself." The monk was bewildered.

Master Rasan was at that time living in a temple on Mt. Daiyūrei. A monk who went to Mt. Daiyūrei reported the above story. Rasan said, "Has anyone answered yet?" The monk said, "No one has got the answer yet." Rasan said, "Go back and tell Sozan: 'If you give the constructor three mon, you will not have the monument built in your lifetime. If you give him two mon, you will both be extending one hand. If it is one mon, you will both lose your eyebrows and beard.'" The monk went back and told this to Sozan. Sozan, with due ceremony, turned in the direction of Mt. Daiyūrei, bowed, and said, "I thought there were no great masters anymore. I never dreamt that on Mt. Daiyūrei an old Buddha is now radiating light which shines all the way to this

place. However, it is a December lotus flower." Rasan heard about that and said, "When I said that, the hair of the tortoise had long before grown several feet."
*As against, "Which is the best thing to do—give the constructor three mon, or give him two mon, or just give him one mon?"*

### ANSWER
"Wow! Thank you for so much!"
*As against, "An old Buddha is now radiating light which shines all the way to this place."*

### ANSWER
The pillar stands, the threshold lies."
*(Quote)*
> On the wide plain a light breeze blows.
> From the sky, scattered rains dimly, dimly.

*As against [Rasan's], "If you give three mon, you will not have the monument built in your lifetime. If you give two mon, you will both be extending one hand. If you give one mon, you will both lose your eyebrows and beard."*

### ANSWER
"The first one is a pine tree at the pond. The second one is a pine tree in the garden. The third one is a drooping pine tree."
*As against, "A December lotus flower."*

### ANSWER
"Well, it's easily done."
*(Quote)*
> The many mountains abide in the one
>     mountain,
> The many voices go to the sea and disappear.

### OR
(According to another school)
### MASTER
In place of the monk, you, say how many mon are to be given.

### ANSWER
The pupil counts, "One mon, two mon, three mon."
*(Quote)*
One, two, three, four, five, six, seven; Daruma does not know how to count.

(133)

As against, "*The radiant light shines all the way to this place.*"

ANSWER

The pupil recites, "The radiant light shines all the way to this place."

## 25. An Iron Cow

Master Fuketsu said, "Buddha-mind is just like an iron cow; if there is movement—there is no progress; if there is standstill—there is stagnation. Well, this 'no-movement-no-standstill,' should one be mindful of it? Should one be unmindful of it?"

At that time a monk by the name of Roha said, "I hold the working of the iron cow. Please, master, I wish you wouldn't be hindered by it." Fuketsu said, "I'm used to catching whales. I thought I had a whale of the great sea on my line, but all it was was a muddy, creepy, small frog." Roha, dumbfounded, was speechless. At that, Fuketsu yelled ["Katsu!"] at him and said, "Why can't you go on?!" Roha was bewildered. Fuketsu then hit Roha with a stick and said, "If you remember what was said, let me hear you say it!" Roha opened his mouth to speak when Fuketsu hit him again.

At that point, a monk named Bokushu said, "The law of Buddha and the law of the emperor are the same!" Fuketsu asked, "What do you mean by that?" Bokushu answered, "Not to cut when one should cut invites disorder." With that, Fuketsu got down from his seat and left.

As against, "*Buddha-mind is like an iron cow.*"

ANSWER

"It's like a stone mill."

MASTER

Why is it so?

ANSWER

"It doesn't move a bit."
(*Quote*)

> Along the hedge chasing a butterfly,
> By the water's side toying with a frog.

*Or:*

> Carrying one's wine bottle to drink the
> village-brewed wine;
> At home, wearing the kimono, be the
> master of the house.

*As against, "If there is movement—there is no progress; if there is standstill—there is stagnation. This 'no-movement-no-standstill,' should one be mindful of it? Should one be unmindful of it?"*

MASTER

[He repeats the above quote and says], If I keep after you in this way, how will you answer?

ANSWER

The pupil slaps his master once.

## 26.  *Similar to a Dream*

Official Rikkō and Master Nansen were conversing. Rikkō said, "The philosopher Jō once said, 'Heaven and earth are of the same root as myself; the universe and I are one.' It is really strange." Nansen pointed at a flower in the garden and said to Rikkō, "When people look at this flower, it is similar to a dream."

MASTER

It is said, "When people look at this flower it is similar to a dream." Now tell me—what's Rikkō's view? [i.e., How does Rikkō see the flower?]

ANSWER

"Like a mortar, like a rice cake."

MASTER

What is Nansen's view? [i.e., How does Nansen see the flower?]

ANSWER

"It has really blossomed beautifully."

MASTER

Distinguish the positions of Rikkō and Nansen.

ANSWER

"Rikkō's state is one of admitting the mysterious working [of Buddhism]. Nansen does not."

MASTER

Distinguish the positions of Rikkō and Nansen as to daily affairs.

"Rikkō, in ceremonial dress, is proper and formal. Nansen, in ordinary clothes, a pipe in his mouth, is just about to go out."

## MASTER
*(Quote)*
To listen, to see, to learn, to know is not all. The mountains and rivers should not be seen through a mirror.

## ANSWER
With his finger, the pupil points at things one by one, reciting, "To listen, to see, to learn, to know is not all." Then saying, "The mountains and rivers should not be seen through a mirror," he gives the appearance of taking all and everything into himself, folds his arms, and looks down.

## MASTER
*(Quote)*
The moon is sinking from the frosty sky, and half of the night is almost gone. With whom can I cast a cold shadow upon the surface of the crystal pond?

## ANSWER
"It's gotten late—well, since there's no one to talk to, guess I'll piss and go to bed."
*(Quote)*

> When Kōsen, king of Etsu, returned after
>     defeating the state of Go,
> The righteous warriors went home all clad in
>     silk,
> And maids were all over the spring palace
>     like flowers,
> But now, nothing but wild birds can be seen
>     flying about.

[In reference to the above quote, the book comments that the first three lines illustrate the bustling characteristic of Rikkō's view. The last line expresses the distinctionless, still position of Nansen.]
*Or:*

> The donkey stares at the well,
> The well stares at the donkey.

(According to another school)

*As against, "Heaven and earth are of the same root as myself."*

ANSWER

The pupil recites, "Heaven and earth are of the same root as myself."

*As against, "The universe and I are one."*

ANSWER

"Be it the floor, be it the charcoal brazier, be it the sliding door, it's all one with myself."

*As against, "It is similar to a dream."*

ANSWER

Nodding his head, the pupil pretends to be asleep.

*(Quote)*

> He saw only the meandering of the stream,
> and the winding of the road
> Without realizing that he was in "peach
> paradise."

*As against, "To listen, to see, to learn, to know is not all."*

ANSWER

"Without a doubt I'm listening, seeing, learning, and knowing."

*As against, "The mountains and rivers should not be seen through a mirror."*

ANSWER

The pupil pretends to look at mountains, rivers. Then, dropping his eyes on his chest, he stops.


MASTER

*(Quote)*

The moon is sinking from the frosty sky and half of the night is almost gone. With whom can I cast a cold shadow upon the surface of the crystal pond?


ANSWER

"It's gotten late. Well, since there's no one to talk to, guess I'll go to bed."


27.  *"Not Affected," "Not Deluded"*

Whenever Master Hyakujō held a meeting, there was always an old man in the crowd listening to him. When the crowd dispersed, the old man went with it. One day, however, the old man did not leave. So Hyakujō asked, "Who is it standing before me?" The old man answered, "I am not a human being. In ancient times I lived on this mountain. A student of the Way asked me if the enlightened were still affected by causality. I replied, saying that they were not affected. Because of that I was degraded to lead the life of a wild fox for five hundred lives. I now request you to answer one thing for me." Thus he asked if the enlightened were affected by causality. The master said, "They are not deluded by causality." The old man was enlightened upon hearing this. He bowed and said, "I am already liberated but my body as a fox is still at the back of this mountain. I am venturing to beg Your Reverend to treat me as you customarily do a dead monk."

The master then ordered the monk in charge of burial to beat the drum so as to announce to the people that there would be a service for a dead monk after the meal. The people started wondering and talking since everybody was safe and sound and there were no patients in the sick room. After the meal the master led the people to a big rock at the back of the mountain. From under the rock he dug out a dead wild fox with his stick and had it cremated.

When night fell, the master told the above story in his lecture. Master Ōbaku [Hyakujō's disciple] said, "The only mistake of the deceased was his answer which made him lead the life of a wild fox for five hundred lives. If he were right in every answer, what should he become?" Hyakujō said, "Come up and I'll tell you." So Ōbaku drew near and gave Hyakujō a slap. Hyakujō clapped his hands, laughed, and said, "I only thought that the barbarian's beard was red, I never realized it was a red-bearded barbarian." *As against, "Not affected by causality" and "not deluded by causality."*

ANSWER

As against "not affected by causality," the pupil says, "Kon, kon" [the cry of a fox]. As against "not deluded by causality," he says, "Bow-wow" [the bark of a dog].

MASTER

In the vast mountain of Hyakujō's, why is there a dead fox?

ANSWER

"Within the boundaries of even this temple there is at least one dead skunk. All the more, in the vast mountain of Hyakujō, there's nothing strange about there being one dead fox."

*As against, "I only thought that the barbarian's beard was red, I never realized it was a red-bearded barbarian."*
ANSWER

The pupil repeats, "I only thought that the barbarian's beard was red, I never thought it was a red-bearded barbarian."
*(Quote)*

> I thought that the yellow lily was sweet like
>     honey,
> But in fact it is honey that is bitter like the
>     yellow lily.

OR
(According to another school)

*As against, "Not affected by causality."*
ANSWER

The pupil takes two to three steps forward, saying, "Kon, kon" [the cry of a fox].

*As against, "Not deluded by causality."*
ANSWER

The pupil takes two to three steps backward, saying, "Bow-wow" [the bark of a dog].

OR
(According to another school)

*As against, "Not affected by causality."*
ANSWER

The pupil, saying, "Kon, kon," acts out the falling into the state of a fox.

*As against, "Not deluded by causality."*
ANSWER

The pupil, lying on his back, draws in his arms and legs, pretending to be a dead fox. Thus he shows the point of breaking loose from the fox's body.

## 28.  Where Thing Does Not Contradict Thing

The four realms of existence of the Kegon sect are: (1) the realm of truth (idea); (2) the realm of things; (3) the realm where truth and things do not contradict each other; and (4) the realm where thing does not contradict thing.

*As against, "The realm of truth."*

"The world throughout is clear. Not a speck of dust."
*(Quote)*
All this stretch of land is but a rod of iron.
*Or:*
In the wide world there is not an inch of land.
*As against, "The realm of things."*

ANSWER

"Each and all things are radiating a great light."
*(Quote)*

> The tidal water in the spring river joins the sea
> and is level with it.
> Over the sea, the bright moon is born
> with the tide.

*As against, "The realm where truth and things do not contradict each other."*

ANSWER

"The flower and moon relate as one, the mountain and river relate as one, night and day, man and woman, monk and layman relate as one."
*(Quote)*

> The mist of sunset sweeps the sky together
> with the lonely duck,
> And the autumn river is of the same color
> with the wide heaven.

*As against, "The realm where thing does not contradict thing."*

ANSWER

"The willow radiates a willowlike light; the flower radiates a flowerlike light; the mountain, a mountainlike light; the river, a riverlike light; man, a manlike light; and woman, a womanlike light."
*(Quote)*
Green is the grass and yellow the willow. Profuse are the blossoms of the peach and fragrant are those of the plum.

OR
(According to another school)
MASTER
Show me the four realms using your hand.

The pupil thrusts his hand forward saying:
1. "To see the hand as a hand is the realm of things."
2. "Not to see the hand as a hand is the realm of truth" [idea].
3. "To be at the point where the hand is not seen as a hand and yet still to see the hand as a hand is the realm of truth and things not contradicting each other."
4. "The one hand immediately becomes heaven, earth; it becomes mountain, river, grass, tree; it becomes each and every thing; each and all things come into the one hand." (This is the realm where thing does not contradict thing.)

*(Quote)*

> The one moon appears on all waters,
> All waters reflect the one moon.

## 29. *What Will You Call It?*

Master Isan said, "When I die, I will be transformed into a male buffalo at the house of the parishioner at the foot of the mountain. On the buffalo's lower left side will be written the five words, 'This is the monk Isan.' If you call it 'Isan,' it's a buffalo. If you call it 'buffalo,' it's Isan. Well then, what will you call it?" Here Kyōzan stepped out, bowed, and walked away.

"My name is so-and-so," the pupil says, giving his own name.
*(Quote)*
Whether you say Kōshi or Kyūchūji [names for Confucius] it's the same thing.

## 30. *Stick!*

Master Shuzan, taking a bamboo stick, said to the people, "If you call this a stick, you fall into the trap of words (or: You must eliminate that which prevents you from calling it a stick); but if you do not call it a stick, you oppose the fact. So what will you people call it?" At that time monk Sekken, who happened to be in the assembly, came forth. He snatched the stick, broke it in two, and threw the pieces down the stairs, saying, "What is this?" Shuzan said, "Blind!"

Master Dai-e added, "Say it quick! Say it quick!"

*As against, "What will you call it?"*
### ANSWER
Clenching his hand into a fist, the pupil thrusts it forward saying, "Stick! Stick!"

### MASTER
If you call a stick a stick, it is like a donkey forever tied to a pole.

### ANSWER
The pupil says, "Then you may call it a night pot or a nightsoil dipper."

### MASTER
What's the use of the stick?

### ANSWER
"It may be a cane, chopsticks, a pestle, or a rice spoon."

### MASTER
"If you call this a stick you fall into the trap of words (or: You must eliminate that which prevents you from calling it a stick)." Handle this.

### ANSWER
The pupil, handling the stick, assumes the pose of putting it away in the corner of the shelf.

### MASTER
*(Quote)*
If it cannot be called "emptiness" ["nothingness"], what should it be called?

### ANSWER
The pupil turns a somersault in front of his master.

### OR
(According to another school)
*As against, "If you call this a stick, you fall into the trap of words."*
### ANSWER
"Stick."

### MASTER
Ha! You trespass [i.e., you violate "nothingness"]!

(142)

"Hmm, it's a piece of wood," the pupil says, throwing it away.

[He says again] Ha! You trespass!

"Stick."

Without falling into the trap of words [without violating "nothingness"]—how will you deal with this?

"Falling into the trap . . . trespassing—what a bore. Break it to pieces, stick it under the bathtub and burn it up!"

Not involving yourself in trespassing, say the phrase.

The pupil quotes, "Originally empty, ultimately empty."
(*Quote*)

> If it is the time of Tō and Gu [dynasties]
>     then we shall have ceremony and music;
> If it is the time of Ketsu and Chū [villain
>     kings] then we shall have only war

## 31. *The Emperor and the Bowl*

[Enō's master decided that Enō would take his place as the next master, and as proof of the authority, he gave him his cloak and bowl. The other monks, displeased with this, chased after Enō. Near Mt. Daiyūrei they caught up with Enō and attempted to steal the bowl from him. However, when they tried to grab the bowl away, they could not lift it.]

One day Emperor Taisō of the Sō Dynasty held up a bowl, turned to his minister Ōzui and said, "Since the monks at Mt. Daiyūrei could not lift the bowl, how is it that I can?" Ōzui gave no reply.

"The holy virtue of the emperor is a vast and magnificent thing. All the surrounding nations are bathed in his glorious presence."

*(Quote)*
The clouds are deep and thick; I'm not supposed to be able to go to the emperor's court; how is it that I am here?

"The holy virtue of the emperor is a vast and magnificent thing. Even the birds and beasts in the depths of the mountain are worshipping His Majesty."
*(Quote)*

> The four seas are completely under the enlightenment
> of the emperor.
> Who dares to invade our boundaries from the
> south, west and north?

## 32. *How Is Your Health?*

Master Baso was not feeling well. The head monk of the temple went to him and asked, "How is Your Reverence's health these days?" Baso said, "Nichimenbutsu, Getsumenbutsu [two legendary Buddhas]."

"Neither Shaka Buddha nor Amida Buddha know anything."

*(Quote)*
When I die it is a good monk who bears not his bereavement for too long.

"A man's life is short lived. Very soon my life too is in danger."

(According to another school)
The pupil turns to the right, saying, "Nichimenbutsu." Turning to the left he says, "Getsumenbutsu."

As against, "*When I die it is a good monk who bears not his bereavement for too long.*"

ANSWER

"Oh, what shall I do? If anything should happen to my master, hereafter under whom am I to study?"

OR

(With certain masters)

ANSWER

"Oh, the pain! The pain!"

## 33. *The Gate!*

At the end of the summer session, Master Suigan said to the people, "I have been talking to you brothers for a summer; see if my eyebrows are still here." Hofuku said, "The thief is afraid." Chōkei said, "It grows!" Ummon said, "The gate!" [or: "Shut!"]. *As against, "Chōkei said, 'It grows!'"*

ANSWER

"It grew! It grew!"

MASTER

What kind of place is the place where it grows?

ANSWER

"From the mountain just beyond, to the place of the hedge, it is covered all over with green grass grown."
(*Quote*)
After it rains, the greenery of the green hills turns greener.
*Or:*

> Clouds stood still after the rain and the day
> had just begun to dawn;
> The few peaks looked picturesque with their
> green height and massiveness.

*As against, "Hofuku said, 'The thief is afraid.'"*

ANSWER

"The thief's heart is beating in fear."
*As against, "Ummon said, 'The gate!'"*

ANSWER

"GAAATE!" the pupil roars like a lion and hits the floor.
*Or:*
The pupil slaps the master once.

(145)

*(Quote)*

> The father is equipped with tricks that can
> persuade his wayward son;
> The son has the fist that can beat his father.

*Or:*

An angry fist does not strike a smiling face.


OR

(According to another school)

MASTER

See if my eyebrows are here.


ANSWER

The pupil looks at his master's eyebrows.


MASTER

Suigan's feeling—what's it like?


ANSWER

"The feathers of the cormorant—not even one can be plucked,
not even one can be added."
*As against, "Hofuku said, 'The thief is afraid.'"*

ANSWER

"Somehow, the fellow who steals cannot relax."
*As against, "Chōkei said, 'It grows!'"*

ANSWER

"It certainly grows."
*As against, "Ummon said, 'The gate!'"*

ANSWER

"This 'gate'—in things good or bad, anything, everything, there
is nothing that is not the 'gate.' It hasn't got a single crack, this
not-even-an-ant-can-crawl-through GATE!"

*(Quote)*

To lose money and be accused of a crime.

*Or:*

An angry fist does not strike a smiling face.

*Or:*

> I stop the vehicle for love-to-sit-in-the-
> twilight-forest-of-maple-trees.
> The leaves under the frost are redder than
> flowers of February.

## 34.  *Unforgivable*

That Daruma knows is forgivable. That Daruma understands is unforgivable.
*As against, "That Daruma knows is forgivable."*
### ANSWER
"Yes, that's okay, that's okay."
*As against, "That Daruma understands is unforgivable."*
### ANSWER
"No, no, that's bad."
*(Quote)*
His cleverness can be matched, but his foolishness is surpassing.
*Or:*
Make me a good courtier, don't make me a faithful courtier.


## 35.  *How Do You Say It?*

Master Kinzan went together with Master Gantō and Master Seppō to see Master Tokusan. Kinzan said, "Master Tennō said it like this. Master Ryūtan said it like this too. [Tennō was the master of Ryūtan, and Ryūtan was the master of Tokusan.] I wonder how you say it?" Tokusan said, "Try and show me how Tennō and Ryūtan said it." This upset Kinzan and just as he was about to speak, Tokusan hit him.

On the way back Kinzan said, "I know he is right, but beating me was too much!" Gantō said, "If that is the way you are, do not ever say you have met Tokusan."


### MASTER
"Master Tennō said it like this. Master Ryūtan said it like this too. I wonder how you say it? Now, you answer in place of Tokusan."


### ANSWER
"I knew you'd ask that."


## 36.  *Discuss Buddhist Law*

Master Nansen said, "Monju and Fugen [legendary Buddhas] discussed Buddhist law until late last night. I gave them each thirty strokes with my stick and sent them to Mt. Nitetchi [i.e., the farthest end of earth]." At that point Jōshū stepped out from the crowd and said, "How shall we have hit you?!" Nansen said, "What have I done wrong?" Jōshū bowed.

### ANSWER
"Yesterday I awoke at midnight and started thinking about home and my family. I thought of this, I thought of that, then SHUNK! quit it and slept soundly till morning."
(Quote)

> To read out the verdict while carrying the
> stolen object in your arms.

Or:

> I cut out all the rights and wrongs of the
> human world,
> And shut the wooden door where white
> clouds lie thick and deep.

### OR
(According to another school)
As against, "Discussed Buddhist law."
### ANSWER
"Since last night my back and shoulders hurt—what a pain!"
As against, "Sent them to Mt. Nitetchi."
"This morning I sent for the masseur and after the treatment I'm completely well."

## 37. Simultaneous Doubt and Enlightenment

Master Nan-in said, "You know only 'simultaneous doubt and enlightenment' [i.e., when a chick is about to come out from an egg, it chirps. In response, the hen will peck at the egg so as to break the shell and free the chick. This process is compared to having doubt and receiving the solution right away] as a thing in itself, but you are not equipped to apply it." A monk came up with the question, "What is the application of 'simultaneous doubt and enlightenment?'" Nan-in said, "The truly great master does not hold onto the mold of 'simultaneous doubt and enlightenment.' One who does is deprived of its working." The monk said, "I still have some doubt." Nan-in said, "What is it that you doubt?" The monk said, "The so-called 'deprived of.'" At that, Nan-in struck him. The monk protested but Nan-in drove him away.

Later, this same monk went to the assembly of Master Ummon and reported the above story. A certain monk said, "So, Master Nan-in broke his stick." With that, the monk came to realization. He went back to see Nan-in, but Nan-in had just passed away. Instead he met Master Fuketsu. The moment he bowed, Fuketsu said, "Aren't you the monk who asked our deceased master about 'simultaneous doubt and enlightenment?'" The monk said, "Yes." Fuketsu said, "How did you understand it then?" The monk said, "At that time I was like one walking by the light of a lamp." Fuketsu said, "You have understood."

ANSWER

"I'm doing all that I can, so please don't worry about me."
*Or:*
"I've grown *THIS* big without the help of others," the pupil says standing up.
*As against, "The application of 'stimultaneous doubt and enlighten-ment.'"*

ANSWER

"When the bell rings—to the meditation hall.
When the gong strikes—to the dining room."

## 38. *Don't You Believe Me Now?*

One day, the official Chinsō along with other officials were climbing up a tall building when they saw several monks coming. One of the officials said, "Those coming are all Zen priests." Chinsō said, "They are not." The official said, "How do you know that they are not?" Chinsō said, "Wait till they come closer. I shall ask them." When the monks came to the front of the building, Chinsō called out suddenly, "Reverend!" [In Japanese, "joza"—a general term for Buddhist priests; not the specific term for a Zen priest.] The monks looked up. Chinsō said to the officials, "Don't you believe me now?"

ANSWER

"I am filled with awe realizing the height of your lordship's wisdom and virtue."

OR

(According to another school)

*As against, "Don't you believe me now?"*

"Don't you believe me now?"

Take the place of the officials and say something.

"Your judgment is truly admirable!"
*(Quote)*

> The cold weather is selfless;
> You should understand even before the
> occasion arises.

*Or:*

> Without great intelligence, how can we get
> this man?

*Or:*

> If you do not have the strength to lift up a
> three-legged giant stove or to root up a
> mountain,
> You will find it not easy to ride the black
> horse that runs a thousand miles a day.


## 39.   *I Never Said a Word . . .*

Master Kassan said, "I have been living on this mountain for twenty years but I never said a word about our sect of religion." A monk then asked, "I have heard you say that you had been living on this mountain for twenty years yet you never said a word about our religious sect. Is it true?" Kassan said, "Yes it is." At that, the monk threw Kassan off his seat. Kassan dismissed the assembly and left. The next day he made the people dig a pit and then ordered his attendant, "Ask the monk who raised the question yesterday to come." When the monk arrived, Kassan said, "I talked of nothing but nonsense in the past twenty years, so I request you to beat me to death and bury me in the pit. If you do not kill me, you have to beat yourself to death and be buried in this pit." The monk gathered his things and sneaked away.

Take the monk's place and say something.

The pupil makes a face. "Ha, ha! Good for you!"

## 40. *Where in the World Are They?*

It is said in our sect that Master Toku-un of Mt. Myōhō never came down from the mountain. Master Zenzai went to see him but was unable to meet him for seven days. However, one day they happened to meet each other on the peak of another mountain. Having met, Toku-un spoke to Zenzai about the truth that a single thought holds the wisdom of all the Buddhas of past, present, and future.

Master Engo commented on the above story, saying, "Since Toku-un never came down from Mt. Myōhō, how come they met each other on another mountain? If he did leave the mountain, then it is contrary to the belief in our sect that Toku-un never came down from Mt. Myōhō. When it comes to this—where in the world are Toku-un and Zenzai?"

ANSWER
"Master and I are facing each other like this."

## 41. *A Bottle Is a Bottle*

When Master Isan was still a pupil under Master Hyakujō, he was in charge of cooking. At that time, Hyakujō founded a temple on Mt. Daii and was about to choose the monk to become the chief priest of this temple. He asked the head monk to call those qualified enough to apply for this position. Then Hyakujō picked up a bottle and put it on the ground. He asked, "If you weren't allowed to call this a bottle, what would you call it?" The head monk replied, "You cannot call it a wooden log." Then Hyakujō asked Isan. Isan kicked the bottle over and walked away. Hyakujō laughed and said, "The head monk lost to Isan." Thus he appointed Isan to be the chief priest of the temple on Mt. Daii.
(*Quote*)

> Rain falling on tree leaves—jadelike beads of
> water turning around,
> And the heron breaks through the misty
> curtain hanging over the bamboo trees.

## 42. A Silver Bowl Filled with Snow

A monk asked Master Haryō, "What is the teaching of the Daiba Sect like?" Haryō said, "A silver bowl filled with snow."

ANSWER

"Such a thing—smash it to pieces!"

OR

(According to another school)
*As against, "Daiba Sect."*

ANSWER

"Don't blab around."
*(Quote)*
Open your mouth and your insides are seen.

## 43. Every Coral Branch Supports the Moon

A monk asked Master Haryō, "What is the sword that can cut a hair blown against its blade?" Haryō said, "Every coral branch is supporting the moon."

ANSWER

"Such a thing—I broke it and flung it into the western sea!"
*(Quote)*
> A broken mirror does not reflect images
> again,
> And it is difficult for fallen flowers to go up
> the branches.

OR

(According to another school)
*As against, "The sword that can cut a hair blown against its blade."*

ANSWER

"When standing, in standing; when sitting, in sitting; when listening, in listening; unhindered, unhampered, freely managing."
*(Quote)*
To howl at the moon and sleep in the clouds.
*Or:*
To sing to the flowers and recite poetry under the moon.

## 44. *An Open-eyed Man Falls into the Well*

A monk asked Master Haryō, "What is the way?" Haryō said, "An open-eyed man falling into the well."

### ANSWER

"Whew! That was close! I almost fell in!" the pupil says as he imitates one narrowly escaping a fall.
*(Quote)*
The pit that entraps people is full every year.
*Or:*
The pitch-dark, deep pit is almost terror-inspiring.


## 45. *In Relation to One*

A monk asked Master Ummon, "What is the real religion that Buddha preached?" Ummon said, "It is in relation to one."

### ANSWER

"In meeting a minister, preaching to a minister; in meeting a beggar, preaching to a beggar; meeting a man, preaching to a man; meeting a woman, preaching to a woman."
*(Quote)*
> In speaking to an inferior official one should
> be pleasant and kind,
> In speaking to a superior official one should
> be pleasant and upright.

*Or:*
Talk of various things by the side of a dung fire.


## 46. *In Opposition to One*

A monk asked Master Ummon, "What if it is neither a happening-right-before-your-eyes nor a thing-right-before-your-eyes?" Ummon said, "It is in opposition to one."

### MASTER

"In opposition to one"—what's it mean? Attach a quote to this.

*(Quote)*

> There are two lines of tears on the coral
>     pillow.
> Half is for thinking of you, while the other
>     half is for hating you.

*Or:*

> I always recall places south of the Yōsukō
>     River in the month of March,
> With the hundred flowers sweetening the air
>     amid the chirping of the small birds.

### MASTER

As against, "What if it is neither a happening-right-before-your-eyes nor a thing-right-before-your-eyes?"—how'd you answer it?

### ANSWER

The pupil solemnly recites, "What if it is neither a happening-right-before-your-eyes nor a thing-right-before-your-eyes." *(Quote)*

> Grab the thief's gun and kill him.

[In reference to the above, the book comments that this is a case of answering through snatching the question.]

## 47. *Are You Alive?*

A monk asked Master Kyōshō, "I am chirping, will my master peck for me?" [i.e., when a chick is about to come out from an egg, it chirps. In response, the hen will peck at the egg so as to break the shell and free the chick. In Zen, this process is compared to having doubt and receiving the solution right away.] Kyōshō said, "Are you alive?" The monk said, "If I were not alive, people would laugh at me." Kyōshō said, "That's quite a guy."

### ANSWER

"Chirp, peck, chirp chirp, peck peck."

## 48. *The One-Piece Tower*

Emperor Shukusō asked his Zen master Etchū, "When you die, what am I to do?" Etchū said, "Build a one-piece tower for me." The emperor asked Etchū for the form of the tower. Etchū remained silent for awhile. Then he asked, "Do you understand?" The emperor said, "I do not understand." Etchū said, "Among my disciples there is the man called Tangen. He knows about it. You may ask him about it."

After Etchū died, the emperor called for Tangen and asked him about it. Tangen said, "It is south of the place called Shō and north of the place called Tan. [On this phrase Master Setchō later said: 'The one hand does not sound of itself.'] Within, it overflows with gold. [Setchō: "A cane in the shape of a mountain."] Under a shadeless tree rests a ferryboat. [Setchō: "The sea is quiet, the river is clear."] There is an emerald palace that holds no Buddhist priest of fame." [Setchō: "He brought it out right in front of your eyes."]

*As against, "To ask the master for the form of the tower."*

ANSWER

The pupil folds his arms across his chest and stands up.

*As against, "Etchū remained silent."*

ANSWER

(Quote)

> North of the River Isui, trees under the
>     spring sun;
> East of the River Yōsukō, the clouds of
>     twilight.

*As against, "South of Shō, north of Tan."*

ANSWER

"Here is the shelf, here is the door."

*As against, "Within, it overflows with gold."*

ANSWER

"In the living room, there is spread a fine carpet."

*As against, "Under a shadeless tree rests a ferryboat."*

ANSWER

"Thus I seat myself down." [So saying, the pupil sits down.]

*As against, "There is an emerald palace that holds no Buddhist priest of fame."*

ANSWER

"In the whole world there is not one who knows my mind."

## 49.  No Meaning

Master Ryūge asked Master Suibi, "What is the meaning of our founder coming from the west?" [i.e., what is the meaning of Zen?] Suibi said, "Hand me the stick." Ryūge handed the stick to Suibi who, upon receiving it, hit Ryūge with it. Ryūge said, "Hit me as you like, at any rate there is no meaning to our founder coming from the west."

Ryūge then asked Master Rinzai, "What is the meaning of our founder coming from the west?" Rinzai said, "Hand me the cushion." Ryūge handed the cushion to Rinzai who, upon receiving it, hit Ryūge with it. Ryūge said, "Hit me as you like, at any rate there is no meaning to our founder coming from the west."

MASTER

"There is no meaning to our founder coming from the west"—what's it mean?

ANSWER

"Starting with the koan on the one hand, I went through the various stages of the [koan] teaching; but what I've gained can't even be pinpointed with a single rabbit's hair."
(Quote)

> Last year we were so poor we had only land
>      as big as a drill-point.
> This year our poverty is such that we haven't
>      even got land as big as a drill-point.

## 50.  It Is Somewhat a Pity

Master Hofuku and Master Chōkei were strolling in the mountains. Hofuku pointed his finger and said, "That is the peak of Mt. Myōhō." Chōkei said, "It is all right, but it is somewhat a pity."

Later Master Setchō commented, "What is it I want touring mountains with this man?" And he also said, "After one hundred years there will be few, but not none." Master Kyōshō commented, "If it were not for Chōkei, skeletons would scatter the wilderness."

As against, "That is the peak of Mt. Myōhō."

ANSWER

Shading his eyes with one hand, the pupil pretends to look afar and says, "What a beautiful view!"

As against, "It is all right, but it is somewhat a pity."

"To be taken in by beautiful scenery can't be helped—before it gets dark let's go. Let's go home !"
*(Quote)*

> Weeping, I held the sleeves of Riryō [a
>     famous general] in my hands.
> The thought of returning home made tears
>     wet the lapels of my clothes.

## 51.  A Few Here, a Few There

Monju [a legendary Buddha representing wisdom] asked Master Mujaku, "Where have you been recently?" Mujaku said, "I have been in the south." Monju said, "How is the teaching of Buddha faring in the south?" Mujaku said, "The teaching of Buddha is declining and monks hardly keep discipline." Monju said, "How many monks are there?" Mujaku said, "Sometimes three hundred, sometimes five hundred. It varies." He then asked Monju, "How are things getting on here?" Monju said, "The people and saints live together. Dragons and snakes mingle." Mujaku said, "How many monks are there?" Monju said, "Three three in front, three three in back" [i.e., a few here, a few there].

*(Quote)*
There are rubies in front and pearls in back.
*Or:*
With upright head and straight tail.
*Popular Saying*
The tail is long, the head is long—a long-tailed cock.
*Or:*
Hiding the head yet forgetting to hide the rear.
*Or:*
Clap the hands, slap the ass—horse market.

## 52.  Where Is the Mind?

Master Banzan left a saying, "There is no existence in the three realms of past, present, and future. Where is the mind?"

"The pillar stands, the threshold lies, the willow is green, the flower is red."
*(Quote)*

> Green is the grass and yellow the willow,
> Profuse are the blossoms of the peach and
> fragrant are those of the plum.

OR

(According to another school)

ANSWER

The pupil slaps his master's face once.

MASTER

"No existence"—what's it mean?

ANSWER

"I ask you to excuse me," the pupil says, bowing his head.

OR

(According to another school)

ANSWER

The pupil stands up, shades his eyes with one hand as he pretends to look afar, and says, "If you look over here you see Mt. So-and-so; if you look over there you see Mt. So-and-so."
*(Quote)*

> Arriving at the river, the territories of the
> state of Go seem to come to an end;
> Yet on the other bank, many are the hills in
> the state of Etsu.

*Or:*

> When evening falls in picturesque spots on
> the river,
> Fishermen wearing straw raincoats are on
> their way homeward bound.

## 53. *A Speck of Dust*

Master Fuketsu said, "Raise up a speck of dust and the nation will prosper; if a speck of dust is not raised, the nation will fall."

Later, Master Setchō said, "Is there no monk among you who will live and die like me?"

*(Quote)*
> Arriving at the river, the territories of the
>    state of Go seem to come to an end;
> Yet on the other bank, many are the hills in
>    the state of Etsu.

## 54.  *Gya!*

One day a monk of the eastern hall and a monk of the western hall had a fight over a cat. Master Nansen saw this so he took the cat and held it up, saying, "If any of you can tell me the meaning of this, I shall not cut this cat." The monks said nothing in reply; Nansen cut the cat into two.

ANSWER

"Gya!" [the cry of a dying cat].

## 55.  *Nyan*

Master Nansen told the previous story to Master Jōshū and asked him about it. Jōshū took off his sandals and put them on his head. Nansen said, "If you were there, you would have saved the cat."

ANSWER

"Nyan" [the cry of a come-alive cat].
*(Quote)*
> When one is angered with another,
>    the sword is drawn. [Nansen]
> To cure a malady, one takes medicine
>    from the chest. [Jōshū]

## 56.  *Come and Eat Your Rice*

Whenever mealtime came, Master Kingyū would himself take the rice pot to the front of the hall, dance and laugh heartily, saying, "Ho, ye children of Buddha! Come and eat your rice!"

Later, Master Setchō commented, "Though Kingyū did that, he did not do it out of good nature."

A monk asked Master Chōkei, "When Kingyū said, 'Children

of Buddha, come eat your rice!' what did he mean?" Chōkei said, "It is very similar to reciting a song of praise for the meal."

MASTER

"Children of Buddha, come eat your rice"—how'd you answer to that?

ANSWER

"I'm full," the pupil says, patting his belly.
*As against, "Though Kingyū did that, he did not do it out of good nature."*

ANSWER

"The rice pot's empty."
*As against, "Chōkei said, 'It is very similar to reciting a song of praise for the meal.'"*

ANSWER

The pupil recites a prayer usually said at mealtimes.

## 57. *Playing Ball on Rapid Water*

A monk asked Master Jōshū, "Has a newborn baby the six senses?" Jōshū said, "Playing ball on rapid water."

The monk then went to Master Tōsu and asked, "What does 'playing ball on rapid water' mean?" Tōsu said, "Thought after thought incessantly flows on."

ANSWER

The pupil draws in his arms and legs, lies on his back and says, "Ga, ga," imitating a baby.

## 58. *Playing with Mud*

A monk asked Master Yakusan, "On the plain where short grass grows, there are herds of deer. What should one do to shoot the deer among deer?" Yakusan said, "Watch out for my arrow!" The monk let himself fall. Yakusan said to his attendants, "Drag out this useless corpse!" The monk then went away. Yakusan said, "This fellow plays around with mud. He knows no limits."

Later, Master Setchō commented, "Though he [the monk] lives while he takes three steps, when he takes the fifth step, he has to die."

*As against, "Watch out for my arrow!"*

ANSWER

The pupil gives the pretense of one fixing an arrow and drawing
the bow.

*As against, "Let himself fall."*

ANSWER

The pupil pretends to let himself fall.

MASTER

"Drag out this useless corpse!" Instead of the monk, you say
something.

ANSWER

"The master has died."

## 59. *The Sturdy Body of Truth*

A monk asked Master Tairyū, "The physical body will rot and
decay, but what will happen to the sturdy body of truth?"
Tairyū said, "The blossoms of the mountain flowers are like
brocade and the brook is deep and looks so blue!"

*As against, "The blossoms of the mountain flowers are like brocade
and the brook is deep and looks so blue!"*

ANSWER

The pupil, folding his arms across his chest, stands up, reciting,
"Mountain flowers." Sitting down again, he recites, "The brook."

MASTER

[In reference to "mountain flowers" he quotes]—[If "mountain
flowers" are the body of truth] when strong winds blow, what
will happen?

ANSWER

The pupil, swaying his body, imitates falling flowers. Then,
plop! he drops himself down.

MASTER

[In reference to "the brook" he quotes]—[If "the brook" is the
body of truth] when the mountain slides, what will happen?

ANSWER

"Chin, don, shan" [chime of bells]. So saying, the pupil gives the
air of a funeral.

You think resentfully of the morning dew, yet in the end your body lying on the grass will pass away like dew.
*Or:*

> On a spring evening coming to the mountain
> temple,
> Together with the evening bells the flowers
> fall.

## 60. *Put Together*

Master Ummon said, "Put a famous master of old together with that pole outside the hall. How does that work?" He answered himself saying, "It gets cloudy south of the mountain, but it is north of the mountain that it rains."

### ANSWER

"I've bought a bag of red pepper for two cents. I also bought turnips, fried bean curd, and potatoes for five or six cents."
*(Quote)*

> Cream and cheese are mixed into one,
> Cake trays and head ornaments are melted
> into one metal.

*Or:*

> A Taoist hat, Confucian shoes, and a Buddhist
> cassock,
> Mix and harmonize them together and the
> three schools become one.

## 61. *"Say Nothing" and Nothing Said*

Yuima [a legendary Buddhist layman] asked Monju [a legendary Buddha], "What is the only way to enlightenment?" Monju said, "Those who have the same idea as I do will say nothing, preach nothing, show nothing, learn nothing about any method. Avoid all questions and answers. This is the only way." Those around also gave their views. Then Monju turned to Yuima and said, "Now that we have each had our say, what is your view?" Yuima was silent.

Later, Master Setchō commented, "What did Yuima say?" Then he added, "I've got it."

"Yuima was silent"—what's the gut meaning of that?

The pupil slaps his master's face once.

The view of Monju—what's it like?

The pupil solemnly recites, "Say nothing, preach nothing, show nothing, learn nothing about any method. This is the only way."

## 62.  Which Is Your Self?

Master Ummon said, "Medicines cure diseases. The whole earth is medicine, but which is your self?"

ANSWER
"TURRNIP of Oari" [a town near Nagoya], the pupil slowly recites.
[In reference to the above the book comments, "It is taking the other by surprise and sending him flying."]
(Quote)
The fusu [name of a plant] of Menshū [name of a place] and the ginger of Kanshū [name of a place].
Or:
When you come once again, it is for no other reason than the misty rain of Ro Mountain and the tide of River Sekkō.

## 63.  Blind, Deaf, Dumb

Master Gensha said, "Our elders always tell us to meet nature and benefit the living. But if suddenly there came the sick of the following three kinds, how would you treat them? There is the blind, who even if you pick up a hammer and wave it before him, sees nothing. Then there is the deaf, who, no matter how you tell him of the wonder of Buddhism, hears nothing. There is also the dumb, who, no matter how you teach him to speak, simply cannot do it. How will you deal with them? If you cannot deal with them, the teaching of Buddha has no effect on you."

Later a monk asked Master Ummon about this. Ummon said, "Make a salute." The monk saluted and rose. Ummon struck with his stick. The monk stepped back. Ummon said, "You are not blind." Then he called him to come near. The monk drew near and Ummon said, "You are not deaf." Ummon then said, "Do you understand by now?" The monk answered, "I do not." Ummon said, "You are not dumb." At that the monk was enlightened.

*As against, "There is the blind, who, even if you pick up a hammer and wave it before him, sees nothing."*

ANSWER

"It's unseen by the eyes, but it's a beautiful flower, isn't it?"
*As against, "There is the deaf, who, no matter how you try to make him hear, hears nothing."*

ANSWER

"The ears can't hear a thing, but the clock is going tick-tock, tick-tock."
*As against, "There is the dumb, who, no matter how you teach him to speak, simply cannot do it."*

ANSWER

"I won't say it with my mouth."
(Quote)

> Only in buildings in the capital or in the big
>    cities can the color of tiles be seen,
> And in the temple of the goddess of mercy
>    nothing but the sound of bells can be
>    heard.

Or:

> Raising the curtain, I saw the snow on top of
>    Peak Kōrō,
> And leaning on my pillow, I heard the peal
>    of the bell in Iai Temple.

Or:

> Morning saw the clouds floating along so
>    freely,
> And evening heard the murmuring sounds of
>    running streams.

64. *Sound*

One day Master Kyōgen was weeding the grass. A piece of

brick hit the bamboo. It made a sound. At that moment, Kyōgen was enlightened. He recited the following: "One stroke and all I know is forgotten. No further learning is needed. I gather myself and give up the old way, untrapped by the stealthy occasion. Not a trace to be found anywhere. Sight and sound make me forget about manners. Those who know the way will say this is an excellent occasion."

ANSWER

The pupil stands up and pretends to clean up, throwing away rubbish. At the same time he utters, "Clunk!," acting out the point of a stone hitting bamboo.

## 65. *What Do You Understand by This?*

Master Gettan said to a monk, "Make a hundred carts. Take off both ends of each cart and get rid of the axle. What do you understand by this?"

ANSWER

The pupil pretends to push a cart from behind up a slope saying, "Creak, creak, rattle, rumble," in imitation of the sounds a cart makes.

## 66. *Not Keeping Silent, Not Using Words*

Master Hōen said, "On the road you meet a man who understands the way. You cannot keep silent and you should not use words. Tell me how you do it."

ANSWER

"In order to get to so-and-so from here, you go out the front gate, pass so-and-so and head in the direction of so-and-so." In this way the pupil, using the temple as the starting point, enumerates the course one takes in going to a place three or four miles away.

## 67. *Taking a Bath*

It is said that when the Bodhisattva called Baddabara was taking a bath, in a flash he attained great enlightenment.

Master Setchō said, "How do you monks understand this?"

The pupil takes the pose of taking a bath. Very quietly he rubs his arms saying, "Suu, suu," expressing the delicate sensation of touch.

## 68.  *Without Cold, Without Heat*

A monk asked Master Tōzan, "How can one escape from winter cold and summer heat?" Tōzan said, "Why do you not go to a place where there is neither cold nor heat?" The monk said, "What is the place without cold, without heat?" Tōzan said, "When it is cold, the cold freezes you. When it is hot, the heat burns you."

"Hot. Cold," the pupil says with force in his voice.
[In reference to the meaning of the above answer the book comments, "If you wholly become cold and heat, there is neither cold nor heat."]

## 69.  *What Do You Have in Mind?*

Master Nansen along with Master Kisū and Master Mayoku went together to pay their respects to Master Etchū. When they were halfway there, Nansen drew a circle on the ground and said, "I shall go if you can tell me what this means." Kisū sat in the middle of the circle. Mayoku played the woman and bowed. Nansen said, "If it is like this, I am not going." Kisū said, "What do you have in mind?"

He draws a circle in front of the pupil, saying, "Well, what now?"

The pupil, saying, "Oh, this is a nice present!" gives the pose of one accepting.

## 70.  *Don't Fancy*

Whenever Master Mugō was asked a question, he would simply say, "Don't fancy!"

The pupil folds his arms and gravely says, "Don't fancy."

## 71. *Buddha's Master*

Master Hōen said, "Even Buddha and Miroku [a legendary bodhisattva] are his slaves. Tell me who he is."

### ANSWER
The pupil enumerates such names as "Gonbē, Hachibē, Ohichi, Osan" [common Japanese names of men and women].

## 72. *Swallow a River?!*

The disciple Hōkoji visited Master Baso and asked, "Who is he that transcends existence?" Baso said, "When you have swallowed the waters of the west river in one gulp, I shall answer you." In an instant Hōkoji realized the answer and said the following: "People from all over come and meet together; each seeks to learn the way of non-doing. This is the place where Buddhas are born. I, having been chosen for holding the heart of nothingness, can now go back."

### ANSWER
"I'll have a cup of tea," the pupil says, taking a cup of tea.

## 73. *Thought of the Moment*

"The boundless world is not even a pinpoint's distance from me. The happenings of ten generations past and present are never absent from the thought of the moment."
*As against, "The boundless world is not even a pinpoint's distance from me."*

### ANSWER
"With a mountain, become one with the mountain; with a river, become one with the river; master and I are one body."
*(Quote)*
Mt. Tendai is the pillow, the footsteps on Mt. Nangaku.
*As against, "The happenings of ten generations past and present are never absent from the thought of the moment."*

"How hateful; how charming; how desirable; how disappointing."
(*Quote*)

> Though my golden bracelet on my arm has
>     grown an inch too loose,
> Yet when meeting people I still tell them I am
>     not in love.

*Or:*

> Only the lines of tears can be seen wetting
>     her face.
> Heaven alone knows on whom her heart's
>     hate is centered.

*Popular Saying*
A woman's single thought can pass through even rock, and if it so desires can cut a golden chain.
*Or:*
Be it rock, be it gold, it pierces right through—the-single-minded-ceaseless-beat-the-bell.

## 74. *Where Is My Rhino?*

One day Master Enkan ordered his attendant, "Fetch me the fan with a rhino on it." The attendant said, "The fan is broken." Enkan said, "Since the fan is broken, then give me back my rhino." The attendant could not answer.

[The following are comments of later masters]:

Master Tōsu said, "I would do anything to bring it out for you, only I am afraid that its head and horn will not be perfect." Later, Master Setchō commented to this, "I want imperfect head and horn."

Master Sekisō said, "If I give it to Your Reverend, then it will be no more." Setchō commented to this, "But the rhino is still there."

Master Shifuku drew a circle and wrote the word "rhino" in the center. Setchō commented to this, "Why didn't you bring it out before?"

Master Hofuku said, "As Your Reverend is advanced in age, I think it is better for you to ask somebody else to do it." Setchō commented to this, "It is a pity that all efforts are in vain."

*As against, "Give me back my rhino."*

"Such a thing! I cracked it in half and threw it out on the rubbish pile."
As against, "*I want imperfect head and horn.*"
"I bought a piece of flower-patterned silk for sixty-five cents."
As against, "*Why didn't you bring it out before?*"
"It was here just a little while ago—now it's gone somewhere."
So saying, the pupil looks all around.
As against, "*All efforts are in vain.*"
The pupil, in a loud voice, weeps.
(Quote)

> Time is against me and my horse refuses to
> budge.
> What can I do now that my horse refuses to
> budge?
> Oh yu! Oh yu! What can I do?

## 75. Ōbaku's Stick

When Master Rinzai was still practicing under Master Ōbaku he performed his duties single-mindedly. The head monk praised him and said, "Though he is young, he is different from the rest." He asked Rinzai, "How long have you been here?" Rinzai said, "Three years." The head monk said, "Have you already met Master Ōbaku and asked him questions?" Rinzai said, "No, not yet. I do not know what to ask." The head monk suggested, "Why don't you go and ask Master Ōbaku what the gist of the teaching of Buddha is?" So Rinzai went and asked. However, before Rinzai could finish his question, Ōbaku hit him. Rinzai returned and the head monk asked him, "How was the inquiry?" Rinzai said, "Master Ōbaku hit me before I could finish my question. I don't understand why." The head monk said, "Just go and ask the master again." Rinzai went to ask Ōbaku and was beaten again. In this way he asked three times and was beaten three times. Rinzai went and said to the head monk, "I am fortunate in meeting you, who were kind enough to send me to inquire. I had asked Master Ōbaku three times but was beaten three times. I have only myself to blame for lacking the qualification to understand his deep meaning. I am leaving this day."

The head monk said, "If you leave you have to bid farewell to Master Ōbaku." Rinzai bowed and left. But before Rinzai got there, the head monk went to Ōbaku and said, "The man who asked you questions is young, but he has discipline. Please be available and see him. We should shape him into a big tree so that it can thereafter give shade to people all over the world." So when Rinzai came to bid farewell to Ōbaku, Ōbaku said, "You may not go anywhere else but to the place of Master Daigu. He will certainly explain things to you."

When Rinzai arrived at Daigu's place, Daigu asked, "Where do you come from?" Rinzai said, "I come from Master Ōbaku's place." Daigu said, "What did Ōbaku say?" Rinzai said, "I asked him three times about the gist of the teaching of Buddha and was beaten three times. I don't know if I have done anything wrong."

Daigu said, "Ōbaku was indeed kindhearted to you in sending you here." Upon hearing this Rinzai was enlightened. He then said, "Ōbaku's Buddhism is really nothing serious." Daigu caught hold of him and said, "You bed-wetting baby! Just now you asked if you were wrong and then you say Ōbaku's Buddhism is nothing serious. What is your reason? Say it quick! Say it quick!" Rinzai hit Daigu in the ribs thrice with his fist. Daigu pushed him away and said, "Your master is Ōbaku. It is none of my business."

Rinzai then left Daigu and returned to Ōbaku. When Ōbaku saw him he said, "What end can there be to this man's coming and going?" Rinzai bowed and said, "Just because your kindness urged me, I went and came back." Ōbaku said, "Where have you been?" Rinzai said, "Yesterday, in compliance with your order, I went to see Master Daigu." Ōbaku said, "What did Daigu say?" Rinzai then repeated the above story. Ōbaku said, "How can I get this man [Daigu] here so that I can give him a sound beating?" Rinzai said, "Why talk of waiting till he is here? You can have it now!" Having said that, he slapped Ōbaku. Ōbaku said, "This crazy man has come here to pluck the tiger's beard." Rinzai shouted at him. Ōbaku said to his attendants, "Take this crazy man to the hall."

Later Master Isan told this story to Master Kyōzan and asked, "At that time did Rinzai get the help of Daigu or the help of Ōbaku?" Kyōzan said, "He knows not only how to ride a tiger's head but also knows how to hold onto the tiger's tail."

"Have the taste of sixty strokes from Ōbaku's stick !"
*(Quote)*

> With a golden cup I come to you.
> Decline me not and fill it to the brim with
> wine.

## 76.  *The Three Sentences of Master Rinzai*

[Continuation of koan 19]

Master Rinzai also said, "Each sentence must hold three subtle gates; each gate must hold the three seals (or elements). To each of these there is its variation and its working. How do you understand this?" With that he stepped down from his seat.

ANSWER

"This one fan—at times it makes a paperweight, at times it holds things atop of it, at times it blows in the wind."

## 77.  *On an Isolated Peak; At the Crossroads*

Master Rinzai said, "There is a man on top of an isolated peak not removed from the world. There is a man at the crossroads looking neither forward nor backward. Which one is in front? Which one is in back? Do not be like Yuima [who meditated in an isolated place], and do not be like Fudaishi [mixing with people in worldly affairs]. Take care of yourselves."

*As against, "A man on top of an isolated peak not removed from the world."*

ANSWER

"Even to Buddha or Amida I would not show my face."

*As against, "A man at the crossroads looking neither forward nor backward."*

ANSWER

"With an old man, old-man-like; with a child, childlike; with each as each is."

OR

(According to another school)

*As against both, "A man on top of an isolated peak" and "a man at the crossroads."*

ANSWER

"The old man goes to the mountain to gather firewood, the old woman to the river to wash clothes."

## 78. *Why Can't the Tail Go Through?*

Master Hōen said, "It is like a cow passing through a window frame. The head, the horns, the four legs have all gone through; why can't the tail go through?"

MASTER

This cow—when was it born?

ANSWER

"It was born before this world began."

MASTER

This cow—what's its form?

ANSWER

"The carpenter—tap, tap [with a hammer]; the plasterer—beto, beto [with a trowel]."
*(Quote)*

> Everything in the southern and northern
> villages is soaked in rain,
> The newly married woman is serving her
> mother-in-law food,
> While her father-in-law is feeding the son.

MASTER

Is it a female cow? A male cow?

ANSWER

"It's a huge-balls-hanging-down male cow."

MASTER

What's its color?

ANSWER

"The cloak is iron-blue, the kimono is gray, the underwear is white."

MASTER

How does it feed?

"For breakfast, wheat porridge; for lunch, the regular meal; for dinner, rice and vegetable porridge."

MASTER

Where is the cow?

ANSWER

*(Quote)*
> I sit by myself in the deep and quiet
>        bamboo forest,
> Playing music and howling out loud.

MASTER

Where is its birthplace?

ANSWER

*(Quote)*
An octagonal millstone spinning in midair.

MASTER

Say the working of the cow.

ANSWER

"I waved up my horns and ran head-on into you."

MASTER

"Why can't the tail go through?"

ANSWER

The pupil holds the master by the nose, slaps his master's rear, saying, "Even if I say giddy-up, he doesn't budge an inch."
*(Quote)*
> Where is the person with whom we came
>        together to appreciate the moon?
> The scenery looks very much the same as
>        that of last year.

OR
(According to another school)
*As against, "A cow passing through a window frame."*

ANSWER

The pupil gets on all fours and like a cow crawls around the room.


MASTER

What's the form of the cow?


ANSWER

Getting up, the pupil moves forward and backward, left and right.


MASTER

What's the height of the cow?


ANSWER

"So-and-so feet, so-and-so inches" [the pupil gives his own height].


MASTER

Is it a male cow? A female cow?


ANSWER

Sticking his nose in front of his master, the pupil says, "Moo——."


## 79. *What Is Jōshū?*

A monk asked Master Jōshū, "What is Jōshū?" Jōshū said, "The east gate, the west gate, the south gate, the north gate."

ANSWER

"Even Buddha or Amida will never see the face—what makes a fellow like you think you will?"


## 80. *A Shell Holding Moonlight*

A monk asked Master Chimon, "What is the essence of the supreme wisdom?" Chimon said, "A shell holding moonlight." The monk asked, "What is the working of the supreme wisdom?" Chimon said, "To bear the child of the rabbit [in the moon]." *As against, "The essence of the supreme wisdom."*

ANSWER

The pupil folds his arms.
*As against, "The working of the supreme wisdom."*

The pupil, his arms still folded, bends forward.

## 81. *It Is Your Hearts That Move*

Master Enō saw a banner fluttering in the wind. Two monks were arguing about it. One monk said, "It is the banner that moves." The other said, "It is the wind that moves." They argued back and forth without ever reaching the core of the matter. Enō said, "It is not the banner that moves. It is not the wind that moves. It is your hearts that move." The monks were stunned.

ANSWER

The pupil stands up, and using the sleeve of his cloak, flutters it like a banner in the wind.

## 82. *The Immovable Cloak*

[Enō's master decided that Enō would take his place as the next master, and as proof of the authority he gave him his cloak and bowl. The other monks, displeased with this, chased after Enō. Near Mt. Daiyūrei they caught up with Enō.]

The monk called Myō was among those chasing Enō. Enō, upon seeing Myō, threw his cloak and bowl on the rock and said, "This cloak represents faith; if it is in your power to lift it, I shall let you have it." Myō tried to lift it but it was as immovable as a mountain. Bewildered and scared, Myō said, "I came here to look for the Way. I did not come for the cloak. Master, I beg you to teach me."

ANSWER

The pupil solemnly recites, "It represents faith."

## 83. *What the Old Woman Meant*

A monk asked an old woman, "Which is the road to Mt. Tai?" The old woman said, "Go straight ahead." The monk had just taken a few steps when the old woman remarked, "This one, too, is no different from the others." Later, a monk reported this to Master Jōshū who said, "Let me ask this old woman for you." He went the next day and asked the old woman the same question.

The old woman answered as before. Jōshū then returned and told the people, "I have got for you what the old woman meant."

ANSWER
"The strong one beneath the porch."
(Quote)

> I only wish my emperor would notice me.
> To be seen, I would climb the tall building
>     several times, my eyebrows painted.

OR

(According to another school)
ANSWER

"Go straight ahead."
(Quote)

> The raising of a great god's hand is nothing
>     serious,
> But it is enough to split the thousand hills
>     of the mountain range of Ka.

OR

(According to another school)
ANSWER

Walking around in the room, the pupil acts out the monk's going and Jōshū's going.

OR

(With certain masters)

ANSWER
"A wrinkled-faced old woman!"

## 84.  The Tortoise Is a Turtle

A monk asked Master Kōrinon, "What is the lamp in the room?" Kōrinon said, "Three men testify that the tortoise is a turtle."

ANSWER
The pupil rubs his head around, saying, "All catch hold of this fellow, saying, 'It's so-and-so, it's so-and-so.'"

OR

(According to another school)

The pupil rubs the straw mat, saying, "It feels like Bingo [a product of the Bingo District] and yet it doesn't feel like Bingo." (*Quote*)

> Please don't show that you dislike the stains
>> on the lapels;
> I, shedding tears, had sewn it in front of the
>> lamp.

## 85. *Cut!*

Master Gantō asked a monk, "Where do you come from?" The monk said, "From the western capital." Gantō said, "After Kōsō [a leader of a rebellion] was gone, can you still get a sword?" The monk said, "Yes, I can." Gantō then stretched out his neck and said, "Cut!" The monk said, "The master's head has fallen." Gantō laughed out loud.

The monk later went to Master Seppō. Seppō asked, "Where do you come from?" The monk said, "From Master Gantō." Seppō said, "What had Gantō said?" The monk told the above story. Seppō gave him thirty strokes and drove him away.

### MASTER

"Gantō stretched out his neck and said, 'Cut!'" Take the place of the monk and say.

### ANSWER

The pupil takes a leap back and, as if in dread, says, "Oh, that's danger! That's danger!"

### MASTER

"Can you still get a sword?" Take the place of the monk and say.

### ANSWER

The pupil, pointing his finger in front of him, says, "Just now it was there. It's gone somewhere."

### OR
(According to another school)
*As against, "Can you still get a sword?"*
### ANSWER
"Such a piece of junk! I threw it out."

## 86.  When the Sail Is Hoisted

A monk asked Master Gantō, "How is it when the old sail is not yet hoisted?" Gantō said, "A small fish swallows a big fish." The monk said, "What becomes of it after the sail is hoisted?" Gantō said, "The donkey eats grass in the backyard."

Later Master Kidō asked Master Nanpo, "How is it when the old sail is not yet hoisted?" Nanpo said, "Mt. Shumi in the eyes of an insect." Kidō said, "What becomes of it after the sail is hoisted?" Nanpo said, "The yellow river flows northward."

*As against, "How is it when the old sail is not yet hoisted?"*

ANSWER

The pupil spreads both sleeves of his kimono and is silent.

*As against, "What becomes of it after the sail is hoisted?"*

ANSWER

"Today is the day of shaving the head, cleaning the temple in and out. When that's done, take a bath."


## 87.  Why Don't People In Know about Out?

Master Kempō said, "The true self has three kinds of diseases and two kinds of light. You have to go through them before you are enlightened." Master Ummon stepped out and said, "Why don't people in the hermitage know anything about the outside of the hermitage?" Kempō laughed out loud. Ummon said, "I still have doubt." Kempō asked, "What are your thoughts?" Ummon said, "I need Your Reverend to tell me." Kempō said, "One has to be like that, observant and meticulous, before one is enlightened." Ummon said, "Yes, yes."

*As against, "The true self has three kinds of diseases and two kinds of light. You have to go through them before you are enlightened."*

ANSWER

The pupil gives a scornful laugh, saying, "Hm!"

(Quote)

> To grab a deer from the mouth of a fierce
> tiger,
> To take a rabbit from under the claws of a
> hungry eagle.


MASTER

Attach a quote that gives the gut meaning of Kempō.

*(Quote)*

> On the surface you see peach blossoms
>     among bamboo trees,
> But deep inside there are briars reaching for
>     the sky.

*As against, "Why don't people in the hermitage know anything about the outside of the hermitage?"*

### ANSWER

The pupil opens the door slightly, saying, "What a nice garden! Over here, stepping stones; over there, a lantern; beyond is the toilet, isn't it? Before it stinks, let's close the door." With that, he slams the door shut.

*(Quote)*

Shun [a wise and virtuous king] had not the land to hold even a drill.

U [a wise and virtuous king] had no more than ten families to gather around him.

### MASTER

This koan is on the "holy body" [of truth]. Attach to it a quote on the "holy body."

### ANSWER

*(Quote)*

> We get our body, hair, and skin from our
>     parents;
> We dare not destroy them; that is the basic
>     requirement of filial piety.

### OR
### (According to another school)
### MASTER

"Three kinds of diseases"—what's it mean?

### ANSWER

"Greed, anger, stupidity."

### MASTER

"Two kinds of light"—what's it mean?

### ANSWER

"With the two lights of serene mind [samadhi] and wisdom, the three diseases of hatred, covetousness, and attachment are brought to salvation."

As against, *"Why don't people in the hermitage know anything about the outside of the hermitage?"*

ANSWER

The pupil opens the door and acts surprised at seeing the daybreak. (Quote)

> Without going beyond the garden gate,
> I can see all the rivers and mountains in their
>     thousands.

Or:

> Together with the fall of night there comes
>     the sound of wind and rain;
> Yet can you tell how many flowers have
>     fallen from their trees?

OR

(According to another school)

ANSWER

As against, "the three kinds of diseases," the pupil enumerates three diseases [such as ulcers, lumbago]. As against, "the two kinds of light," he pulls at both eyes.

## 88. *Where Is the Old Man Going?*

Master Seppō was in charge of meals under Master Tokusan. One day the meal was late. Tokusan, carrying his bowl, came down to the dining hall. Seppō said, "The bell has not yet rung, neither has the drum been struck. Where is the old man going carrying his bowl?" Tokusan was silent, He bowed his head and returned to his room. Seppō told this to Master Gantō. Gantō said, "Tokusan does not know the last sentence" [the ultimate truth]. When Tokusan heard of this, he ordered his attendant to summon Gantō to his room. He said to Gantō, "You will not let me go at that, will you?" Gantō in a whisper revealed his intention. The next day when Tokusan came to the hall to give a lecture, he behaved in an unusual way. Gantō clapped his hands, laughed, and said, "I am glad that the old man knows the last sentence. From now on, people the world over will not know how to deal with him. However, he has only three years to live." After three years, Tokusan died.

*As against, "Tokusan returned to his room."*

ANSWER

The pupil stands up and gives the pretense of leaving.
*(Quote)*

> It has just gone away with the fragrant grasses,
> Yet returns again, chasing after the falling
> flowers.

MASTER

Gantō said, "Tokusan does not know the last sentence"—
instead of Seppō, you answer Gantō.

ANSWER

"You talk big, but you yourself don't know, do you?"
*Or:*
"You stupid monk! You think there's such a thing as the last
sentence?!"
*(Quote)*
A single hair pulling a weight of a thousand jun.
*As against, "Gantō in a whisper revealed his intention."*

ANSWER

"There's something there. There's something there."
*(Quote)*
The father shelters for the son and the son shelters for the father.
*As against, "He has only three years to live."*

ANSWER

"Can you foresee everything? That's pretty terrific what you
know."

MASTER

What would happen if he didn't die?

ANSWER

"No matter what you say, life may end tonight."

MASTER

"The last sentence and the first sentence are not the same sentence"—how about that?

ANSWER

"You ever blab about last sentence, first sentence and I'll beat
you to death!"

## 89. Yet I Should Not Be Rash

After Master Tokusan arrived at the place of Master Isan he, still in his traveling clothes, walked around the hall from east to west, west to east, looking around right in front of Isan and said, "Mu. Mu" ["Nothing. Nothing"]. Then he walked away. [Master Setchō commented, "He has got it!"] But when Tokusan reached the front door he said, "Yet I should not be rash." Thus with proper dignity and ceremony he went in again to meet Isan. Isan was sitting. Tokusan said, "Master!" Isan reached for his stick and Tokusan shouted ["Katsu!"]. With a sweep of his long sleeves, Tokusan went out. [Setchō commented, "He has got it!"] Tokusan, with his back to the lecture hall, put on his sandals and left. When night came Isan asked the head monk, "Where is the one who newly arrived?" The head monk said, "He has long before turned his back to the hall, put on his sandals, and walked out!" Isan said, "Later this fellow will go to the peak of Mt. Ko, build himself a hermitage of grass, and will set to scolding Buddha and our masters." [Setchō commented, "To add frost on top of snow."]

As against, "He has got it!" [Setchō's first comment].
                                                ANSWER
The pupil, raising his voice says, "He has got it!"
(Quote)
Gall is bitter to the root.

As against, "He has got it!" [Setchō's second comment].
                                                ANSWER
The pupil, raising his voice, says, "He has got it!"
(Quote)
Melon is sweet clear through.

As against, "To add frost on top of snow."
                                                ANSWER
"It is the laughter of a monkey's bottom."
(Quote)
The prisoner tells everything honestly.


## 90. Every Day Is a Good Day

Master Ummon said, "About the fifteen days before [i.e., before enlightenment] I do not ask you. Now that fifteen days have passed, come, say something." Nobody answered. Ummon himself said, "Every day is a good day."

"The fifteen days before," one sentence—say it.

"The grocer." (Or: "How about some vegetables?")

"The fifteen days after," one sentence—say it.

"The bean curd man." (Or: "How about some bean curd?")

"The just fifteenth day," one sentence—say it.

"Yes, today is a fine day, isn't it?"
*As against, "Every day is a good day."*
"Yesterday Hachibē from near the front gate got hurt. This morning again, I heard that Ohachi is sick. Just now a cable from the country arrived saying that a relative has died."
*(Quote)*
> When flowers bloom there is lots of rain and
> wind.
> In life there are enough partings.

*Popular Saying*
With no wife, no parents, no child, not even a house—with all this, wouldn't it be better to die?


## 91.  *Without Caring, Go Straight*

The head of the hermitage, Master Renge, picked up his stick and said, "Why didn't the people before us like to stay here?" Nobody answered. Then he answered the question himself, saying, "Because they didn't rely upon the teaching of a superior master." Then he said, "But how is it finally?" Again he answered himself, saying, "To carry the stick on your shoulders and without caring for others, go straight into the thousand hills" [i.e., monastery].
*As against, "Strike the ground with the stick once."*

[The one stroke of the stick symbolizes the realization of the answer to which the people could not reach.]

ANSWER

"Goton!" [the sound of a stick striking the ground]. Here the master comments, "The whole universe is just the one 'goton!' It resounds from the highest sphere of heaven down through the bottom of the deepest layer."

*As against, "Because they didn't rely upon the teaching of a superior master."*

ANSWER

"By dropping your bottom steadfast into the evenness of the plane of enlightenment you cannot save the people."

*As against, "To carry the stick on your shoulders and without caring for others, go straight into the thousand hills."*

ANSWER

"To leap into the rabble of this world and lead the masses to salvation."

*Or:*

"To meet up with favorable circumstances without halting there; to meet up with adversity without halting there. Such a fellow is an all right Zen priest."

## 92. *Seven*

A monk asked Master Ummon, "What is the true self?" Ummon said, "It does not hold six things."

ANSWER

The pupil, moving his body a bit, recites in a stern voice, "One, two, three, four, five, six, seven."

MASTER

Say it in reference to the "other."

ANSWER

"The two next-door neighbors and the three across. The nandin tree is three feet high and the wall is five feet high."

## 93. *I Have a Lot of Things to Do*

Master Sanshō asked Master Seppō, "I wonder what the small fish that can pass through a small net eat." Seppō said, "I shall tell you if you bring me a net." Sanshō said, "Does any of the thousand and five hundred wise [of the past] understand what I have said?" Seppō said, "I have a lot of things to do."

ANSWER

"If you're hungry, have some wheat porridge; if you're thirsty, drink some tea."
As against, "I have a lot of things to do."
ANSWER

"You know today I'm busy so I've got no time to mess around with you."

## 94. Rice in a Bowl, Water in a Bucket

A monk asked Master Ummon, "What is all-the-wonders-hidden-in-a-small-dust-particle?" Ummon said, "Rice in a bowl, water in a bucket."

ANSWER

"The bean paste barrel is filled with bean paste to the top; in the pot, boiling potatoes are going 'gutsu, gutsu.'"

## 95. I Have a Headache Today

A monk asked Master Baso, "Without using the four sentences [concerning the division of existence], without resorting to the hundred negatives [to describe the nature of nirvana], tell me directly the meaning of Zen." Baso said, "I am tired today, I cannot tell you anything. Go and ask Master Chizō." The monk asked Chizō, who said, "Why don't you ask Baso?" The monk said, "But the master told me to ask you." Chizō said, "I have a headache today. I cannot tell you anything. Go and ask Master Ekai." The monk asked Ekai, who said, "But I do not understand this far." The monk told this to Baso. Baso said, "Chizō's head is white. Ekai's head is black."

MASTER

"Chizō's head is white. Ekai's head is black"—what's it mean?

ANSWER

"Should the parent be a shit dropper, then the offspring is a bed wetter."

*(Quote)*
The king behaves like a king, while his courtiers behave like courtiers.
*Or:*
The father shelters for the son, the son shelters for the father.


## 96. *"All Over"; "Throughout"*

Master Ungan asked Master Dōgo, "What are the many eyes and hands of Daihi Buddha [Kannon Buddha, representing compassion] for?" Dōgo said, "It is like people twisting their hands back to grope for their pillows in the middle of the night." Ungan said, "I've got it!" Dōgo said, "What do you understand?" Ungan said, "It means that the body is eyes and hands all over." Dōgo said, "You got only eighty percent right." Ungan said, "How would you say it then?" Dōgo said, "The body is eyes and hands throughout."


MASTER

"It is like people twisting their hands back to grope for their pillows in the middle of the night"—what's it mean?


ANSWER

The pupil rubs his hands together, saying, "Shall I pound your back for you; shall I rub your legs?"
*As against, "All over the body and throughout the body."*
ANSWER
"It's the same thing, but it may be called 'sensu' and it may be called 'ōgi'" [Japanese synonyms for "fan"].


## 97. *Why Is That Thing Not You?*

The scripture of Ryōgon says, "When I do not see, why cannot I see what I do not see? If you can see what you do not see, naturally that is not something which cannot be seen. If I cannot see what I do not see, that thing naturally is not an object." Why is that thing not you?
*As against, "That thing is naturally not an object. Why is that thing not you?"*

Looking left and right, the pupil says, "That thing is naturally not an object. Why is that thing not you?"
*(Quote)*
> There was dazzling light when Zōmō arrived,
> And there were sky-high waves wherever
> Rirō went.

## 98.  *Go and Have Some Tea*

Master Chōkei said, "It is not good to say Buddha has two languages [one for the initiated, one for the laymen]. I will not say Buddha has no language, only that he does not have two languages." Master Hofuku said, "What is the language of Buddha?" Chōkei said, "How do the deaf hear?" Hofuku said, "[You missed!] Say it the other way." Chōkei asked, "What is the language of Buddha?" Hofuku said, "Go and have some tea."

"Only he does not have two languages."
*Popular Saying*
Looking from the top of a high mountain down to the bottom of the valley, the melon and eggplant are blossoming.
*(Quote)*
> There were five or six adults, six or seven
> children.
> We bathed in the river, sang to the dance music,
> played when people prayed for rain,
> And then went home reciting poems.

## 99.  *Made a Fool Of*

The Kongōkyō [the Diamond Sutra] says, "When a person is made a fool of by others, the sins of his former lives are the cause. But at this point of falling into adversity, by being made a fool of, the sins of his former lives are erased."

The pupil curses, "Stinking fool of an asshole!"
*Or:*
"This stupid bald head of a monk—get out! get out!"

*(Quote)*

When two persons are quarreling, meddle in.
When two persons are spitting at each other,
splash water over them.

### 100. *"Wrong!"*

When Master Tenpyō was a traveling monk, he visited Master Saiin. Tenpyō always used to say, "Never say you understand the teaching of Buddha. If you look for anyone who understands this, you will not find him." One day Saiin saw Tenpyō from afar and called out, "Tenpyō!" Tenpyō looked up and Saiin said, "Wrong!" Tenpyō moved two or three steps and again Saiin said, "Wrong!" When Tenpyō drew near Saiin said, "The two 'wrongs' just now, are they meant for you or for me?" Tenpyō said, "It is Tenpyō that is wrong." Saiin said, "Wrong!" Tenpyō was silent. Saiin said, "Stay here for the summer so that I may discuss with you the two 'wrongs.'" But Tenpyō left right away.

Later when Tenpyō became a permanent temple resident, he told the people, "When I was a traveling monk I was carried by the wind of destiny to the place of Master Saiin. He said 'wrong' twice and asked me to stay for the summer in order to discuss it with me. At that time I did not know exactly where I was wrong, but as soon as I set foot for the south, I knew I had made a mistake."

Later, Master Setchō commented on the above, "Tenpyō, thinking about what happened at Saiin's place, felt regret at being wrong. That is wrong."

#### MASTER
In what way is the mistake of Setchō similar to that of Tenpyō?

#### ANSWER
"Setchō's mistake is like dung, Tenpyō's mistake is like bean paste."

### 101. *Tread on the Head of Buddha*

Emperor Shukusō asked his teacher, Master Etchū, "What is Buddha?" Etchū said, "Tread on the head of Buddha." The emperor said, "I do not understand." Etchū said, "Do not think of yourself as pure, true self."

*As against, "Tread on the head of Buddha."*

ANSWER

"I am Buddha."
*As against, "Do not think of yourself as pure, true self."*

ANSWER

"Though the body is covered with all sorts of beautiful clothing, the bowls are filled with piss and shit. Though ruler of heaven and earth, it's the same as Gonbē or Hachibē" [common names of the lower class].

MASTER

Now you, as a monk, how do you say it?

ANSWER

"Gonbē, Hachibē, anyone holds the nature of Buddha."

## 102. *The Body Emits Autumn Wind*

A monk asked Master Ummon, "What happens when trees wither and leaves fall down?" Ummon said, "The body emits autumn wind."

MASTER

*(Quote)*
Don't you understand what it is to waste away languishing in love, yearning? This love song, where did it come from?

ANSWER

"The garden of the ancestors has become bleak and desolate. Hmm, how can we get it back to its former state?" the pupil says, heaving a deep sigh with an air of lamentation.

MASTER

What does it finally come to?

ANSWER

"Now [time], here [space] are interwoven."

## 103. *The Mind as It Is*

Master Daibai asked Master Baso, "What is Buddha?"
Baso answered, "The mind as it is, is Buddha."

The pupil, raising his eyes in a glare, says, "Hateful!"
*Or:*
"Hot! Cold!"
*(Quote)*
The angry Nata [a mythical figure] struck at the emperor's bell.
*Or:*

>When it is cold, the cold freezes you.
>When it is hot, the heat burns you.

*Popular Saying*
Even the thought of an ant can reach the sky.

## 104. *No Mind, No Buddha*

A monk asked Master Baso, "What is Buddha?" Baso said, "It is no mind, it is no Buddha."

### ANSWER
"At the railroad crossing a frog is squashed by a train."

## 105. *One*

>One hair swallows the big sea.
>One seed holds Mt. Shumi.

### ANSWER
"One cup of tea, one piece of rice cracker."

## 106. *Take Care!*

Master Kanzan said, "Take care! Take care! Past, present, or future, you may at any time fall to hell."

### ANSWER
The pupil, clapping his hands in rhythm, says, "From here to Edo [Tokyo] it's three hundred miles. Such a trip, is it possible to take it naked?"
*(Quote)*

>In the morning, I go out of Fuyōki. At night,
>    I stop at Fuyōki.
>Two or three nights I have stopped at Fuyōki.
>I have never really left Fuyōki at all.

What's your present karma?

The pupil, taking the pose of a beggar, says, "If you have any leftover food, I'd be grateful if you'd give it to me."
*Popular Saying*
Last night, where did I sleep? Tonight, I'm here. Tomorrow, I'll sleep in the rice field with the footpath as my pillow.

OR
(According to another school)
ANSWER
"From the age of sixteen or seventeen, wearing a monk's cassock, handbox hanging from my neck, I left home and went to Oshū in the east, Kyūshū in the west, Shikoku, Saigoku, Chichibu, Bandō [districts in Japan]; not leaving out anywhere, I traveled all over Japan making the rounds of pilgrimage."
*Popular Saying*
Hey you, going here, going there, traveling monk! From here to Edo it's three hundred miles. Such a trip, is it possible to take it barefooted?

OR
(According to another school)
ANSWER
The pupil, clapping his hands in rhythm and walking around the room, from time to time recites, "Take care! Take care! Past, present, or future, you may at any time fall to hell."

## 107. *What Will You Do after Three or Four Shouts?*

Master Bokushū asked a monk, "Where have you been recently?" The monk shouted ["Katsu!"]. Bokushū said, "I am shouted at once by you." The monk shouted again. Bokushū said, "What will you do after three or four shouts?" The monk was speechless. Bokushū then hit him and said, "You empty-headed fool!"

ANSWER
At shouting, "Katsu!" the pupil hits the floor with his hand. [In reference to the above answer the book comments, "The answer shows the simultaneous working of the stick and the shout."]

## 108.  Non-Attachment

What is real insight? Master Rinzai said, "No matter whether you are a commoner or a saint, or in the state of attachment or enlightenment; in whatever realm of existence, everywhere you can see the formation, the existence, the corruption, and the passing into nothingness of the world. Buddha came into this world to teach. He entered into nirvana but we cannot see his coming and going. It is impossible to investigate into his life and death. If you realize this, then you enter the realm of nothingness; you may roam every corner of its territories. There you see that every existence is no real existence at all. All is but nothingness. You come to realize that you who are now listening to the truth of non-attachment are the source of all Buddhas. Therefore a Buddha is actually born from non-attachment. If you can understand non-attachment, then all the Buddhas are nothing—such understanding is real insight."

ANSWER

"To pass through the forest of thorns without setting the foot down on one's own ground—that is my view."
(Quote)

> On a night when cold frost falls, the moon as
> it is glides into the valley in front.

MASTER

Finally, what is it like?

ANSWER

"On 'u' ['being'], on 'mu' ['nothing']—to halt not the foot."

## 109.  Calamity! Calamity!

When Master Rinzai went up to the hall to give a lecture a monk asked him, "What if under the threat of a blade?" Rinzai said, "Calamity! Calamity!"

ANSWER

The pupil takes three to four steps; then abruptly he makes himself fall as one who dies, head cut off.

*Or:*
"Oh! Danger! Danger!" the pupil says, as if in fear.
*(Quote)*

> When waves are three stories high and fishes
> change into dragons,
> The simpleton is still measuring the water of
> the country pond with a bucket.

*Or:*

> Because a piece of white cloud lay across the
> entrance to the valley,
> Many homeward-bound birds lost their way
> to their nests.


110.   *Use the Air as Paper*

Master Hōen said, "If one uses the air as paper, the sea as an inkstand, Mt. Shumi as a brush, can he write the words: 'The meaning of our founder coming from the west?' If any of you can, I shall give you the seat and bow to you in due ceremony."

ANSWER

"The wily old fox!" says the pupil.
*(Quote)*

> I let my hands go beyond the broad
> firmament.
> People of the time are all unaware of it.

*Or:*
The pupil with his finger writes in the air in big letters: "The meaning of our founder coming from the west."

OR

(According to another school)

ANSWER

The pupil, in pretense, rubs the ink stick, spreads out paper, takes a brush, and on the floor writes a large numeral "one."


111.   *What Is Your Feeling at This Moment?*

There was an old woman who looked after a hermit. For twenty years she always had a sixteen-year-old girl bring him rice and wait on him. One day she ordered the girl to hug the man and ask, "What is your feeling at this moment?" The hermit said,

"The old tree leaning against the cold cliff has no warmth in the winter months." The girl went back and reported this to the old woman. The woman said, "For twenty years of support I get only a good-for-nothing fellow." So she drove the man out and had the hermitage burnt down.

As against, *"What is your feeling at this moment?"*

ANSWER

"Good-for-nothing tramp! When the old woman says 'Jump!' she jumps. What a mess!" So saying, the pupil pushes the master away.

*(Quote)*

> When light and darkness overlap each other,
> Who can see me emerging beyond the sky?

*Or:*

"Ah! That's a beautiful kimono you're wearing today! Is it muslin? Is it printed silk? Who made it for you? Did your mother make it for you?"

As against, *"Had the hermitage burnt down."*

*(Quote)*

The crocodiles are dead, the people are appeased.


## 112.   *Of a Different Color*

A monk asked Master Sōzan, "The snow covers a thousand hills, but why is only the one peak not white?" Sōzan said, "You should know the absurdity of absurdities." The monk asked, "What is the absurdity of absurdities?" Sōzan said, "Being of a different color from the rest of the hills."

ANSWER

The pupil, stroking his head around, says, "Ah, my hair too has lately been growing white."

*(Quote)*

Once I had great ambitions, but dilly-dally, I have reached the age of white hair.

OR
(According to another school)
ANSWER

The pupil, as if standing in the midst of falling snow, pretends to shake the snowflakes off his hair.

Finally, what's the gut meaning?

ANSWER
The pupil, pretending he can't stand the cold, brings his frozen
hand to his mouth, blowing on it to warm it up.
*(Quote)*
>             Try to shake the snow off the branches,
>             You are sure to find flowers of the night.

*Popular Saying*
In the top of the pine tree, the-monkey-jumped-at-one-branch
looks especially green.

## 113.  *Beard*

Master Wakuan said, "Why doesn't Bodhidharma have a
beard?"

ANSWER
The pupil reciting, "Why doesn't Bodhidharma have a beard?"
pretends to stroke his beard.
*(Quote)*
Sōsō and Kanu [two generals] bear golden hair.
*Or:*
"I'm afraid that the razor blade is not sharp."


OR
(According to another school)
ANSWER
The pupil, stroking his chin, says, "At the last shaving day I had
my beard shaved, but here it's already grown back."
*Or:*
[With certain masters] "It was getting on my nerves so I shaved it
off." So saying, the pupil strokes his chin.
*(Quote)*
>             The wild fire cannot burn it out completely.
>             With the blowing of the spring wind they
>                      come to life once more.

*Or:*
Weeds cannot be hoed up entirely.

## 114. *It Is Here*

A monk asked Master Kenpō, "I wonder, where is the road to Buddha [enlightenment]?" Kenpō took up his stick, drew a line in the air, and said, "It is here."

Later, the monk asked Master Ummon for his view. Ummon took up his fan and said, "This fan jumps up to the thirty-third heaven, hitting the nostril of Buddha. Give the carp of the eastern sea a stroke of the stick and rain will come down in torrents."
*As against, "I wonder, where is the road to Buddha?"*

ANSWER

The pupil slaps his master once.

MASTER

"Buddha"—what's it mean?

ANSWER

Surveying his surroundings, the pupil says, "The realm of Buddha."


## 115. *Is There? Is There?*

Master Jōshū went to a hermitage and asked its master, "Is there? Is there?" The master raised his fist. Jōshū said, "This shallow water is no place to anchor my boat." He went away. He went to another hermitage and asked the master, "Is there? Is there?" This master also raised his fist. Jōshū said, "It can give, it can grab, it can kill, yet can make alive." He bowed.
*As against, "It can give, it can grab, it can kill, yet can make alive."*

ANSWER

The pupil recites, "It can give, it can grab, it can kill, yet can make alive," simultaneously raising up his fist.
*(Quote)*

> In places south of the Yellow River there is
>     the small orange,
> In places north of the river there is the
>     trifoliate orange.

*Or:*

> The plum blossoms in the cold clearly
>     demonstrated the meaning of [the
>     founder] coming from the west.

> One petal flies toward the west while
>> another flies toward the east.

*Or:*

> The same tree bathed by the spring wind has
>> two different states:
> The southern branches facing warmth,
>> the northern ones facing cold.

*Popular Saying*
When the place is changed, the thing changes—in Naniwa [Osaka] it is reed; in Ise it is rush.
*Or:*
Doing-this-doing-that-going-through-life-man—what an empty dream. Doesn't he know that it's the same as the reed of Naniwa?


## 116.   *Where Do You Come From?*

In a small meeting Master Tokusan said, "I shall not answer any questions tonight. Anyone who asks will receive thirty blows of my stick." Then a monk stepped out and bowed. Tokusan beat him. The monk said, "I have not yet even asked, why do you beat me?" Tokusan said, "Where do you come from?" The monk said, "I am from Shinra [Korea]." Tokusan said, "It is high time to give you thirty strokes before you step into the boat." On hearing this the monk was enlightened.

Later, Master Hōgen commented, "The words of Tokusan are broken into two halves." And Master Enmei said, "Tokusan started well but ended badly."

In reference to the above comments of Hōgen and Enmei, Master Setchō said, "Though the two elders are good at cutting from the long in order to mend the short, giving up the heavy in order to take up the light, it is still impossible for them to know Tokusan. Why? It is because Tokusan is like one holding power over places outside the imperial city gate. He possesses the sword of quick decision. Do you people want to know the monk from Shinra? He is but a blind man who has knocked himself against the pillar outside the hall."

ANSWER
The pupil takes the master by the neck and gives thirty blows of the stick.

MASTER
How would *you* take the thirty blows?

ANSWER
"I truly ask your forgiveness."

OR
(According to another school)
MASTER
*(Quote)*
"Whether you have anything to say or not—thirty blows"—
what's it mean?

ANSWER
While hitting the master on his back the pupil recites, "Whether
you have anything to say or not—thirty blows."

MASTER
Forget about Tokusan for awhile—the blows of my stick, how
would you take them?

ANSWER
Springing back, the pupil pretends to be in fear, and bringing
his hands together he pleads, "Forgive me! Forgive me!"

MASTER
Let's forget Tokusan for awhile—how does your stick work?

ANSWER
"What rubbish! I don't carry such trash around with me!"

## 117. *One Got It, One Missed It*

A monk came to consult Master Hōgen before mealtime.
Hōgen pointed to the curtain with his hand. At that, two monks
simultaneously went to pull the curtain up. Hōgen said, "One
got it. One missed it."
*As against, "One got it."*

ANSWER
The pupil takes hold of the stick and thrusts it in front of his
master.
*As against, "One missed it."*

The pupil drops the stick on the floor.


## 118. *Yes*

Master Etchū called his attendant three times and three times the attendant answered back. Etchū said, "I thought I had done you wrong, but in fact it is you who had done me wrong."

"When called a thief of a monk, answer as a thief of a monk; when called a fool of a monk, answer as a fool of a monk; when the crow cries 'Caw!' answer 'Caw!'"

OR

(According to another school)
The master, taking the place of Master Hōgen, turns to the pupil, saying, "Attendant!" The pupil responds, "Yes!" This is repeated three times.
*(Quote)*

> Only the wild monkey knew the traveler's
>     sorrow.
> On the waterway of Ekiyō I heard it wail a
>     third time.


## 119. *Three Pounds of Flax*

A monk asked Master Tōzan, "What is Buddha?" Tōzan said, "Three pounds of flax."

"One, two, three," the pupil acts as a fish peddler taking count.
*(Quote)*
It looks like flax, and it looks like millet too.


## 120. *Even Up Till Now*

Bibashi Buddha [a legendary Buddha] has been practicing since very ancient times. In spite of this, he does not know the deep meaning, even up till now.

"On the slope the sun shines hot; at Suzuka [name of a place] it is cloudy; in Tsuchiyama [name of a place] it rains."

## 121. *One Finger*

Whenever Master Gutei was asked a question, he would simply raise one finger.

ANSWER

The pupil raises one finger.

MASTER

What if I cut this finger off?

ANSWER

"Even if you cut it, it cannot be cut. From the top of the thirty-third heaven down to the deepest layer of earth, it is the one finger."

*(Quote)*

> The one thing communicates with all natures,
> The one existence includes all existences,
> The one moon appears on all waters,
> All waters reflect the one moon.

*Or:*

A cut that cuts all cuts.

*Or:*

My way is run through by one single principle.

*Or:*

All this stretch of land is but a rod of iron.

## 122. *It Is Important that the World Be in Peace*

When Buddha was first born, he pointed with one hand to the sky, and with the other to the earth. He walked seven steps in a circle and, looking in the four directions, said, "I am the only one to be honored in and below heaven."

Master Ummon said, "If I were there I would have killed him with a stroke of my stick and would have given him to the dogs to eat. Because it is important that the world be in peace." On this, Master Rōyakaku commented, "Ummon says that one should offer one's body and soul to this world. This is called repaying the favor of Buddha."

ANSWER

The pupil stands up, and, pointing one finger toward the sky and the other toward the earth, says, "I am the only one to be honored." *As against, "It is important that the world be in peace."*

ANSWER

"Mister, mister, please bestow your favor on the blind," the pupil says, acting out a beggar.
*(Quote)*
Rain falling on tree leaves—jadelike beads of water turning round.

## 123. *Mother and Father*

Prince Nata [a mythological figure] tore up his flesh and returned it to his mother, broke up his bones and gave them back to his father. Then he revealed his original body, and, exercising great magical power, preached the truth for his parents.

ANSWER

"I have made the pilgrimage to Ise seven times, to Kumano three times, to Atago [all Shinto shrines] I go every month," the pupil says, singing and dancing around the room.
*(Quote)*

> Silk dresses and jeweled sashes were untied for
>     thee,
> En [district] songs and Jō [district] dances
>     were performed for thee.

OR
(With certain masters)

ANSWER

"Father, you must be tired. Mother, you must be tired. Shall I rub your shoulders for you?"

## 124. *The Eastern Mountain Walks on Water*

A monk asked Master Ummon, "Where is the place of origin of Buddha?" Ummon said, "The eastern mountain walks on water."

"In the monks' quarters the fuzui [the monk in charge of daily
affairs] welcomes the guests and prepares the welcoming dinner,
the tenzo [in charge of cooking] boils the rice, the densu [in
charge of sutra reading] reads the evening chapter, the attendant
cleans the place up. It is very busy."

OR
(According to another school)
ANSWER

The pupil folds his arms across his chest and, while wandering
about the room, says, "Shush, shush," pretending to walk along
a valley stream.

## 125. *Youngsters Like You Never Know of That*

Master Hōun said, "In the third year of Kinei, I held the post
of the official in charge of papers and accounts in Hōshō Prefecture.
In that year, there was a great landslide at Mt. Ka and villages
within a span of eighty miles were completely buried. Youngsters
like you never know of that."

ANSWER

"Well, well, we are indeed fortunate to have heard such a bene-
ficial lesson. We shall remember it for the rest of our lives.

## 126. *The Guy Understands This Time*

When Master Kassan first lived in the temple of Keikō, a monk
asked him, "What is the body of truth?" Kassan said, "The body
of truth is formless." The monk asked again, "What is the eye
of wisdom?" Kassan said, "The eye of wisdom is blemish-free."
At that time Master Dōgo burst out laughing from his seat.
Kassan then dispersed his followers and went to see Master Sensu.
There he reached enlightenment. Later, he went back and gathered
his followers once more. Dōgo then sent a monk to ask Kassan,
"What is the body of truth?" Kassan said, "The body of truth is
formless." The monk asked again, "What is the eye of wisdom?"
Kassan said, "The eye of wisdom is blemish-free." The monk
returned and reported the whole thing to Dōgo. Dōgo said, "The
guy understands this time."
*As against, "The body of truth is formless."*

"The incense tray is formless, the mat is formless, the table is formless, the pillar is formless, the wall is formless, each and every thing is formless."

As against, *"The eye of wisdom is blemish-free."*

ANSWER

"A round thing is round, a square thing is square."

*(Quote)*

Curved is the squash and straight is the cucumber.

## 127. *How Can We Go Through Without Interfering?*

A monk asked Master Fuketsu, "We are in constant contact with existence and its workings whether we talk or keep silent. How can we go through without interfering with it?" Fuketsu said, "I always recall places south of the river in the month of March when the small birds sing amid the fragrance of a hundred flowers."

MASTER

"How can we go through without interfering?"—what's it mean?

ANSWER

The pupil looks around him.

MASTER

"I always recall places south of the river in the month of March when the small birds sing amid the fragrance of a hundred flowers"—what's it mean?

ANSWER

The pupil just recites the above.

## 128. *Peach Blossoms*

Master Reiun saw the peach blossoms and was enlightened. He recited a selection that goes: "I am a traveler who has been looking for a master for thirty years. Time and again leaves have fallen and new shoots sprouted. But ever since I saw the peach blossoms, I have never doubted again."

Later he told this to his master, Isan. Isan said, "Those who are destined to join us will never fall back or be at a loss. Go on protecting and keeping your faith."

Master Gensha heard about this and said, "It is certainly very true, but I am sure that you [Reiun] are still not thoroughly clear." Master Ummon said, "Say nothing of thorough and not thorough again. Study thirty years more!" Afterward, Master Daisen was asked by a monk about the poem mentioned above. Daisen said, "The thief trembles within."

ANSWER

"If the seer is a flower, the seen is a flower too." [This can also be translated: "If you see a flower, it's a flower that is seen."]

## 129.  I Have Nothing to Hide from You

One day the poet Sankaku was conversing with Master Maidō. Maidō said, "There are a few sentences in the book [*The Analects of Confucius*] that you know of which go: [Confucius said] 'You fellows, do you think that I am hiding something from you? I have nothing to hide from you.' It is exactly the same with the affairs of Zen. Do you know this?" Sankoku said, "I do not know." Later, Maidō and Sankoku were walking in the mountain. Maidō asked, "Do you smell the fragrance of the flowers?" Sankoku said, "I do." Maidō said, "I have nothing to hide from you." At that moment Sankoku was enlightened.

Two months later, Sankoku again went to see Maidō. Maidō asked Sankoku, "When you and I die and are burned into two piles of ashes, when and where shall we meet?" At that Sankoku, bewildered, could do nothing. Later, at a certain place, Sankoku was taking an afternoon nap. The moment he opened his eyes he was greatly enlightened. He realized the working of Maidō. Thereafter his mind was perfectly free.

*As against, "When you and I die and are burned into two piles of ashes, where and when shall we meet?"*

ANSWER

"Oh, this must be the house where Rikiyo [a male figure in a Kabuki play] lives. I don't know why, but I feel a little shy."

## 130.  Bamboo Shoots Sprout Sideways under a Rock

A monk came to Master Nansen. Nansen said to him, "Now I am going up to the mountain. You stay here and cook the meal.

When you have finished, carry my share of the meal to the mountain." Saying this, he left. The monk cooked the meal, ate it all up, then he broke all the dishes, and he went to lie down on the bed. Nansen waited for the monk for a long time. As the monk did not show up he went back to the hermitage and saw the monk lying on the bed. Nansen lay down beside him. The monk got up and went away. After Nansen had come to live in a temple he said, "Before, when I was still living in a hermitage, there was a clever monk. But I have never seen him again up till now."

Later Master Kidō commented, "If Nansen did not recognize the monk, the monk could not have gotten up and left. However, bamboo shoots will sprout sideways under a rock, and flowers will grow down on an overhanging cliff." Kidō added, "Clad in short breeches, long gowns, and white linen headbands, people are noisily, hurriedly pushing their carts under the sun. Those one meets on the roads of Rakyō City are all merchants and businessmen."

*Popular Saying*
I've been waiting and waiting, but no word from him. I wonder what he's doing now.
*(Quote)*

> The white plain is desolate under the autumn
>     sky,
> But someone is coming east on horseback.
> Do you know who he is?

*Or:*

> There are thousands of miles along the river.
> How can I meet my wise and holy king?

## 131. *Not Enter Nirvana, Not Fall into Hell*

In the Mahahanya scripture preached by Monju [a legendary Buddha] it says, "Chaste practitioners will not enter nirvana, and monks who violate the rules will not fall into hell."

MASTER
"Chaste practitioners will not enter nirvana"—what's it mean?
*As against, " The four classes of warrior, farmer, artisan, and merchant."*
ANSWER
"The soldier with his rifle on his shoulder is drilling; the farmer

with hoe and plow is plowing the field; the carpenter with the plane is shaving a board; the merchant with the abacus is doing business."

### MASTER
"Monks who violate the rules will not fall into hell"—what's it mean?

### ANSWER
"The rooster from early morn crows the time, the dog all night long guards the gate, the cat catches mice."

### MASTER
Why isn't there falling into hell?

### ANSWER
"Already in hell, what's this talk about falling or not falling?" (*Quote*)

> When spring is warm, the singing of
>     nightingales seems so smooth;
> When the world is peaceful, people put on
>     smiling faces.

*Or:*

> The white herons go down to the fields in a
>     thousand dots of snow,
> The yellow birds fly up the tree to form a
>     bunch of flowers.

*Or:*

[Master Hakuin's poem on this koan]

> The leisured ants fight to drag the dragonfly's
>     wing while young swallows rest together
>     on the willow twigs.
> The silkworm raiser carries a leaf-filled
>     basket; her face reflects the blueness of
>     the leaves.
> The village boy, to steal some bamboo shoots,
>     crosses over the sparse fence.

*Popular Saying*

The ayu fish in the shallow waters of the river stays, the bird in the tree dwells, man in the midst of feeling lives.

(According to another school)

MASTER

The "chaste practitioners"—where are they?


ANSWER

"Right here," the pupil says, pointing to himself.


MASTER

The "monks who violate the rules"—where are they?


ANSWER

"Right here," the pupil says, pointing to his master. Then he switches the order. Pointing at his master he says, "Chaste practitioners"; pointing to himself he says, "Monk who violates the rules."


MASTER

Now, this "chaste practitioner" and "monk who violates the rules"—distinguish them in the affairs of everyday life.


ANSWER

"The tongs are stuck in the charcoal brazier; the knife is on the cutting board."


## 132. *High Rank, Low Rank*

Once upon a time, Monju Buddha went to where the gods met. It so happened that the gods had all returned to their own places. There was only a woman sitting near the seat of Buddha in deep contemplation of quietude. Monju said, to Buddha, "Why is this woman allowed to sit near you when I am not?" Buddha told him, "You just wake this woman. Rouse her from her contemplation and ask her yourself." Monju walked around the woman thrice, snapped his fingers, and carried her to a high sphere of heaven. Yet despite all his efforts, he could not get her out of her contemplation. Buddha said, "Even if there were hundreds and thousands of Monjus, they still would not be able to get her out of her contemplation. You go to the lower sphere where Mōmyō [a Bodhisattva of low rank] is. He can rouse this woman from her contemplation." Then Mōmyō gushed out from the ground. He bowed to Buddha, who commanded him to stand in front of the woman. Mōmyō snapped his fingers once, and the woman woke from her contemplation and stood up.

MASTER

Why couldn't Monju rouse the woman?

ANSWER

"Monju is an extremely distinguished Buddha. He holds the source of wisdom. Therefore, 'rousing,' 'not rousing' is not the problem."

MASTER

Why could Mōmyō rouse the woman?

ANSWER

"Mōmyō is a Bodhisattva of low rank, functioning in the sphere of cause and effect. It is in this realm that he saw the reason for rousing the woman."

MASTER

The enlightenment of the Buddha and the enlightenment of Daruma [Bodhidharma—founder of Zen]—how are they distinct?

ANSWER

"By the enlightenment of the Buddha—'What a fine rosary!' By the enlightenment of Daruma—'This rosary is made from such-and-such tree, it is painted in gold leaf and attached with a tassel of silk. It's a fine thing!'"
(*Quote*)

> Wild geese flew over the city wall against a
> night sky sparingly dotted with faint
> stars.
> A long drawn note of the flute arose and
> someone was leaning on the balcony.

*Or:*

> Light boats are floating on the lonely waters.
> The purple flowers of the water plant are
> growing on the clear pool.

When night falls those who gather in the
    overlooking pavilion are mostly
    fishermen.

MASTER

The following quote was composed as a comment to this koan:
"The Buddha together with Monju and Mōmyō entering into the
deep mountain bush." How about that?

ANSWER

"The view of making all equal is of no use."

## 133. *The Oak Tree in the Front Garden*

A monk asked Master Jōshū, "What is the meaning of our
founder coming from the west [i.e., the meaning of Zen]?"
Jōshū said, "The oak tree in the front garden." The monk said,
"Master, please do not show people the place your heart has
roamed to." Jōshū said, "I will not." The monk said, "What is
the meaning of our founder coming from the west?" Jōshū
said, "The oak tree in the front garden."

Afterward Master Hōgen asked Master Kakutesshi [Jōshū's
disciple], "I have heard that Jōshū said something about an oak
tree, didn't he?" Kakutesshi said, "My deceased master had never
said that. Do not slander him!" Hōgen said, "The real offspring
of a lion can roar like a lion."

ANSWER

The pupil folds his arms, stands up, and says, "Oak tree."
*(Quote)*
    The pine trees in the cold are of the same
        color,
    Yet the span of a thousand years has lapsed.
*Or:*
Pine trees will be green for a thousand years.
*Or:*
The withered trees flourish in the winter months.
*Popular Saying*
The good luck young pine—its branches flourish wide and far,
its leaves grow thick and green.
*As against, "Do not slander the deceased master."*

The pupil folds his arms, stands up, and says, "Oak tree."
(*Quote*)

> Bamboo shoots will sprout sideways under a
> rock,
> Flowers will grow down on an overhanging
> cliff.

*Or:*

> The whale swallowed up all the water in the
> sea.
> Thus coral branches were exposed.

MASTER

Give a quote expressing Kakutesshi.
(*Quote*)
A good son never uses his father's money.
*Or:*
A filial son knows that the father is kind.
*Or:*

> The trees in the garden, knowing not that all
> the people had gone,
> Still put forth the same flowers as in olden
> days.

MASTER

Give a quote for this koan as a whole.
(*Quote*)
The oak tree in the front garden.

MASTER

The root of the oak tree—how far does it go?

ANSWER

"Horizontally it stretches across the ten directions [of space].
Vertically it reaches the end of the three worlds [of time]."

MASTER

The leaf of the oak tree—what is its color?

ANSWER

"The peach tree is so fresh-looking, its leaves are so profuse."

(According to another school)

*As against, "Oak tree."*

ANSWER

The pupil stands up, makes an angry face, and, spreading his arms out wide in a slight angle upwards, he gives the form of an oak tree.

MASTER

This tree—when did it grow?

ANSWER

"It's about five or six years."

MASTER

If I ask you [about the meaning of our founder coming from the west]—how'd you answer it?

ANSWER

"I guess I'd say pine tree."

## 134. *That Is Still Not Enough*

Master Haku-un said to Master Hōen, "Once there came a few guests from Mt. Ro. Every one of them was enlightened. When they said something it was perfect. When asked about a koan, they understood it. They also attached the right quote to their answer. But that is still not enough."

ANSWER

"In every and anything, he is a well-rounded monk, isn't he?"

## 135. *Give, Grab*

Master Bashō said, "If you have a stick, I will give you a stick. If you do not have a stick, I will grab your stick."

ANSWER

"Master, here's tea for you, 'cause I'm taking a cake." So saying, the pupil pretends to take the cake box.

What's the gut meaning of Basho's "give and grab"?

"When giving, give even the maggots in the toilet; when grabbing, of course, not to mention the ashes under the stove, don't even leave a single hair of an ant behind."

## 136. *The Three Sentences of Master Busshō*

The three sentences of Master Busshō are:

1. If the way upward [to enlightenment] is shared with all [saints] alike, why then did [the man called] Chōtatsu fall to hell?

2. Daruma did not come to the east. And Master Niso [the second patriarch] did not go to India. Why did Master Gensha bruise his toe?

3. Where will those who have broken through the void rest themselves?

*As against, "The way upward is shared by all [saints] alike."*
"'The way upward?!' What're you doing, dilly-dallying, messing around—what's the good of it?"
*As against, "Daruma did not come to the east."*
"Take care!"
*As against, "Those who have broken through the void."*
"Now, right now, right here."

## 137. *Which One Is Real?*

[Once there was a woman named Seijo whose body and spirit were split apart. The one Seijo eloped and married her lover Ōchū, while the other Seijo remained in her parents' home ill and speechless in bed.]

Master Hōen asked a monk, "The body and spirit of Seijo are split apart. Which one is the real Seijo?"

"Which one is real?"

(*Quote*)
A single spark of the lightless flame [the world of bondage]
will temper big men of the human race.

MASTER

The state of Seijo's existence—what's it like?

ANSWER

"Regrettable! Desirable! Hateful! Charming!"
(*Quote*)
>                 Though my golden bracelet on my arm has
>                 grown one inch too long,
>                 Yet when meeting people I still tell them I am
>                 not in love.

## 138.  *Only There Is a Word That Is Not Very Proper*

Once during a general meeting, Master Eimei heard a log fall
to the ground with a sound. He was enlightened. He said, "It is
not other things that fell, it is not dust that rushes this way and
that. Rivers, mountains, and the big earth all reveal the body of
truth."

Master Kidō commented on this, "Eimei is just like a small
Confucian scholar who went up to the big city which made him
completely satisfied. Only there is a word [in what he said]
that is not very proper."
*As against, "There is a word that is not very proper."*

ANSWER

The pupil points at his master's nose.

## 139.  *Functions Like Theft*

Master Kanzan said, "The story of the oak tree functions like
theft."

ANSWER

"When I think of you, the sunny day goes cloudy, the clear
moonlit night turns pitch black."
(*Quote*)
Yojō [a robber] hid himself and swallowed charcoal.

*Or:*

> Only after it snows can the goodness of pines
>  and oaks be known.
> And only a difficult experience can reveal the
>  heart of man.

### 140.  *The Four Shouts of Master Rinzai*

Master Rinzai asked a monk, "Sometimes a shout ["Katsu!"] is like a precious sword molded from the hardest of gold. Sometimes a shout is like a golden-haired lion crouching on the ground. Sometimes a shout is like a fishing rod with floating weeds [in the shadow of which fish gather]. Sometimes a shout does not function as a shout. What do you understand by this?" Just as the monk was about to speak, Rinzai shouted at him.
*As against the first three shouts.*

ANSWER

The pupil goes, "Katsu! Katsu! Katsu!"
*As against, "The shout that does not function as a shout."*

ANSWER

The pupil with all his might shouts, "KAATSU!" shaking heaven and earth.

[In reference to the above answer the book comments, "From the highest heaven down to the lowest layer of earth—the one 'katsu.'"]
*(Quote)*
From blue sky and bright sun, angrily the thunder rolls.

### 141.  *First, Second, Third*

If you got the first sentence you will become the master of Buddha. If you got the second sentence you will become the master of men and gods. But if you got the third sentence you will not be able to redeem even yourself.

ANSWER

"Standing, she is a gladiolus; sitting, she is a peony; walking, she is a lily"

### 142.  *Host and Guest*

One day Master Rinzai went to the town of Kafu. When the host Ōjōji asked Rinzai to take his seat, Master Mayoku stepped out and asked, "Kannon Buddha has a thousand hands and eyes; which is the eye proper?" Rinzai said, "Kannon has a thousand hands and eyes; which is the eye proper? Say it quick! Say it quick!" Mayoku dragged Rinzai down from his seat and seated himself. Rinzai drew near and said, "How are you doing?" Mayoku was about to say something in reply when Rinzai dragged him down from his seat and sat down again. Mayoku then went out and Rinzai stepped down from his seat.

ANSWER

"Sometimes you are the host [subject], sometimes you are the guest [object]. It is not set."
(Quote)

> The mist of sunset sweeps the sky together
>     with the lonely duck,
> And the autumn river is of the same color
>     with the wide heaven.

## 143.   The Dragon Bitten by a Snake

Master Ungo was at [the place called] "the gate of dragons." One day a monk had his foot bitten by a snake. Master Butsugen asked Ungo, "If this is 'the gate of dragons,' why was the monk bitten by a snake?" Ungo said, "Of course, he is great as expected."

Later, Master Engo heard of this and commented, "Since there is such a monk in 'the gate of dragons,' the teaching of Master Hōen [Butsugen's teacher] will not yet die out."

ANSWER

The pupil, stretching one leg, says, "It hurts! It hurts!" pretending to have been bitten by a snake.

## 144.   Zen

Master Kotoku said, "Say one sentence where intelligence does not tread."

ANSWER

"Good morning, Master."

# PART FOUR
# NOTES AND COMMENTARY

# NOTES AND COMMENTARY

## NOTES TO PART ONE

### The Koan on the Sound of the One Hand
### and the Koan on Mu

### The Way of the Inzan School

A:  *The Koan on the Sound of the One Hand*  (pp. 47–51)

This koan was composed by the Japanese Zen Master Hakuin (1686–1769). It is either this koan or the koan on "mu" which the novice receives as his first koan upon entering the monastery. The pupil is usually expected to "contemplate" his first koan for a long time. It may take him up to three years to reach the answer. In the meantime, the master rejects all the answers that do not correspond to the answer of "thrusting one hand forward." However, the master may guide the pupil in various ways. For instance, if the pupil comes up with an answer such as, "It is half" (namely, half the sound of clapping both hands), the master may reject the answer, explaining that the pupil is taken in by "two" (i.e., dualistic thinking). The master may also hint at the answer in a more concrete way. He may say, for instance, "Think of handing over your ticket upon entering the train" (i.e., extending one hand forward). In this case however, there is the danger that the pupil, through guessing, reaches only the correct *form* of the answer without really realizing its "meaning."

It will not be of much use trying to "explain" the koan. The state of mind which it embodies is not fully understood if we take into consideration only its philosophical, or rather anti-philosophical (anti-rational) aspect. The formation of the koan and its answer are to be viewed in relation to *zazen* (Zen meditation).

In the "clapping of both hands" the phenomenon ("sound") is the outcome of the interaction between two (or more) factors. It is thus possible, through distinction and differentiation, to trace its "reason" in other phenomena. In rational thinking we are always concerned with the *relation* of one "thing" with the "other." When "the sound of the one hand" is "heard," not a thing has been excluded. Every thing *is* ("u") in as far as it cannot be denied. However, its raison d'être does not lie in any "other" thing, nor does it lie in some principle or truth beyond the thing itself. The essence of a thing is no-thing or nothing ("mu"). Thus the one who has heard "the sound of the one hand" has realized "mu" without denying "u."

## ANSWER

The seemingly paradoxical requirement to hear the sound of the one hand is answered through an act of extreme simplicity. To reach this height of simplicity, the pupil's mind undergoes a process of ever-growing sophistication. Yet however sophisticated rational thinking may be, its basic function is still that of adding one to one. Through seeing each one in itself and all as one, the pupil abandons rational thinking as a mode of being. This does not of necessity imply that logical thinking can no longer be employed for pragmatic purposes.

The pattern of response in the answer may be expressed in the following way:

Question: "What is the sound of *two* hands?"

Answer: Clapping *both* hands.

Question: "What is the sound of the *one* hand?"

Answer: Extending *one* hand forward.

Or to give another example—no one in the usual state of mind would ever answer three successive calls in the same manner. Now imagine the following exchange:

| Hey you. | Yes. | |
|----------|------|---|
| Hey you. | Yes. | Same intonation, same pitch |
| Hey you. | Yes. | |

In this manner of response, there is such an extreme immediacy between every call and its answer that it is impossible to describe the situation as a process developing according to normal "reason."

(It may start anywhere and it may end anywhere.) If we apply the above to the koan, we get the following pattern:

Question: "Two hands!"

Answer: Extending (or clapping) *two* hands.

Question: "One hand!"

Answer: Extending *one* hand.

## DISCOURSE

1. ★The pupil is not taken in by "prove it." He evades explanations by simply implying "that's it."

2. The pupil is not taken in by "enlightenment–non-enlightenment." The answer implies "here, now."

3. The pupil is not taken in by "existence–non-existence." Through the immediacy of his response, the pupil implies "here, now." The "after death" notion exists only while one is alive.

4. Suimo sword—the sharpest of all swords. "Suimo" is composed of the characters meaning "blow" and "hair"; namely, the sword that is so sharp that it cuts a hair that is blown against it.

There is nothing to be cut. Cut (or divide) no-thing and you still have nothing ("mu"). The third answer, because of its immediacy, is the best.

5. Surprisingly enough, the pupil responds to the "why" with a "philosophical" answer. However, it should be assumed that the response (if genuine) is of a more immediate nature than in the usual process of philosophical reasoning. The answer implies "non-distinction."

6. No comment necessary.

7. Similar to note 3. The pupil is not taken in by "life–death." The notion of "before life" is artificial and can be entertained only while alive (i.e., here, now).

8. The "essence" of a situation is the situation itself and nothing beyond it. When asked, 'What is actually happening now?" there is no way of answering the "what is actually" phrase. All that can be said is to repeat the "happening now." Thus the pupil responds to "summit" in a natural way by describing the view from the summit.

9. There is no need to speculate too much about the "meaning" of quotes. The pupil simply responds to "summit" and quotes a Chinese poem on a landscape viewed from a summit.

10. This question is a trap. The master tests whether the pupil

---

★ The note numbers correspond to the numbers in the text.—Translator.

is taken in by distinction or not. The "sound of the one hand" is not to be located spatially. Nevertheless it is not unrelated to space. Both answers imply that whether from the back or from the front it is just the same. However, it seems that through the second answer the pupil also implies that he has seen through the master's trap.

11. The pupil answers according to his own situation. As for the reader, the answer would be, "I'll go on reading" (or anything else he intends to do).

12. The pupil answers the challenge of the trap-question by slapping his master. By slapping he also implies that the master should not underestimate his understanding of the koan.

13. Again, a simple trap-question. The "one hand" is not to be located in space, but the pupil naively responds to the question within the frame of common sense.

14. This trap-question is intended to test if the pupil is taken in by distinctions of time or phase (beginning, middle, end) as to the "sound of the one hand." The answer implies "there is not much difference," no more than the simple difference of before a certain fixed limit and after that limit. More concretely, in terms of "beginning, middle, end," the answer is a simple response showing "this end" (right hand), "that end" (left hand), and "middle" (both hands together).

"Before-the-fifteenth-day" and "after-the-fifteenth-day" is sometimes also used as a set phrase for "before enlightenment" and "after enlightenment." This question may also be interpreted in such a way which does not differ much from the above interpretation. In such a case however, the reader should not read into the bringing of the hands together on the "fifteenth day" (the time of enlightenment) as an overtly abstract philosophical meaning (such as "unity" or "non-distinction"). The question is of the same pattern as question 10. Thus, instead of the answer in the book (extending right hand, then left hand, then bringing hands together), the pupil may, as in question 10, answer through sound imitations of three animals, or through the enumeration of three examples of any other phenomena of the same category.

15. The trap lies in the notion of "sublime." The expectation of a supermundane experience is perhaps the greatest obstacle in the way of Zen enlightenment. Through his answer, the pupil implies that he is not taken in by the distinction of "sublime–mundane."

16.   The pupil's action is an imitation of the Japanese style of greeting. Through the omission of the words which usually accompany the greeting ceremony, the pupil simply responds only to the word "soundless" in the master's question.

17.   In the demand to explain what it is "truly" like, the question entails a trap. Asked what it is "truly" like (i.e., its "essence"), the pupil has to answer that it is "truly" nothing ("mu"), for to define "truth" in positive terms is mere illusion. In his answer, the pupil rejects the master's demand to define the "ultimate truth" as something of illusory nature. If the pupil responded philosophically—for example, "everything exists, yet ultimately it is nothing"—he would be ridiculed by the master for the denial of existence.

18.   To define the "source" of things is similar to the definition of their "ultimate truth." The answer suggests that the emptiness (or void) of "mu" is the "source." The answer and the attached quotes express the mood of "mu" by using the symbols of far-extended time and space, serenity, and evenness.


B:   *The Koan on Mu*   (pp. 51–54)

This version of the koan is recorded as the first koan in Master Mumon's (1183–1260) *Mumonkan* ("The Gateless Gate"). An earlier and larger version of this koan by Master Jōshū (778–897) is found in *Jōshūgoroku* ("The Sayings of Jōshū"). It seems that the shorter version has purposely been chosen for the koan teaching. Some of the master's questions in the discourse on this koan are related to points of doctrine discussed in the earlier version of the koan. However, the purpose of the koan in this book is not so much the problem of "Buddha-nature" (i.e., "dharma-nature"—the potentiality of self-realization or enlightenment) in its doctrinal aspect; as a point of doctrine, it is more or less expected that the question, whether a dog has Buddha-nature, be answered in the affirmative. And indeed, we find that in the fuller version of the koan, Jōshū *also* answers in the affirmative ("u") to the very same question. In the version of *Jōshūgoroku*, Jōshū explains his negation ("mu") and affirmation ("u") on doctrinal grounds.

The presentation of the koan in this book, the answer to the koan, and the discourse on it, make it evident that the point to be realized is not "Buddha-nature" in relation to the dog, but the nature of affirmation and negation. The monk expects an answer *either* in the affirmative *or* in the negative. But Jōshū's "mu" is neither "no" nor "yes." Like the "sound of the one hand," Jōshū's "mu" includes and at the same time excludes both "yes" and "no" (or "being" and nothing"). "Mu" is not a response to the contents of the question but to its logic.

It is perfectly legitimate to ask whether a dog has a tail. If the pupil says he would not answer the question about the tail because he does not recognize the dog (it is "nothing"), the master would stick the dog's tail into his mouth. Jōshū has nothing against the dog; it is actually the monk's enlightenment which is put into question. The monk may be well versed in Buddhist doctrine, but he knows little about dogs and still less about himself. With his "mu," Jōshū challenges the monk's logic and at the same time makes the utmost effort to kindly answer the "question" to the limit that language permits. Thus we would do best to read Jōshū's "mu" as "void" (in the sense of "null and void").

### ANSWER

The pupil takes up Jōshū's answer, yelling "Mu——!" with all his might. In doing so, he adds to Jōshū's "mu" the urgency of "see! see!"

## DISCOURSE

1–3. Similar to the corresponding questions and answers of the koan on the "one hand" (see p. 47).

4. As explained above, Jōshū's "mu" and the pupil's "Mu——!" are not the negative ("no"). In his answer, the pupil does not object to Jōshū's "u" (see below, note 6) but implies the rejection of the affirmative–negative mode of reasoning.

5. In "Mu——!" the pupil implies that he is not taken in by the distinction between the "karmic state" and the "enlightened state."

6. In the earlier version of the koan, when asked by the monk why he responded in the affirmative ("u") to the question on whether a dog has Buddha-nature, Jōshū answered, "Knowing yet trespassing." In the earlier version, this phrase could mean that the state of a dog is of the same karmic cycle as that of human beings (namely, it is of a self-conscious nature and therefore belongs to the realm of moral retribution). However, in our version of the

koan, it seems plausible that Jōshū's "knowing yet trespassing" should be understood as "knowing the truth of 'mu' yet purposely saying 'u.'" Namely, Jōshū admits that by answering in the affirmative he knowingly trespasses the "mu" (i.e., the negation of the affirmative–negative mode of reasoning). In this, Jōshū admits that his "u" answer is a trap intended to test if the monk is still taken in by the categories of "yes–no." Only if one takes Jōshū's "mu" as "no" does his "u" ("yes") appear as contradictory. The answer implies that the pupil is not taken in by the trap of interpreting Jōshū's "mu" as one of negation.

7.   Master Mumon was given this koan by Master Getsurin. After six years, when he suddenly came to realization, he composed the "poem" that goes:

Mu! Mu! Mu! Mu! Mu!
Mu! Mu! Mu! Mu! Mu!
Mu! Mu! Mu! Mu! Mu!
Mu! Mu! Mu! Mu! Mu!

The pupil's answer (any quote consisting of twenty characters) implies that he is not taken in by "mu" in the sense of negation (nor in any other sense).

8.   The pupil's action implies "it's me."

9.   The concept of "working" is usually brought into relation with "essence." "Essence" is the "truth" of things, whereas "working" is the function or mode of operation. Having pointed at himself as the "essence" of "mu," the pupil implies that the working of "mu" is his own activity. In immediate response to the call of the moment, the activity of the (enlightened) self is not hampered by anything—it is absolutely free.

10.   The pupil is tested whether he is taken in by the distinction between "enlightenment–non-enlightenment." In the description of a course taken from a certain place and back to that same place, the pupil implies that one ends up exactly where one has started from. He thus rejects the distinction between "holy" and "mundane."

11.   The quotes simply refer to the course "to and back" of the previous answer.

12.   Similar to the question and answer concerning the source of the one hand" (see p. 223, note 18).

# The Way of the Takujū School

A:  *The Koan on the Sound of the One Hand* (pp. 47–51)

There are only minor differences between the Inzan School and the Takujū School. In order to avoid repetition, I have refrained from including notes where the two schools are identical or similar in pattern. It should be noted, however, that the presentation of the koan on the one hand is made somewhat easier for the pupil through the addition of the word "soundless." It also appears that there is a greater tolerance in the Takujū School regarding the answer to the koan. The alternative verbal answer is not as sharp and clear as the answer of "thrusting one hand forward," but the reader may benefit from it if he is still in need of help in words.

## DISCOURSE

5.  Through this action the pupil implies "it's me," not taken in by the spatial aspect of the word "shape."

9.  The pupil is not taken in by the seemingly paradoxical request to "grind the one hand into powder"; if the "one hand" may be "grasses, trees, cows, horses" (as in the alternative answer to the koan), it may as well be red pepper and noodles.

10.  Having answered question 8 on the "Mt.-Fuji-summit-one-hand," this question is too simple a trap to be caught by.

11.  The question is phrased so that it may be understood both as the "high-one-hand" (in contrast to "low" or "valueless") and as the "lifted-one-hand." The pupil is not taken in by the trap of "high–low" in the evaluative sense, and simply responds with an act of lifting the hand to the mouth the way traveling peddlers do when calling out their merchandise. The examples from everyday life also imply the rejection of the "high-one-hand" in the evaluative sense.

12.  In question 9, "Grind into powder and swallow it," the master refers to a useful action that is indeed performed in everyday life. Here, however, the master's requirement is simply nonsensical and nothing more than a trap. The pupil sees through the trap and responds accordingly.

14.  In the discourse of the Inzan School, the pupil responds to the question on the "source of the one hand" with an attempt

to answer verbally (see p. 223, note 18). However, such a question is better regarded as a trap. The pupil's response implies that he has seen through the trap and that the question does not deserve an answer.

16. The Zen monk is of course in no special position where the "one hand" is concerned. My "one hand" is to be writing this book, the reader's "one hand" is to be reading it.

18. The quote simply refers to the "one" of the "one hand."

## B: *The Koan on Mu* (pp. 51–54)

### DISCOURSE

1. The pupil is not taken in by affirmation negation. But that does not mean that he transcends common sense. When something is not "no," it is simply "yes."

2. The response is simple and immediate. After all, the only distinction that can be made between "being" and "non-being" is that of "is" and "is not."

3. The pupil does not respond to the "u" and "mu" of the question. In his answer he simply refers to "how far." Instead of pointing out the "mixing of categories" in the master's question, he naively responds within the category that can be dealt with without trespassing common sense (i.e., distance).

9–13. The pupil implies that he has become "mu."

14. This question deals with the "essence" and "working" of things (similar to the Inzan School on the "essence" and "working" of "mu"—p. 225, note 9). "Knowing" a thing is simply seeing it. The "working" of a thing lies in its function or usage.

17. The question is nonsensical. The pupil naively responds to each of the master's demands without being bothered much about their meaning.

19. In the answer, the pupil simply responds to "selling articles" without being bothered about the distinction between "u" and "mu." The quotes imply that "u" and "mu" are of the same origin.

21. Another possible translation of the master's question can be: "Say Jōshū's 'mu' like this."

22. This original, striking question can, I believe, be considered an outstanding koan. It does not necessarily have to deal with Jōshū's "mu." The pattern of the question is: "What if . . . (any

fact) . . . had never happened?" The answer may, in any of the possible applications, be the same "mu——" (see note on the koan of "mu," Inzan School, pp. 223–224).

23. The one-footed Persian—Nata Taishi, a legendary figure in Buddhist folklore. Nata Taishi, having three faces and eight arms, symbolizes authority and freedom of action. It is difficult to make sense of Ryōfu's poem. The pupil, not taken aback by inconsistencies, naively responds to the parts of the poem without caring for its overall meaning. Note also how the pupil responds to the master's "Explain!" in the last part of the answer. If the master is not enlightened, he might attain enlightenment through the pupil's answer.

27. The answer would, of course, also be correct if the pupil said, "If you're 'mu' then I'm 'u.'" The point here is that the master asks for a "distinction" and the pupil provides him with one.

28. Identical to question 3 (see p. 227, note 3).

29–30. The pupil, not taken in by the demand to explain Zen, provides the master with an example of the correct usage of words.

31. The phrase "rush [or get into] this leather [or skin] bag" appears in the earlier version of the koan on "mu." When Jōshū answers in the affirmative to the question of whether a dog has Buddha-nature, the monk asks, "How did it [Buddha-nature] get into this skin bag [the dog's body]?" The pupil, who apparently knows the origin of the quote, implies in his answer that the skin bag (himself) holds everything.

32. In his answer, the pupil rejects the "source" question as a trap. The quotes however, hint at the "source" of mu. In the first and third quotes, we have a description of natural scenery; while the second quote speaks of "man's heart."

33. The answer sounds somewhat artificial. The pupil seems to imply "the essence of karma is karma" or simply, "karma is karma."

34–35. The reference to attachment in answer 34 does not necessarily imply non-enlightenment. Non-enlightenment does not lie in the karmic states themselves but, as mentioned in answer 35, in the making of a distinction between "u" and "mu."

36. The answer "u" implies, "Well, if you say Jōshū and 'u,' he must have said 'u'" or, "If you wish it to be 'u,' then let it be 'u.'"

37. The pupil implies that the view of things as "u" ("is," "existence") is the common sense view of the world. It should be noted that the answer does not entail any evaluation of this view.

38. The state of "consciousness of one's deeds" is a state of freedom. Although one cannot escape the karmic consequences of one's deeds, one can *disregard* them. The first answer expresses the freedom which disregards the karmic consequences of one's deeds, whereas the second answer implies the absolute freedom that disregards the limitations of common sense.

# NOTES TO PART TWO

## Miscellaneous Koans

When the pupil has answered his first koan (either the "one hand" koan or the "mu" koan), the discourse on the koan (Part One) takes relatively little time. The pupil usually sees his master for "dokusan" (private meeting) twice a day. During "sesshin" (concentrated zazen practice usually taking a week), the pupil may meet his master three to six times a day. During each meeting, which lasts for about three minutes, the master asks the pupil one or two questions, more or less according to the order in this book. When the pupil is asked to attach a quote to his answer, he looks for a fitting quote (most of them from *Zenrinkushu*, a collection of Zen sayings) and presents it at the following meeting. When the pupil has answered all the questions of the "discourse" on his koan, the master presents the pupil with the "miscellaneous koans" of Part Two of this book. The koans in Part Two are presented to all pupils—that is, those who answered the "one hand" koan and those who answered the "mu" koan. As the "one hand" koan and the "mu" koan are ultimately the same thing, the "miscellaneous koans" do not differ much from the "discourse," but whereas the questions of the "discourse" are phrased in accordance with the language of the koan (either that of the "one hand" or that of "mu"), the miscellaneous koans are of a wider scope, not being restricted by any specific frame. In answering the "miscellaneous koans" the pupil demonstrates his ability to apply his realization of the first koan in thought and action in various situations.

## The Koans

1. The question can also be translated as "your face before your father and mother were born." In his answer, the pupil implies "it's me," thus avoiding the trap of an unanswerable question.
2. The "body of truth" ("Dharma-body"; in Japanese,

"hosshin") is here referred to in the sense of "the body of enlightenment" or "the state of enlightenment." In ancient times ships
were made of wood; "a metal ship floating on water" was considered a paradox. The metaphor hints at the quasi-paradoxical
state of being enlightened yet still remaining in this world (of
karmic existence). The pupil responds with "it's me"—identifying
himself with "body of truth."

3.   The question about the meaning of Bodhidharma, the
founder of Zen, coming from the west (from India to China) is
identical in meaning to the question, "What is the meaning of
Buddhism?" or, "What is Zen?" Such a question is a "trap-question" for it should not and cannot be answered according to the
phrasing of the question (i.e., in abstract terms). In his question, the
master already hints at the futility of the question, presenting it
as a "question in a dream." The pupil's answer disregards the
question and responds only to "dream." When saying, "You
think that answers it?" the master tries the same trap again. In
the Japanese popular saying, there is a simple response to the word
"sleep." Through the Chinese quote, the pupil distinguishes between the state of sound sleep in which no silly questions can be
asked, and the state of awakening in which no questions remain,
for everything has become clear.

4.   If one is bothered with the thought of how to reach a
destination, even a straight way is curved; free of delusion and
doubt, the curved way is straight.

5.   A more extreme version of the previous question. Jumping into the water without getting wet is similar to going straight
in a curved way. If you do not care about the curves—you go
straight; if you do not care about the water—you do not get wet.

6–7.   The distinction between subject and object exists only
as long as there is self-consciousness. When you forget yourself,
you become one with the stone you are picking up. In such a state,
even if the stone lies at the bottom of the sea, you pick it up without
getting wet.

8–11.   As in the case of the "curved mountain road" or the
"stone," once you respond to a situation in an absolutely immediate
way, you become the situation and the situation becomes you.
Consciousness of movement exists only as long as there is consciousness of a static self. By becoming a boat you stop its movement, by joining the fight you stop the (consciousness of) quarrel,
and by becoming the bell you stop the sound.

12.   One cannot respond to four different sounds at once, but

by responding to each sound in its turn, ultimately all the sounds are one sound. This also answers the koan on the "sound of the one hand."

13. The pupil disregards the absurd request to exert influence over a distance of a "thousand miles" and simply responds by "blowing out" the lamp at home.

14. The pupil, disregarding the absurd request to draw out a mountain from the medicine case, presents the master with what is in the case—that is, medicine.

15–18. The pupil disregards the condition of "not using hands" and simply refers to his or the master's "getting up." He disregards "Mt. Fuji" and simply "walks"; he cannot "grind a mill in a duck egg" but he can do the grinding. The four questions are of the same pattern—demanding an action yet posing an absurd condition. The pupil performs only the desired action. Through the immediacy of his response, he makes the absurdities vanish.

19. The existence of legendary figures or even that of historical figures is not anything beyond one's self. This answer should not be interpreted idealistically. The pupil does not imply that "the world is consciousness"; like in the previous answers, he simply disregards the unanswerable and responds within the limits of his immediate knowledge.

20. In his answer the pupil rejects the theoretical systematization of "principles" or "virtues."

21. Being in a room the pupil cannot see the sky. Thus his answer can reach no further than where his eyes reach.

22–23. A somewhat artificial version of the "become one with the object" theme. In the popular saying, by referring to the woman's attachment to her lover, the pupil seems to be simply responding to the idea of "unity." These two questions and the saying may also refer to the absolute determination required of the novice in his pursuit of enlightenment.

24. The same pattern as questions 14–18. (See above.)

25. The pupil disregards the connotation of "blasphemy" in the question. In his answer, he becomes "Buddha" (which he actually is), and presents the commonplace situation of being shitted upon by a bird.

26–27. The pupil disregards the absurdities of "wooden cock crowing" and "straw dog barking" and simply responds to "cock" and "dog."

28.  A purposely grotesque presentation of the principle of "holding everything within oneself."

29.  The pupil disregards the peonies in China and simply refers to the peonies in front of his eyes.

30.  Disregarding the absurdity of walking in one day from India to China and back, the pupil simply "walks."

31.  This is another version of the koan on "the sound of the one hand." The master's quote suggests non-distinction between "u" (is) and "mu" (is not). It should be noted, however, that the answer does not imply the elimination of common sense. Repeating the master's quote, the pupil hits a piece of wood, which of course makes a sound, and hits the air, which of course makes no sound. There either is a sound or there is no sound; ultimately however, there is the "sound of the one hand." The pupil's answer equates all sounds (the sounding-sound of wood and the soundless-sound of air) with the "sound of the one hand."

32.  The pupil disregards the absurd condition and simply "holds the spade."

33.  The master poses the contradictory demand of "walking while riding." The first answer implies "walking," the second answer implies "riding," whereas the third answer (riding on the master-buffalo) turns the master into the victim of his own trap-question.

34.  After a series of trap-questions based on "contradiction," the master poses the trap of "simplicity." The pupil has proved sophisticated enough to react to "contradiction-questions" in a simple way. Now he proves that his mind is also simple enough to react to a simple question in a simple way.

35.  This is not a trap-question. The bridge stands still only in relation to water, whereas water flows on only in relation to the bridge. The attribution of qualities to things is done through the comparison of one thing to another. Seen beyond their relations, things are just what they are. A bridge is a bridge and water is water. The answer of pretending to be a "bridge" or "running water" is too dogmatic. This quote deserves a better response.

36.  The question is intended to test the pupil's attitude to magic as a means of "salvation." The Zen concept of "salvation" rejects magical and superstitious beliefs. The pupil, in his answer (imitation of a revengeful spirit) reacts naively to the master's story. In that, however, he does not answer the master's question. The master is asking for the pupil's reaction as a "Zen monk."

Therefore, the pupil's answer should perhaps better be interpreted as an ironical reaction to the question. That is, in making a farce of the master's story, the pupil ridicules "spirit–salvation" as nonsense.

37. In ordinary thinking, "space" or "void" is understood as an abstract concept and is distinguished from "matter" or "things." It is through this distinction that the differentiation between "u" ("being") and "mu" ("nothing") originates. As against this common sense distinction, the *Hannya-Shin-Gyo*—a summary of the *Prajñāpāramitā Sutras* ("the wisdom sutras," a group of sutras setting forth the doctrine of sūnyatā, kū, or "void")—argues "shikisokuzekū, kūsokuzeshiki"—"matter is void, void is matter." Therefore, by handing over any object to the master, the pupil at the same time also hands over "space" (or "void"). In this the pupil implies that his standpoint is one of non-distinction between "void" and "matter" (or "nothing" and "being").

38–39. More concrete implications of the previous problem. In accordance with the master's request, the pupil presents him with space in the form of "salad" and "powder."

40. Shōki—a god of Japanese folk religion who chases away the devils of sickness. The belief in this god originated in China. In fact, Shōki is neither one of the Shintō gods nor does he belong to Buddhist tradition. The pupil, through his answer, makes it clear that he is not taken in by superstitious beliefs.

41. The pupil suggests that his view of Buddhism does not entail the belief in magic and superstition. In Zen Buddhism, there is no reliance on external powers for "salvation." Enlightenment is entirely a matter of self-realization.

42. The pupil is not taken in by the historical situation. As far as he is concerned, his master is not the historical Buddha but the Zen master in front of him. The painting of Buddha's death expresses the deep sorrow of Buddha's followers. In contrast to the historical situation, the pupil presents the situation he would find himself in should his master pass away.

43. The pupil is not taken in by an abstract or supernatural interpretation of Buddha's entrance into nirvana. His answer simply suggests the state of death. The master's repeated question and the pupil's holding his breath is somewhat overdone.

44. There is indeed a cat in the painting referred to. However, the question, "Why is there a cat?" is a trap. There is a cat in the painting because the painter painted a cat. The problem is really

that of "why" and "because." In his answer the pupil demonstrates that his mind is clear enough (i.e., free from speculation) to avoid a "because" where "why" is nonsensical.

45–46. Similar to question 41. The pupil rejects the belief in mythological powers, implying that the "source" of everything is the self. The answers may also be interpreted as the pupil "becoming" the mythological figures. The meaning, however, is the same in as far as the mythological figures are not taken to be *external* powers.

47–48. Disregarding the myth of creation by external powers, the pupil simply responds to "give birth to a mountain," "give birth to a land."

49. The pupil disregards the "statue of Buddha" and implies that his concern is only with the "human Buddha."

50. In his answer to the master's story, the pupil disregards the absurdity of receiving fire as a gift, and simply responds to the situation of receiving a parting gift.

51. The tea ladle suffers no pain from heat and cold because it has "no-mind." The pupil's answer seems to suggest the "no-mind" state of the enlightened. "The mind of the moment"—"when hot, hot! when cold, cold!"—is, in effect, "no-mind" because it does not form a problem outside of the situation (i.e., it responds to the situation in an absolutely immediate way). Of course, this does not exclude the sensations of pain from heat or cold, only the mind's dwelling upon these sensations when the stimulus is over.

52. The pupil avoids the temptation to respond to the abstract "after death" and simply responds to "go."

53. Mt. Godai in China was a "holy" mountain. The metaphor of "clouds steaming rice" is employed for the poetical impact of the landscape description. The pupil's answer may suggest that the "rice-steaming clouds" are there because the monks of the monastery on Mt. Godai are cooking rice. It may also be read as a simple response to "rice." In either case, through the daily action of "cooking rice," the pupil implies that he is not taken in by the concept of "holiness."

54. As far as the dog is concerned, there is no difference between an old Buddhist temple and a telephone pole. Both are perfectly suitable to urinate on. The pupil's view is not much different from that of the dog.

55–56. The quotes of the master describe absurd situations.

The pupil responds only to those parts of the quotes that imply common situations ("fry" and "toss coins").

57–58. The quotes suggest freedom from the common pattern of thinking in terms of "cause–effect." The pupil's response apparently implies freedom from the "subject–object" mode of thinking. The answer may, however, be interpreted as an ironical response to the master's quotes.

59. It is no wonder that nothing is heard about the clay cows, for clay dissolves in water. The pupil's answer may simply imply "searching for" (the clay cows). This question–answer is not quite clear.

60. Suiō and Tōrei were the disciples of Master Hakuin, who composed the koan on "the sound of the one hand." This trap-question is, of course, not to be answered and the pupil acts accordingly.

61. By responding to the master's silly request to count the hairs of the nose, the pupil implies that he is not taken in by distinctions of value. As trivial and valueless as something may appear, one should not care about its "significance" and like a simpleton respond without hesitation.

62. The master's question is an imitation of the story on Master Kyōgen's enlightenment upon hearing a piece of tile hit the bamboo. (The original version appears in *Kattōshū*, a collection of Zen stories on various masters. In this book it appears in Part Three, p. 164, koan 64, under the title SOUND).

The master changes the original version: (1) instead of Master Kyōgen, he speaks of "two young monks"; (2) the sound of the tile does not occur in a natural way, as in the original version, but is artificially performed by one young monk to "test" the other.

The pupil is not taken in by the seemingly "deep meaning" of the story; his reaction implies that he has seen through the trap.

63. It is the reliance on "light" that puts one in the situation of "darkness." It is the clinging to the concept of "enlightenment" that makes one consider a "non-enlightened" state. In the first answer the pupil implies that all things are originally perfect the way they are—there is nothing wrong with "the maid's washing clothes at the well" and "the servant pissing in the field." Also, the alternative answers of "digging up the burdock root from the back field" and "pulling the cow out from the back shed" imply

everyday situations. The other two answers can be understood as a simple response to "darkness."

64. Similar to question 49. (See p. 235, note 49.)

65. If one responds to things in a simple and immediate way, there is no room for distinctions of value. All that can be said about excreta is "it stinks." There is nothing "unholy" about it. The same attitude is implied in the quote. The stupid person has his value as stupid, while the wise one has his value as wise.

66. The pupil implies that he is not taken in by "might" or "authority" (in "lion" or "master") and simply does what he is told to do.

67. The answer implies "here, now!"

68. It seems that the master's question is better understood as a nonsensical trap-question. However, the pupil takes "pillar of the house" in its allegorical meaning as the "central figure."

69. To "enter" the incense burner is of course nonsensical, but, by handling the incense burner in the way an incense burner is to be handled, the pupil in a sense "becomes" the incense burner.

70. The pupil evades an abstract philosophical answer by simply responding to "come from" and "return."

71. The pupil implies that he is not involved with problems that are not of his immediate concern. He does not know where the waters of the river go, but he knows where his own waters go.

72. In popular belief, the bones of a saint (in Japanese, "shari") are given various magical qualities. As the master hints with the word "living," the pupil is expected to disregard the historical and legendary "Buddhas" and refer only to the "human Buddha" (see also p. 235, note 49; and above, note 64). In presenting the master with his own ear wax, the pupil himself becomes a Buddha. Reacting to the "body of a saint" through his own ear wax, the pupil also implies a disregard of the connotation of "holiness."

73. The master's question is an artificial imitation of the Zen theme of "say it without words." However, "without words" does not necessarily mean "with your mouth shut." The pupil sees through the trap and in his witty response turns the master into the victim of his own question.

74. The pupil disregards the theoretical "where would you start working on it?" by simply "working." His action also implies that he is not concerned with a situation far removed in time and space (an ancient bridge in China) but only with what is in front

of his eyes (the master). By quoting the popular saying concerning "beautiful" and "ugly," the pupil suggests that he is not taken in by distinctions of value (such as ancient China or present-day Japan, a stone bridge there, or a wooden bridge here).

75.   Same pattern as question 74.

76.   See p. 237, note 66.

77.   A trap-question of the kind, "Have you stopped hitting your parents?" or, "Is the present king of France bald?" In answering such questions directly, you are bound to say the wrong thing. The pupil's answer also implies that he is not taken by metaphysical speculations.

78.   Not being able to count the hairs in the back of his own head, the pupil simply counts the hairs of the master's head. For the significance of the counting see p. 236, note 61.

79.   Same pattern as koans 37–39 (see p. 234). Through the popular saying, the pupil humorously combines "color" with "wind." The quotes simply refer to "color."

80.   The pupil is not taken in by the speculative nature of the question and responds only to "rain." In the last alternative answer, the pupil disregards "rain" and simply responds to "where from," displaying the concrete attitude of common sense.

81.   The quote is taken from *Hekiganroku* (No. 3). In the original, however, the stress is on negation ("mu" or "kū"—"void"). In contrast to the original, the pupil's answer seems to imply affirmation of all ways: "You can do it this way, you can do it the other way. This or that are all possible."

82.   The "deliverance" of the ink stick is in using it.

83.   The pupil is not taken in by the metaphysical problem of "life–death" and simply responds to "flower."

84–86.   The same pattern as the questions on counting the hairs of the nose (koan 61), or of the head (koan 78). The master's demands are both silly and impossible. By naively responding to the silly and the impossible, the pupil proves what he is supposed to prove.

87.   The pupil evades the trap of "why" and simply responds to "turtle."

88.   By using the wine flask as a wine flask should be used, the pupil may be said to have "gone in and out" of the wine flask.

89.   There is no clear answer as to which of the eight dragons of Indian–Buddhist mythology makes the rain fall. Even if there were, the pupil is not concerned with it. In his answer, the pupil

does just what the dragon does (i.e., "making the waters fall").

90.   If you stand still against the wind, you "move" (i.e., your mind is taken in by the attitude of resistance). If you move *with* the wind, you really do not move (see p. 235, note 51).

91.   The pupil disregards the nonsensical "bean curd" condition and simply acts as requested.

92.   The pupil's answer implies "that's all I know" or "that's all I can see." Another possible answer to the same question may simply be, "Are you the elder or the younger sister?"

93.   The question is similar to koan 88. The answer ("becoming a smoking pipe") is, however, somewhat artificial. It would be better to respond by using the smoking pipe.

94.   The pupil rightly disregards the condition of "the day before yesterday." However, the answer ("becoming cigarette ashes") is overdone.

95.   In Japan, gates are usually made of wood. The "stone gate" condition is brought in to exclude the possibility of breaking through by oneself. The pupil answers in the most obvious and natural way that can be thought of. It would, however, be a mistake to expect everybody to respond to this question in such a natural way. People who are taken in by speculative thinking often miss the most obvious.

96.   Similar in pattern to Part One, Inzan School, the koan on "mu," discourse questions 8 and 9; and the Takujū School, the koan on "mu," discourse question 14. (See p. 225, notes 8 and 9; and p. 227, note 14.)

In this case, however, the definition of the "essence" of the wind as its blowing is not good. "Blowing" is the wind's function and should be put under "working."

97.   In Zen, the concept of "reincarnation" is usually not taken in its literal sense (i.e., as a real happening), but rather used in a metaphorical sense for "spiritual" influence. The pupil is not taken in by the esoteric implication of the question. His response may mean "becoming" one with the masters of the past (in the spiritual sense), or it may simply imply that his concern with personal histories does not go beyond his own life.

98.   The answer seems to refer to "kū" in the philosophical sense of "shikisokuzekū" ("the matter is void," see p. 234, note 37), but kū may simply imply the empty space of the room.

99.   The pupil's first answer to the master's absurd request is a response to "tie up." Instead of tying up a "mountain" with a

"lamp wick," the pupil ties up his head with a "headband" the way Japanese (especially workers) do when going out. In the alternative answer, the pupil challenges the master himself to do the impossible.

100. Originally, Tokyo was a conglomeration of hundreds of towns and villages. It is, of course, impossible to see all of Tokyo through one's sleeve. In response, the pupil tells what *can* be seen when looking into the sleeve.

101. The answer may imply that Zen rejects the beliefs in magical powers of omniscience. However, it is better taken at its face value meaning, "There's no use speculating. To see what is inside the box you simply have to take its cover off and look."

102. Similar to koan 78. (See p. 238, note 78.)

103. The pupil disregards the metaphysical implications of the "after death" problem and simply responds to "meet."

104. The quote (taken from a collection of Zen sayings, *Kaisekiroku*) metaphorically refers to the spiritual power of the Zen master. The pupil's response to "turn heaven" by turning a somersault hints at the "turning" possibilities of humans, thus implying the rejection of the quote as an overstatement.

105. The pupil demonstrates a speculation-free attitude by responding simply to the phrases of the poem.

106. The pupil's answer may imply that he refuses to speculate on the concept of "the realm-of-no-thought" in its Buddhist meaning of "realm of enlightenment." Through the enumeration of personalities who passed away he suggests that the realm of "no-thought" is "death." In enumerating personalities from the secular world as well, the pupil may suggest that "the realm-of-no-thought" (this time in the sense of "enlightenment") is not restricted only to practitioners of religion.

107. In his answer, the pupil implies that he refuses to attribute supernatural or magical powers to the "greatly enlightened." The pupil's quote suggests the natural course of things. In the search for enlightenment and in the attainment of enlightenment, there is nothing transcendental.

108. The pupil wisely evades the question concerning the "ultimate truth." He agrees, however, with what has been suggested in the master's quote, that one achieves nothing through the search for the transcendental.

109. The answer may suggest that the simile is wrong because you cannot hit the sky the way you hit a drum (it affords no resis-

tance and therefore makes no sound). Such an answer is quite uncommon in its alertness to details. Most people would perhaps be taken in by the vast dimensions of the master's example and respond in a speculative, philosophical way.

110. The story appears in the collection of Zen stories, *Keitokudentōroku*. In his question concerning the wisdom of Buddhism, the emperor expects a metaphysical answer. In his response, Master Etchū ridicules the emperor's speculative frame of mind and aims at shocking him into enlightenment. Some may interpret the pupil's imitation of a floating cloud as a reference to "non-attachment" (to concepts). However, I think it is best taken simply as "a cloud is a cloud."

111. The story appears in *Keitokudentōroku*. It takes place in China. Monk Daiji (or Daijisanzō) was an Indian Buddhist who possessed the magical art of omniscience. The story does not imply a complete denial of Monk Daiji's mind-reading power. However, the final winner in this contest is Zen Master Etchū. Daiji can read Etchū's thoughts only as long as they are purposely brought forth in order to test Daiji. The pupil's answer suggests that where Etchū responds with the natural reaction of frustration and grudge, Daiji failed to read his mind. The simple and immediate reaction to a situation, whatever that reaction may be, is the "mind of the moment" or "no-mind" (see p. 235, note 51). Therefore Daiji can read Etchū's thoughts only where Etchū is not himself, but his powers do not reach to where Etchū is simply Etchū.

112. The quote implies that the moment one "inquires" (i.e., speculates) about a situation, one's mind is split into the "two halves" of "subject" and "object" or "active" and "passive." With the mind "broken into two halves," one misses the moment of spontaneous action. The pupil, in his answer, refers only to the actual happening—to where there is no doubt (the glittering of the sword). In this he implies a simple, immediate response to the situation.

113. In Buddhist legends, Monju (Manjusri) and Fugen (Samantabhadra) often appear as the attendants of Buddha. Monju, the left-hand attendant of Buddha, rides a lion; Fugen, the right-hand attendant, is mounted on a white elephant; whereas Buddha, in the center, is on foot. The pupil disregards history and mythology and through his answer suggests that the only Buddha he knows are those present (himself or the master).

114. As an alternative answer, the pupil could as well imitate

the form of a teapot, or, even better, demonstrate the correct usage of a teapot.

115. The answer implies "non-distinction." The attitude of an evenness of mind as to the distinctions between "nirvana" and "samsara," or "holy" and "mundane," answers the master's question.

116. The answer simply implies fulfilling one's duties when one is called upon. It relates to the theme of the previous question 115 in suggesting that along with the "religious" duties (meditation, sutra reading, etc.) there are the common everyday occupations, such as preparing food and managing household affairs.

117. Although the question may suggest the theme of question 115 in the philosophical sense of "the realm of light" (enlightenment) and "the realm of darkness" (non-enlightenment), it is better taken at its face value. The pupil evades the speculative suggestions of the question by simply describing what one does in the morning.

118. The phrase "know that there is" is a translation of "know 'u.'" This, however, does not mean that the racoons and the white oxen do not know "mu." One could "explain" the animals' "knowledge" through references to the "natural," "spontaneous," etc., but it would be better to leave this koan as it is.

119. The pupil's response to the quote may sound somewhat artificial, but it does strike a true note in reminding us that the nature of clouds and rivers is not the only "nature." Human life as it is, with its daily occupations and with its wars, is also "nature."

120. To carry a heavy weight and lightly float about is against the nature of human existence. This may be intended as a reminder to those seeking "liberation" from human bondage.

121. Almost identical to question 112. (See p. 241, note 112.)

122. The wisdom of the enlightened does not mean a disregard for worldly affairs, but the proper handling of them.

123. The quote is a saying of the Japanese Zen master Daitō-kotushi (from *Daitōkokushisantengo*); the same theme as koans 115 and 116. (See above, notes 115, 116.)

Instead of dealing with the "problem" of whether it is good or bad for a practitioner of Buddhism to be involved in social relations, the pupil simply points to the fact that *right now* he is in that situation.

124. The theme of non-distinction between samsara and

nirvana. In Zen, enlightenment is not, as in the Hinayana tradition, detachment from passions. Attachment is inevitable. One should not, however, be attached to one's attachment. The popular saying refers to the attachment of "love" in a melancholic mood typical of the Japanese mind.

125. A wise paradox. Freedom of action does not only mean always hitting the center of the target. When absolutely free, one is also at liberty to miss the center of the target. The one who is free to do only "good" is not really free. Only when one is free to also do "bad" can one be said to be absolutely free.

Some may interpret the quote as suggesting that there is nothing absolutely perfect. I believe, however, that the above interpretation is more fitting. The pupil's response simply suggests "missing the center of the target."

126. The same pattern as question 95 (see p. 239, note 95). For further reference, see question 51 (p. 235, note 51).

127. The quote simply suggests that the teaching is the same although the techniques may be different. This is also suggested in the pupil's quotes. The reader should not be taken in by a value distinction between "milk" and "poison." As far as the snake is concerned, "poison" is perfectly all right.

128. While this quote may originally imply philosophical idealism, the pupil's answer makes it perfectly clear that in the Zen context it is not meant to be interpreted in such a way. The pupil's response, rather than suggesting that the world is the *product* of consciousness, implies that human existence is centered around the common affairs of the human world. "Time" is, as far as we are concerned, our "yesterday, today, and tomorrow." "The Buddhas" are people around us, and "existence is the creation of mind" in so far as we plan our activity and act according to our intentions.

129. The pupil is not taken in by the master's trap-suggestion to deny the distinctions between "high" and "low" in their physical sense.

130. The quote implies—though it is ultimately "mu," it is to be admitted as "u." The answer is the same as in the discourse on koan 37 on "mu," Takujū School, (see p. 228, note 37). The world may ultimately be "nothing," but if you say a table is not a table, you are simply an idiot.

131. A clever trap-question. The pupil's answer simply implies

that he has seen through the trap and refuses to speculate. I think, however, that the pupil also suggests that the "problem" is not in the sutra but in himself (and the master).

132.   This quote does not differ in meaning from the quote of koan 130. Yet in suggesting that "knowledge" is not to be reached at through the senses, it puts a stronger stress on the "mu" aspect. The pupil's response is somewhat artificial.

133.   The pupil wisely evades the philosophical problem of "time." In the first answer there is a simple response to "eating" (after all, people *do* eat). The alternative answer suggests the pragmatic conception of time as expressed in the framework of common activity (see p. 243, note 128).

134.   "The mind does not dwell on any thought" does not mean that the mind is void of thought but means "the right thought at the right moment" (see p. 235, note 51). The pupil's answer suggests that a father acts in a fatherlike way, and a mother in a motherlike way. There is nothing wrong with that. It is only in a motherlike father and a fatherlike mother that there is no "true mind." The popular saying and the alternative answer suggest an immediate response to the situation.

135.   The pupil simply responds to the poem without searching for its "deep meaning." Hakuin's "What do you hear?" may be understood as "What do you understand?" or, "In what way are you enlightened?" This is a trap intended to find out once and for all whether the pupil does not indeed attach a "meaning" to the poem. The pupil sees through the trap and responds to "hear" in its simple sense of hearing with one's ears.

# NOTES TO PART THREE

## The One Hundred Forty-Four Koans

The one hundred forty-four koans of Part Three are not intended for all the novices but only for those who aim to become Zen masters. In Japan, those who aim for the lower qualifications of a Zen priest end their monastic practice within a period of about three years. Usually such novices have to answer their first koan (the "one hand" koan or the koan on "mu"), the discourse on the first koan, and the miscellaneous koans. A novice who is quick in finding the answers may also receive a part of the koans of this chapter within the period of three years.

A simple priest of the Rinzai sect is supposed to live in one of the temples belonging to the sect, perform the religious duties of burial, say prayers for the dead on memorial days, and look after the temple and the burial grounds attached to it. In Japan, the temple is usually passed on through heredity. Correspondingly, most of the novices who train to become Zen priests are usually the sons of Zen priests.

However, in order to be qualified as a Zen master the novice has to stay in the monastery and practice under his master for many more years. The average period of training to become a master is about ten years. In order to be qualified as a master, the novice has to go through all the one hundred forty-four koans of this section. It is expected that once the pupil grasps the meaning of his first koan (including the discourse on it) and the miscellaneous koans, he will hit upon the answers to all the one hundred forty-four koans with relative ease. However, the time required for each koan depends, after all, on the personality of the pupil. Some may answer on the spot whereas others may "contemplate" one koan for a month or even more. Only someone who has become a Zen master is qualified to pass the koans on to a new generation of novices.

The original Chinese versions of the one hundred forty-four koans are to be found in *Mumonkan*, *Kattōshū*, *Hekiganroku*, and *Rinzairoku* (for the sources of each koan see Appendix A, "Sources to the Koans Part Three"). Some of the koans have been translated from Chinese into old or modern Japanese; there are also English translations of some of the koans of this section. The pupil is not supposed to look for sources, translations, interpretations, or historical commentaries. All this is absolutely beside the point. As most Japanese novices are not versed in Chinese, the master usually translates the koan into Japanese, thus presenting it (as far as the words are concerned) in such a way that the pupil does not have to do any further research into it.

In the translation of the koans, I have omitted many expressions which are not essential for the understanding of their meaning (such as the full Chinese names of Zen masters, honorific titles, names of places in China, etc.). I have also tried to make the translation of the Chinese Buddhist terms (such as the many expressions for "Buddha," "wisdom," "enlightenment," etc.) as simple as possible for the Western reader. Such a rendering of the koans is perfectly in accordance with the practice of koan teaching in Japan. Most of the Zen novices have little scholarly knowledge of Buddhist history or doctrine, and a good Zen master would avoid any reference to such matters as much as possible. In the notes, I have referred to matters of history or doctrine only where such comments seemed necessary for the understanding of the koans' meaning.

The pattern of most koans is that of a question or series of questions to which the Chinese Zen master answers in words or in action. The "answer" to the koan is thus already within the koan itself. However, as most of these "answers" seem strange and paradoxical, they are hard to understand without further clarification. The answer which the Japanese novice is supposed to provide is therefore, in most cases, no more than a clarification of what is already included in the koan. Such "answers" are by nature somewhat artificial. In some cases, the answer simply consists of a repetition of the essential phrase within the koan. In other cases, it adds a somewhat different variation of what is already implied in the koan. The best answers are those which through an unexpected phrase or action provide a flash of insight into the koan's meaning.

1. *The Man up the Tree*

It is plausible to assume that a man who holds onto a tree with his teeth would fall away. Answering or not answering the question is not his most urgent problem. What he needs is not philosophy, but somebody who is kind and courageous enough to help him down.

Commentaries by later masters are either: (1) criticisms of the koan or of the personalities appearing in the koan; (2) attempts to clarify the koan's meaning; or (3) in some cases simply implications of the mood of the later masters in relation to the koan. Setchō's quasi-paradoxical comment implies that the concrete problem of being caught up in a tree (i.e., being in danger) is not to be confused with abstract speculations about "the meaning of the founder of Zen (Bodhidharma) coming to China" (i.e., the meaning of Zen).

ANSWER

The answer is a simple response to the situation of being "on a tree" and its natural result (if one clings to a branch with one's teeth) of falling "under the tree."

## 2.   The Man in the Well

Shōkū's reaction to the question concerning the meaning of Zen ("getting a man out of a deep well without the use of a rope") suggests that the answer is no less impossible than the question. The monk, not satisfied with this, hints that monk Ō is superior to Shōkū and that *he* might be able to answer his question. Shōkū's reaction to this is quite natural.

Shōkū created the "problem" of the well and Kyōzan was caught up in it. Fortunately, Kyōzan's masters were kind enough to help him out. Tangen provided him with the "principle" (or "truth") in suggesting that there was no man in the well and therefore no one in need of being saved. Isan, by calling out "Kyōzan!" actually whisked Kyōzan out of the "well" he imagined himself to be in, thus providing Kyōzan with the "use" (or "working"). The general meaning is that we are all already enlightened, or at least quite perfect the way we are. However, let nobody be taken in by this.

ANSWER

The first and third answers (imitating the situation of having fallen into a well) miss the point. If the pupil responds with the second answer, he proves he has realized what Kyōzan did. Namely, that he is not in the "well," but right there in his master's room.

## 3. Why a Monk's Garment?

The trap in this koan lies in the word "wide." It is wrong to assume that to be free in this "wide" world means to exploit all the possibilities of life. To be free is to do what one is supposed to do without caring for what one could have done if. . . .

### ANSWER

The answer suggests that a monk is free in being a monk-like monk. The quotes refer to the same idea, implying that if one answers the call of the moment without the slightest hesitation, there is no room to be unfree.

## 4. The World a Grain of Rice

This is on the same theme as, "Even though it is not a world, it is called a world" (Part Two, koan 130; see note on p. 243), and "Bind up space with a rope" (Part Two, koan 37; see note on p. 234). Seppō, with a touch of humor, drives the "mu" ("nothing," "void") aspect of the world ad absurdum.

### ANSWER

Both the first answer with the attached quote and the alternative answer put the emphasis on "u" ("being," "matter"). Whatever the "ultimate truth" of the world may be, we are bound to live its common sense truth of "things are just what they are."

## 5. The Three Gates of Master Ōryū

Ōryū's questions are intended to test if Ryūkei is taken in by "mu." Should Ryūkei answer the question concerning his "origin" through the "mu" aspect, he would deny himself. Ryūkei thus refuses to speculate about his "origin" and presents himself as the "hungry monk" he actually is. He disregards the distinction between his own hand and that of Buddha and simply responds to "hand." In his answer to the third question, Ryūkei implies that though as far as "mu" is concerned all is the same ("a heron standing in the snow," i.e., both white), speaking "u"—Ōryū's foot is Ōryū's foot and a mule's foot is a mule's foot ("not of the same color"). It is noteworthy that Ryūkei resists the temptation to identify Ōryū with a mule. By "passing the gate and going straight on without caring for the gatekeeper," Ōryū implies that the "problem" of "u" and "mu" is answered not by solving it but by making it disappear.

*As against, "Where is your origin?"*

The first answer suggests "mu," whereas the alternative answers imply "u." To the question, "What are you?" the only reasonable answer would be to say what you *are* ("u") and not what you are not ("mu"). The quotes suggest the same attitude. In the poem on the bird and the monkey, however, we feel the undertone of "mu."
*As against, "How is my hand when compared with that of Buddha?"*

The first answer, humorously suggesting that "a leg is a leg," makes it perfectly clear that "a hand is a hand." The quotes are a simple response to "hand."
*As against, "How are my feet when compared with those of a mule?"*

Like in the above answer, through the example of "hand" the pupil suggests that "a foot is a foot." The quotes are a simple response to "foot."

## 6. *Where Do the Snowflakes Fall?*

In stating that "snowflakes do not fall on any particular place," Hōkoji suggests "mu" ("nothing," "void"). There is nothing really wrong with the monk's question; it is just that he sees the "u" of the snowflakes a little too naively. Hōkoji seems to be overly conceited where his insight of "mu" is concerned and his violent reaction to the monk's simplicity of mind is overdone. Hōkoji's understanding of the "mu" of snow is perhaps supreme, but there is something lacking in his understanding of the "u" of the monk. Setchō rightly suggests that the slapping and the scolding of the monk is unnecessary. If the monk is not conscious enough to the "truth" of snow, let him have some snow and he will understand.

The first answer and the quote on a snow landscape simply suggests "snow." The master's question as to the meaning of Hōkoji's remark actually requires an explanation concerning in what way "snow" is "non-snow." By slapping his master, the pupil reveals his attitude toward the master's demand to put "mu" into words. The last two questions of the master concern "hitting." The pupil refuses to speculate on the meaning of "hitting," suggesting that "to hit is to hit."

## 7.   Round Are the Lotus Leaves

This poem is taken from a collection of poems by Zen Master Dai-e. It is fairly plausible to assume that the poem was not intended as a problem to be answered and has no special "meaning" besides what it says. The attempt to turn this poem into a koan is artificial and may only lead to unnecessary speculations which the Zen practitioner is supposed to avoid.

ANSWER

The master picks up the forms "round" and "pointed" and asks the pupil to apply them from the standpoints of "self-centeredness" and "other-centeredness." These concepts respectively imply the nature of Arhat (the ideal of sainthood in Hinayana Buddhism) and Bodhisattva (the ideal of sainthood in Mahayana Buddhism).

In his answer, the pupil points at himself for "self-centeredness" and at the "other" for "other-centeredness." In his reaction to the last phrase of the poem, the pupil contrasts his own situation, which is after all the only situation that concerns him, with the natural scenery described in the poem.

The first three answers under "according to another school" are somewhat less speculative. However the master's last question, asking the pupil to compare the phrases of the poem to the four social classes, is almost grotesque in its artificiality.

It is hard to imagine that the pupil can hit upon such far-fetched answers on his own. It is thus plausible to assume that the master provides the pupil with the traditional answer and passes on to the next koan. The high regard for tradition, so typical of the Japanese, may have its merits, but the preservation of such artificial "koans" is a sign of the stagnation of institutional Zen.

## 8.   The Sound of Rain

The monk's answer to Kyōshō's "What is the sound outside?" is in itself quite natural. However, in Kyōshō's remark, "To put it into words is difficult," he may have suggested that there is still something wanting in the monk's answer.

The pupil, in his imitation of rain, probably suggests that the monk's answer of "It is the sound of rain" is perhaps correct, but that by words we do after all only comment *on* things. We should not confound "rain" with rain.

## 9. *The Three Questions of Master Tosō*

1. This is a trap intended to tempt the pupil into explaining "mu" ("nothing," "void") using words.
2. Transcending "life" and "death" (or "u" and "mu") is fine as long as one is safe and sound. Yet, what becomes of the question of "life" and "death" when it is not just a matter of doctrine, but actually being on the brink of death?
3. The same trap as in (1) only here it is applied to the physical realm.

*As against, "Now where is human nature?"*

The pupil, in giving the pretense of searching, may be simply responding to "where." However, it may also suggest that "human nature" is everywhere (even in the situation of searching for it). The master's additional remark seems irrelevant. The aim of Tosō's question is to uproot the "philosophical disease" of searching for the abstract, whereas the master's remark can only direct the pupil's attention from the concrete to the search of the "self" in the abstract. "Searching for" is the common theme of all the attached quotes. Note that in all of the quotes the object of the "search" cannot be directly grasped.
*As against, "On the brink of death."*

The pupil's response and the quotes attached to it express the actual situation of being "on the brink of death." Through this response, the pupil suggests that "escaping from the circle of of life and death" does not imply that one can transcend death or the pain and horror involved in dying.
*As against, "When the four elements are separated, where will you go?"*

Through his response, the pupil simply implies that, being dead, one turns into a corpse. The attached quotes suggest that when a thing has fulfilled its function, nothing but its useless remains are left to be seen. The last answer ("with certain masters") on "gone away" and "return again," suggests that everything takes its natural course.

## 10. The Sentence of Being and the Sentence of Nothing

Ran-an's simile of "the wisteria vine twining around a tree" entails a trap. If the "wisteria vine" is distinguished from the "tree," one is inclined to distinguish "u" from "mu." Or rather, if one still distinguishes between "u" and "mu," one is bound to view the "wisteria vine" and the "tree" as separate. Sozan is caught up in the trap. He imagines the tree to "fall" and the wisteria vine to "wither," which makes Ran-an laugh. When Sozan implores with Ran-an to explain to him where he is wrong, Ran-an kindly enough hints that Sozan is taken in by "two" (i.e., dualistic thinking) and that he will not understand unless he becomes "single-eyed." When Sozan reports the discourse with Ran-an to Meishō, Meishō immediately sees what Ran-an saw and praises him ("Ran-an is a straight man from head to toe"). Meishō is kind enough not to "explain" to Sozan where he was wrong, upon which Sozan is enlightened.

Like Sozan, Dai-e too is caught in the same trap. His master, Engo, is patient enough to let Dai-e understand by himself. When Dai-e, absorbed in the chopsticks, forgets about the rice, Engo suggests that Dai-e's mind is still split. Chopsticks are there to be used for eating rice. This remark of Engo's is not unlike Ran-an's suggestion to Sozan to become "single-eyed." When Dai-e desperately implores Engo to enlighten him on the truth of Ran-an's simile of "u" and "mu," Engo suggests that Dai-e forget about the whole thing ("It is no use to make a sketch of it"), for it is all the same ("They come in succession"); upon this, Dai-e is enlightened.

ANSWER

The answer and the quotes imply that the "two" (the "tree" and the "wisteria vine," "u" and "mu") are "one."

## 11. Subject, Object

The shout "katsu" cannot be translated into words. When the master shouts "katsu" at his pupil, he is transmitting his satori (the Japanese term for "enlightenment" or "realization") to the pupil in a direct, immediate way. In some cases, the "working" of "katsu" can be compared to an electrical shock used in the treatments of psychotics, aimed at a sudden shaking up of the patient's whole constitution (see Part Three, koan 140, p. 214). The novice may sometimes "katsu" his master, and novices may "katsu" each other. "Katsu" is the concrete form with which one's mind, as if in a sudden burst, is turned inside out.

The two head monks shouted at each other at the same moment. This situation is used by the monk to question Rinzai on the relation of "host" (subject) and "guest" (object). The theme of "host–guest" is dealt with in many of the koans of Master Rinzai (see Part Three, koan 18, p. 124; and also koan 19, p. 126). Generally speaking, we may distinguish four possible relations between "host" and "guest":

1. The "guest" in the "host"—to create the concept of object" from the standpoint of the subjective (or "self").
2. The "host" in the "guest"—to create the concept of "subject" from the standpoint of the objective or "world").
3. The "guest" in the "guest"—there is no subject. The world (including one's own existence) is absolutely objectified.
4. The "host" in the "host"—there is no objective world; the subject is in complete unity with itself.

In states 1 and 2 there is a distinction between the "self" and the "other," whereas in states 3 and 4 this distinction has been eliminated. State 4 may be said to be that of a child acting spontaneously in perfect accordance with the movement of his will. The same is true for state 3; but whereas state 4 is a state of freedom of "self," state 3 is the "enlightened" freedom of "no-self." The difference between these two states should not, however, be overemphasized. In the final account, both are the same in as far as the distinction between "subject" and "object" does not exist. Zen satori is often defined as a state of "non-distinction" between "subject" and "object." However, in the actual situation of Zen training, any such verbal definition carries the danger of being turned into some kind of "truth" which the practitioner tries to understand or to realize in an overly conscious way. When one thinks of a situation in terms of "non-distinction" between subject and object, it only proves that one's mind is taken in by the "subject–object" mode of reasoning.

Rinzai is not concerned so much with the situation of the

two head monks who simultaneously shouted at each other. His answer is directed at the monk who raised the "subject–object" problem in relation to the situation. His answer is best understood within the framework of common sense. There certainly is the one who shouted (subject) and the one shouted at (object). How could it be otherwise? In giving this answer, Rinzai implies that in order to be free from "subject–object" distinctions, there is no use in trying to become "just subject" or "just object." One should freely move between the two in accordance with the situation. When shouting, one is the subject; when shouted at, the object.

### ANSWER

The answer and the two quotes of the first section suggest acceptance of the natural order. Things are just what they are and it is only ridiculous to suggest that a "mountain is not a mountain." Things also stand in certain relation with each other. There is the "high" and the "low," the "green" and the "red," the "straight" and the "crooked." The two alternative answers are a more direct response to the problem of the koan. The pupil suggests that because there are master and pupil (or any two other related people), there is also naturally a subject–object relation between them. There is no use in denying the obvious.

## 12. *The Unrankable Being*

"The unrankable being" may be understood as "the undefinable being." In the realm of "u" ("being") things are rankable, whereas "mu" (nothing," "void") is unrankable. Rinzai may have referred to "mu" but it is better to take his remark at face value, as simply suggesting that the "self" cannot be defined. The "self" cannot be identified with the physical body, neither can it be separated from it. It has to be realized not through words but immediately ("See it! See it!"). In spite of Rinzai's warning, the monk still asks for a definition. In his reaction to the monk's stupidity, Rinzai suggests that whatever the "unrankable being" ("self") may be, in the case of the monk it is no more than "dry dung."

### ANSWER

The answer of "placing one's hand on one's forehead" is a response to Rinzai's "See it!" This answer misses the point. The attached quotes simply suggest the theme of "seeing."

The same is true for the first answer under "according to another school." The pupil's dramatization of "See it!" ("fall down in surprise") only proves that he has misunderstood Rinzai. What Rinzai meant to be "seen" is nothing to be surprised at. The pupil's refusal to "say it" is perfectly in place.

### 13. *A Flower in Bloom*

The concept "pure body of truth" (in Japanese, "hosshin") stands for the absolute nature of the Buddha-mind—the supreme wisdom embodying all perfections. The monk's first question concerns the "essence" of the "body of truth," whereas his second question refers to its "working" or its form of appearance in the enlightened one. Ummon answers both questions using symbolic terms which suggest the "beautiful."

ANSWER

The pupil is not taken in by the suggestion of "beautiful" or "holy," and responds to both of Ummon's phrases by contrasting the "beautiful" with the so-called "ugly." Of course, the pupil does not imply that he prefers the ugly to the beautiful, but that his Buddha-mind is not taken in by the distinction between "beautiful–ugly" and "holy–mundane." The quotes suggest the same attitude through the enumeration of "ugly" or commonplace things together with "beautiful" things. The last answer (imitating a lion's roar) is simply a response to "lion," but it may have its merit in diverting the attention from the lion's "golden fur" to the lion's natural "working."

### 14. *Will IT Be Destroyed?*

"IT" refers to the "pure body of truth" (see note to koan 13, Part Three, above). The monk seems to be suffering from the "philosophical disease." He distinguishes the world and the self (in their "becoming" aspect) from the "eternal truth" or the "permanent essence." Faced with such a question, Daizui understands that the "problem" is not the nature of the world or of the self, but the monk's way of seeking for "salvation." Thus, whatever his view on the matter may be, Daizui is concerned above all with the "destruction" of the monk's dualistic thinking.

The answer may be understood as a simple demonstration of Daizui's words. However, I believe it also suggests the enlightened "no-mind" response to a situation (see Part Two, koan 51, note on p. 235).

## 15. Where Will ONE Return To?

The monk has understood the "one in the many," but he does not understand the "many in the one." If we change the Taoist phrasing of the question into Buddhist terms, we may say that the monk realizes that all things are ultimately "mu" ("nothing," "void"), but he does not realize that "mu" is ultimately "u" ("existence," "the-many-things"). Jōshū directly answers the monk's question. By reminding himself (and the monk) of the very concrete fact of the "cotton dress weighing seven jin," Jōshū suggests that the "one" ("mu") returns to the "many" ("u"). When the pupil is taken in by "mu," it is the master's duty to remind him of "u." When the pupil is absorbed in "u," the master reminds him of "mu."

ANSWER

In an unoriginal, abstract way the pupil simply responds to Jōshū's phrases. The two quotes suggest that there is a relation between the "one" and the "many," whereas the popular saying implies the nature of this relation.

## 16. There Is No Such Thing as Holy

The lessons implied in this koan are: (1) that one should not be taken in by "holy"; (2) that it is futile to try and define the "self."

ANSWER

In the first answer to "There is no such thing as holy," the pupil hints at himself. This might simply suggest an affirmation of the phrase, but it may also mean that the (enlightened) self holds everything in perfect evenness.

The alternative answer ("covered with mud, working") implies that there is "holiness" even in the most commonplace situation. The same is suggested in the attached quote through the description of an everyday situation. In the remainder of the dialogue, the master tries to make the pupil answer what Daruma himself refused to answer (What is the "self"?). The pupil is wise enough to avoid the temptation of answering in terms of "mu" ("non-self"). He does not say he knows "nothing" (or "mu," which is a positive statement) but simply that he knows not. The quotes attached to "I do not know" may suggest that that which cannot be known is not of necessity non-existent.

17. *Words*

Jōshū suggests that the opposite of enlightenment is "choice" (reasoning in terms of affirmation and negation). However, using words does not necessarily imply that one is taken in by "choice." The element of "choice" enters only where words are used to speculate with. A non-speculative usage of words does not stand in contradiction to "understanding" ("enlightenment"). Yet it is not good to be conscious of one's "understanding." Such consciousness indicates that one is still taken in by "choice" (between enlightenment and non-enlightenment). This is why Jōshū says he is "not in the realm of understanding." The monk rightly suggests that if this were so, Jōshū would not be conscious of his "not being in the realm of understanding"; for if Jōshū is "enlightened," why should he make a problem out of it? Jōshū wisely enough says he does not know. Jōshū's "I do not know" is not only a refusal to argue, but also an answer to the monk's question. Namely, Jōshū's statement on "not being in the realm of understanding" might have been too speculative, but he is not taken in by his own words. The monk takes Jōshū's "I do not know" as merely a refusal to argue and presses Jōshū to explain himself. In his answer, Jōshū suggests that being asked "words" he answers "words"; that's all. The monk would do best to become less clever.

ANSWER

*As against, "Reach the way."*

By pointing at himself, the pupil suggests that "the way" is not anything exterior to the (enlightened) self.

*As against, "Not difficult."*

The answer suggests that the "simplicity" of the way lies in recognizing the world *as it is.*

*As against, "The only setback is choice."*

The answer ("What a pity! I want! . . .") presents a state of "choice," but this "choice" is not to be confused with the "choice" Jōshū referred to (i.e., the "choice" of speculative thinking). The quote ("I only love to read . . . .") simply repeats the theme of the answer.

In response to the master's "I am not in the realm of understanding" (i.e., I am enlightened), the pupil simply accepts the master's statement and thanks him for his teaching. This answer should be contrasted with the skeptical attitude of the monk to Jōshū's enlightenment.

"Words reach from edge to edge" may seem to stand in contrast to what Jōshū says concerning "choice" in words. Yet Setchō's quote does not suggest "words" in their speculative function. What the quote implies is that in the enlightened state of mind (that is, when one is not overly conscious of one's enlightenment), "words" are used in a natural way and are therefore perfectly all right. If the pupil attempts to "explain" this quote, he would only prove that he is taken in by the "choice" (speculation) of words. His response in "Shut up!" is not unlike Jōshū's "I do not know." For the last quote ("*ONE* has many varieties, but *TWO* has got none") and its answer, see Part Three, koan 15, note on p. 256.

## 18.  *The Four Ways of Master Rinzai*

"Man" stands for the subjective and "land" for the objective. These terms more or less correspond to "host" and "guest" in koan 11 of Part Three (see note on pp. 252–254). The four possible relations between "man" and "land" indicate four states of mind viewed from the standpoint of "subject–object" relations:

> 1. "Take away the man without taking the land"—to "take away" means to eliminate or to negate. This state refers to an attitude of mind in which the objective dominates the subjective.
> 2. "Take away the land without taking the man"—the emphasis is on the subjective; the objective world is negated.
> 3. "Take away both the land and the man"—the "emptiness" state (of meditation) from which both the subjective and the objective have been eliminated.

4. "Take away neither the land nor the man"—this is "the return to the common world" of Zen satori, in which both subject and object are recognized to be "just what they are."

ANSWER

The meaning of the answers should be clear from the above. Whereas the answers of the first school to the four states (using the hand as "land" and body as "man") simply consist of an abstract, symbolic demonstration, the answers of the second school express the four states in words. The quotes attached to the answers of both schools suggest, respectively, only "nature" ("object"), only "man" ("subject"); neither "nature" nor "man"; both "nature" and "man."

## 19. *The Three Sentences of Master Rinzai*

This koan is unclear unless we understand what the monk is asking for and what Rinzai gives in reply. When the monk asks for Rinzai's "three sentences" he is in search of the "truth" (or contents) of Rinzai's teaching. Rinzai avoids reference to the contents (or meaning) of his teaching, and refers instead to the "working" (or function) of the Zen master. To say it in simpler words, the monk asks Rinzai, "Will you teach me the truth?" To this Rinzai answers, "Don't ask questions. Have trust in me and follow me."

Rinzai's first sentence on the seal and ink suggests that even though you may not be able to *read* the script, the "working" through which brings it into being is clear. The master's role is to "seal" ("host" or "subject"), whereas the pupil's role is to be "sealed" ("guest" or "object"). In his second phrase Rinzai suggests that one would do best not to be taken in by the "ideal" aspect ("essence" or "truth") of things; it is enough to know their "working." The third sentence implies that although it may not be clear to the onlooker, as in the puppet show, there is the one who "pulls" (the master) and the one that is "pulled" (the pupil).

ANSWER

The answers of both schools suggest that the meaning of the "three sentences" is exactly the same.

## 20. Before and After

Chimon's answers are contrary to truth. The lotus before it appears above water is a leaf. After it has appeared it is a flower. Zen satori is in a way a "return" to the world of common sense; yet although the "enlightened mind" admits common sense, it is not taken in by it. In order to "return" to common sense, it is necessary that one first "leave" it. Chimon's paradoxical phrases suggest the negation of common sense distinctions. Such "turning of the world upside down" is a teaching device of the Zen master used to make the pupil realize that distinctions can be played around with freely. However, if the pupil gets attached to such games, he falls into the trap of denying the natural order of the world. In the final account, the enlightened person is supposed to know what every child knows—namely, that the lotus is a leaf under water and a flower above water.

ANSWER

In his nonsensical answers the pupil suggests that he can play the same game. If one wishes to read deeper into the answers, they may be interpreted as also meaning "it is all the same."

## 21. To Beat the Drum

The quote on "mon," "rin," and "shin" is taken from the scripture Hōzōron, written by the Chinese Buddhist philosopher Sōjō (384–414). "Mon" suggests "study." "Rin" suggests coming near to "shin" ("truth" or "enlightenment") through the cutting off of study. Quite naturally the monk is, above all, curious about the meaning of "shin" ("truth"). He tries to make Kasan define "truth," which Kasan refuses to do. In his question on "the-mind-as-it-is-being-Buddha" (sokushinsokubutsu) and "no-mind-no-Buddha" (hishinhibutsu), the monk attempts to make Kasan speculate on the difference between these two concepts (both suggesting "enlightened mind") in relation to "truth" (see Part Three, koan 103 and koan 104). In answering "To be able to beat the drum" to all of the monk's questions, Kasan implies that he refuses to fall into the trap of defining "truth" (or "enlightenment"). This answer may also suggest the "working" of things (in contrast to their "essence").

By imitating the sound of the drum, the pupil suggests that he is "able to beat the drum." The attached quote suggests Kasan's thoroughness.


## 22. No Great Masters?

In saying that "there are no more Zen masters in China," Obaku urges his pupils not to rely on others for enlightenment. By interpreting Ōbaku's remark as a reference to the condition of institutional Zen in China, the monk misses the point.

*As against, "Do you know that there are no more Zen masters in China?"*
By indicating his self-sufficiency, the pupil proves that he has understood the meaning of Ōbaku's saying. The quote suggests the power of one man.
*As against, "I did not say there is no Zen anymore, only that there are no great masters!"*
In his answer, the pupil may be taking the place of the monk. By "I was wrong," the "monk," as it were, admits that he has misunderstood Ōbaku's meaning. The attached quote suggests the theme of the power of one man.

In the answers "according to another school," the pupil naively responds to the phrases of the koan. However, in answering this way the pupil, like the monk, takes Ōbaku's words at their face value and thus misses their meaning.


## 23. Where Did Nansen Go after His Death?

By making Shū ask Chōsa where Nansen went after his death, Sanshō sets a metaphysical trap for Chōsa. Chōsa's answer of Master Sekitō meeting Master Enō may be a historical fact, yet it has nothing to do with the question on Nansen. However, in answering this way, Chōsa does exactly what Shū has done. Namely, he mentions a fact of the past which bears no relation whatsoever to the present situation, and is nothing of the sort he or Shū have to occupy themselves with.

Shū misses the point of Chōsa's response and presses him to answer the question on Nansen, at which point Chōsa sends him to the right place to ask such a question. Shū's remark on the pine and the stalagmite is not quite clear. He may have meant to suggest that Chōsa's Zen, although unshakably strong, is not delicate enough; or that Chōsa's Zen may be perfect but it is not clear enough (or detailed enough) for the hearer to understand. At this, Chōsa is silent; he also keeps silent when Shū thanks him and Sanshō praises him. Silence is, after all, the only wise answer to the "after death" kind of metaphysical trap.

ANSWER

*As against, "When Master Sekitō was a young priest he met Master Enō."*

The quote deals with personalities who have already died. By mentioning the monk who has gone to buy bean curd, the pupil implies that he does not make any special distinction between "death" and "life" beyond the common distinction of regarding those who have died as dead and those alive as alive. His own concern is naturally with the living.

*As against, "I didn't ask anything about Sekitō's young priesthood. I asked, 'Where did Nansen go after his death?'"*

This answer suggests exactly the same thing as the previous answer above.

*As against, "The master was still silent."*

The pupil's silence and his "Shut up" have the same meaning as Chōsa's silence. He implies that the "after death" question is nonsensical and that the questioner had better shut up. All of the quotes attached to this answer suggest the natural course of the world, which goes quite a way toward answering the question on where one goes after death.

*As against, "Go and ask Nansen!"*

In "I wonder where he's gone," the pupil responds "naively" to the demand to go and search for the deceased Nansen. The first and the third quotes suggest the usual course of nature. If one insists on attaching meaning to the second quote, one may perhaps interpret it as suggesting a parallelism between the "life–death" states and the "dream–awakening" states. The popular saying simply refers to "searching for [Nansen]."

OR

(According to another school)

*As against, "Where did Nansen go after his death?"*

The answer, "I'm going to buy some sandals" disregards the "after death" part of the question and responds only to "go." Through the commonplace example of buying sandals, the pupil also suggests that there is not much difference between "going to buy sandals" and "going after death." Both are quite natural provided we regard them as such. As to the master's urging to forget the sandals, the pupil wisely responds with "paper." The quotes are a simple response to "where," suggesting "searching for."

*As against, "When Master Sekitō was a young priest he met Master Enō."*

The answer is unclear. Perhaps it is a simple response to "young."

*As against, "Go and ask Nansen!"*

The pupil suggests that he is not concerned with the non-existent (the deceased Nansen), but with the immediate occurrence as it presents itself moment after moment.

## 24. *One, Two, Three*

Sozan's question, "How much will you give the constructor?" is still within the commonplace situation of evaluating a piece of work and paying for it. The monk, instead of being concerned with the matter of construction, pays respect to his master. In response, Sozan fools the monk, embarrassing him with the "one, two, three" mon question. Rasan's nonsensical response to Sozan's question indicates that he has understood Sozan's mind. In dealing with daily affairs, one is certainly faced with distinctions and evaluations. However, this does not mean that one has to speculate beyond the actual situation as it presents itself. One has to pay the due price, that's all.

Sozan appreciates Rasan's answer and praises him for it. Yet, by "It is a December lotus flower" (i.e., out of season), he suggests that Rasan's phrases are perhaps superb but he would rather have the due answer at the right moment and forget about the whole matter. Rasan responds to the "December lotus flower" with the "hair of the tortoise" (the tortoise of course has no hair). By this he indicates that the whole matter (including Sozan's praise) is indeed outdated and even somewhat superfluous.

ANSWER

*As against, "Which is the best thing to do—give the constructor three mon, or give him two mon, or just give him one mon?"*

The pupil takes the place of the constructor and expresses his thanks for the money. By this he indicates that in paying a generous sum, one receives due thanks.

*As against "An old Buddha is now radiating light which shines all the way to this place."*

In contrast to Sozan's exquisite praise of Rasan, the answer suggests the commonplace.

*As against (Rasan's), "If you give three mon, you will not have the monument built in your lifetime. If you give two mon, you will be both extending one hand. If you give one mon, you will both lose your eyebrows and beard."*

The three pine trees differ in location and form but they are, after all, the same (in being pine trees). This answer indicates that, be it pine trees or money, one should not be taken in by "one," "two," "three"; when it comes time to pay, one simply pays.

*As against, "A December lotus flower."*

As against the "rare" and the "beautiful" the answer suggests the easy and the commonplace. This may refer both to the monk's not answering Sozan's question and to Rasan's answering it. The quote on the "many" and "one" provides a clue to the solution of the "one," "two," "three" problem. Once you realize the relations between the one (or "mu") and the many (or "u"), you simply stop speculating when things ought to be done.

OR
(According to another school)

By "Daruma does not know how to count," the pupil suggests that there is no need to speculate when counting. It is easy to count to three, or to seven, or to a million, provided you know what you are counting for. Ones does not need "special knowledge" for that.

*As against, "The radiant light shines all the way to this place."*

The pupil simply recites the phrase. Rather than attach "meaning" to this kind of answer, it would perhaps be better to consider what else the pupil could have done.

## 25. An Iron Cow

"If there is movement, there is no progress"—that is, if taken in by "u" ("existence," the world of "becoming") one loses sight of "mu" (the immutable aspect of "nothing," or "void"). There is thus "no progress" toward "enlightenment."

"If there is standstill, there is stagnation"—that is, taken in by the static aspect of "mu," one cannot move freely in the world of things ("u"). The "iron cow" stands for "no-movement" (being of iron), and "no-standstill" (being a cow). The problem Fuketsu raises in connection with "iron-cow-like-Buddha-mind" concerns the consciousness of "enlightenment." Being conscious of one's enlightenment (or of one's "iron cow" state of mind), can one really be said to be enlightened?

The monk declares that he is "enlightened" ("I hold: the working of the iron cow") and tells Fuketsu not to be bothered about it. By saying this, however, the monk only proves that he is too conscious of himself. In the example of the frog, Fuketsu suggests the narrowness of the monk's understanding. Fuketsu yells at the monk, hits him, and urges him to repeat what has just been said. When the monk opens his mouth to speak, Fuketsu hits him again. In thus treating the monk, Fuketsu draws out from the monk the consciousness of his own consciousness, and makes him return to what he originally is.

Bokushu's remark is an explanation of Fuketsu's "working" on the monk—when things get complicated and tangled up, there is a need to "cut." Fuketsu's getting down from his seat and leaving might simply mean what it says, but it is not unreasonable to assume that by leaving, Fuketsu "cuts" (the argument) for his own peace of mind.

ANSWER

*As against, "Buddha-mind is like an iron cow."*

A "stone mill" does indeed "not move a bit" as an object in itself, but its "working" is its movement. Through "stone mill" the pupil provides another, perhaps better, metaphor for the "no-movement-no-standstill" quality of Buddha-mind. The quotes attached to this answer suggest that the natural "working" of the mind means responding to the occasion as it presents itself.

*As against, "If there is movement—there is no progress, if there is standstill—there is stagnation. This 'no-movement-no-standstill,' should one be mindful of it? Should one be unmindful of it?"*

In his answer, the pupil indicates that he understands what the monk did not understand. Namely, that if one says one is "not mindful" of something it only proves that one is. By slapping his master, the pupil "cuts" through the entanglement of "consciousness of consciousness."

## 26. Similar to a Dream

Rikkō is taken in by the Idealistic view that "the void is consciousness." (The quote expresses the standpoint of "idealistic monism" held by a group of the Yogācāra School philosophers). Nansen in his answer ridicules Idealism, suggesting that a flower is not a "dream" (the product of consciousness), but simply a flower.

### ANSWER

The pupil's first two answers suggest that according to Rikkō's view a "flower is not a flower" (it is like a "mortar" or a "rice cake," everything being equally "dream stuff"), whereas Nansen regards the flower as a flower ("it has bloomed beautifully"). The following two answers concerning the "positions" of Rikkō and Nansen metaphorically suggest that Rikkō's standpoint is esoteric and metaphysical whereas Nansen's standpoint is that of common sense (or at least that which allows for common sense).

"To listen, to see, to learn, to know is not all," suggests that besides the subject there is the object as it is in itself; we do not "create" the things around us, we only perceive them. "The mountain and rivers should not be seen through a mirror" implies a rejection of the Idealistic standpoint which sees in the external world no more than its reflection on the "mirror of consciousness." In repeating the quote and demonstrating its meaning, the pupil misses the point. The pupil is not supposed to see things from Rikkō's standpoint but from Nansen's.

The master's following quote ("The moon is sinking from the frosty sky . . .") suggests solipsism (the inevitable result of Idealistic philosophy). This time, the pupil's reaction is in accordance with Nansen's view. He responds to the "being alone" suggestion of the quote as simply "there's no one to talk to." The pupil's (and Nansen's) standpoint is "realistic," both in the philosophical sense and in its ordinary sense ("I'll piss and go to bed"). However, philosophically speaking, it is not "naive realism." The last phrase of the attached quote—"But now, nothing but wild birds can be seen flying about"—suggests that along with the "u" aspect of things ("When Kōsen, king of Etsu . . . all over the spring palace like flowers") there is the "mu" ("nothing," "void"). It should be noted that my interpretation of the poem is not in accordance with the author's remark, which regards the poem as a representation of Rikkō's and Nansen's position. I find it hard to see what the author's interpretation is based upon. The quote on the donkey and the well suggests that "subject" and "object" are in harmony, interacting in accordance with the situation.

OR

(According to another school)

At first reading, the pupil's response to the phrases of the koan seems to represent the standpoint of Idealism. However, the pupil's quote on one wandering around without realizing he is already in the "peach paradise" (i.e., the "perfect" state), and his response ("guess I'll go to bed") to the Idealistically-mooded poem ("The moon is sinking from the frosty sky . . .") imply a rejection of the speculative attitude of the Idealistic mind.

Given this clue, we may interpret the answers to the first two "as against" phrases of the koan as suggesting "harmony with the world," not in the Idealistic sense (of the "world as consciousness"), but in the common sense of being "at peace" with the world. The pupil's reaction to the third "as against" phrase (pretending to be asleep) is a simple response to "dream," whereas in his answer to "to listen, to see, to learn, to know is not all," the pupil suggests that he understands that although all of these are functions of the "subject," this does not mean that the "subject" is the whole world. There is the act of seeing and there is the object seen, each in its own right. It is no use denying that the "object" of our mind is "out there," independent of the perceiver; the denial would estrange us from our surroundings and from the people we live with.

## 27. "Not Affected," "Not Deluded"

The old man fell into the state of a fox because he had sought his "enlightenment" in detachment from the natural order ("not affected by causality"). The "not affected" viewpoint is that of the old Theravada tradition, in which nirvana is regarded as a state of total liberation from (or "extinction" of) the natural process of cause and effect. Hyakujō suggests that everything is of necessity "affected" by causality. In his view, "enlightenment" does not mean freedom from the causal order but its total acceptance. In resisting the natural order, we are "deluded by causality." Zen satori consists not in the rejection of the world but in admitting it to be what it is. In the realization of this truth, the old man is delivered from his foxhood.

There is nothing wrong with Hyakujō's answer as far as Zen "doctrine" is concerned. The only flaw in the story is the suggestion that a "word" (or a "doctrine") carries much weight. Arguing on the difference between "affected" and "deluded" is futile no matter whether you side with "non-affected" or "non-deluded." The moment you are taken in by such speculations you become foxy anyway. Both Hyakujō and Ōbaku seem to have understood this. That Ōbaku understands we learn from his slapping of Hyakujō. That Hyakujō understands we learn from his paradoxical saying on the "red-bearded barbarian." The difference between "non-affected" and "non-deluded" suggests the saying, is more or less the same as between "it is a fine day today" and "today is a fine day." This does not necessarily mean that there is no difference, only that we had better forget about the whole argument.

#### ANSWER
*As against, "Not affected by causality" and "not deluded by causality."*

The pupil's answer suggests "it is all the same." However, if we interpret this answer as implying that there is no difference between "non-affected" and "non-deluded" we perhaps go too far. It would be better to take it as a refusal to argue about the matter. In his answer on the "fox" question, the pupil may suggest that in any Buddhist temple there is at least one silly monk who would never miss the opportunity to argue "Buddhist doctrine."
*As against, "I only thought that the barbarian's beard was red, I never realized it was a red-bearded barbarian."*

If the quote on "sweet" and "bitter" was carefully chosen, it might imply a warning not to interpret Hyakujō's saying on the "red-bearded barbarian" as suggesting that "not affected" and "not deluded" are exactly the same. After all, it makes some difference whether one tastes "sweet" or "bitter."

The answers of the second school are identical with those of the first school. In the answers of the third school, the pupil simply demonstrates the phrases of the koan. In answering thus, the pupil seems to have missed the point of the second half of the koan. However, such a response may also imply that the pupil takes a naive (non-speculative) attitude to the story.

## 28. Where Thing Does Not Contradict Thing

The philosophy of the Chinese Kegon school of thought was introduced to Japan around the middle of the eighth century. Although the doctrine of Kegon was widely studied in Japan, the sect did not prosper as a living religion. The philosophy of Kegon deals with the relation of the "world as a whole" to particular phenomena. The central concept of this philosophy is that every particle, no matter how infinitesimal, reflects the whole phenomenal world. In the answers, the Kegon philosophy on the "realms of existence" is given a Zen interpretation.

ANSWER

(The answers of the two schools are reviewed together)
*As against, "The realm of truth."*

If we consider the "truth" of the world ("mu" or "kū"—"nothingness" or "void") in itself, we lose sight of "u" ("existence" or "the particular thing"). The view of "truth" as "kū" or "mu" is a Zen interpretation of the quote. In the doctrine of Kegon, "truth" means the "law" (or "order" of) the phenomenal world.

*As against, "The realm of things."*

The answer of the first school seems to equate this realm with the realm "where thing does not contradict thing." Therefore, the difference between these two realms is better expressed in the answer of the second school—"to see the hand as a hand." "The realm of things" is the realm of "u" viewed in itself.

*As against, "The realm where truth and things do not contradict each other."*

This is the realm where "truth" and "things" are viewed as harmoniously interrelated; but where "mu" ("truth") and "u" ("things") are still distinguished as concepts. This is the realm where one "knows" that the particular and the whole are the same, however this knowledge has not yet been realized in fact.

*As against, "The realm where thing does not contradict thing."*

Whereas in the "realm of things" there is only the realization of a particular thing for what it is ("to see the hand as a hand"), in this realm each and every thing is realized for what it is. "Mu" and "u" are not only *thought* of as one, but indeed *become* one (in the "enlightened" mind). Note that the answer of the second school to this realm is identical with the answer of the Takujū School to the koan on the sound of the one hand.

## 29. *What Will You Call It?*

This koan is intended to test whether or not the pupil is taken in by speculations concerning the essence of things. The problem exists, of course, even if we disregard the Buddhist doctrine of rebirth—am I the same now as when I was a child, or a year ago, or a moment ago?

ANSWER

By simply giving his name, the pupil implies that he is concerned neither with existence in the past or future, nor with "essence." When asked, "Who are you?" one should give one's name; but when asked, "Who are you really?" one had better keep one's mouth shut.

## 30.   *Stick!*

Shuzan suggests that, viewed as "mu" ("nothingness," "void"), a stick is not a stick, and viewed as "u," a stick is perhaps too much of a stick. But his question, "What will you call it?" is a trap. The realization of "mu" should not prevent one from calling things by their name. By breaking the stick and throwing it away, Sekken seems to imply that if Shuzan wants him to do away with the (word) "stick," he has to get rid of the stick. Shuzan's reaction ("Blind!") is unclear. It seems to me that Sekken answered the challenge in a perfect way and set a trap for Shuzan of his own. But as suggested in the answers, Shuzan seems to have expected the demonstration of the correct "usage" of the stick (as a proof of having transcended the problem of whether the stick is a "stick" or a "non-stick"). Therefore, Shuzan might have interpreted Sekken's act as implying the elimination of the stick (together with the word "stick"). Such an interpretation would suggest that in his insistence on "mu," Sekken is "blind" to "u" (of simply using the stick as a stick is to be used).

ANSWER

In the first school, the correct answer to the problem of the stick is "putting it away in the corner of the shelf" (where the stick of the Zen master is usually put). The same is implied in the second school by "stick it under the bathtub and burn it up." The rest of the discourse is a clarification of the aspect of "mu" and "u" concerning names of things. The last answer of the first school (turning a somersault) is somewhat artificial.

## 31. *The Emperor and the Bowl*

This koan may imply criticism of the story of Enō and his miraculous bowl. In lifting the bowl, the emperor does not act out of vanity. Through this act the emperor (and the composer of this koan) seem to suggest their ironical attitude to the supernatural.

### ANSWER

The answers and the quotes are best understood from the position of Minister Ōzui. In the koan, Ōzui keeps silent. Whatever Ōzui's real attitude to Buddhism and its miracle-stories may be, as the emperor's minister he is supposed to serve his emperor and praise him. Those who feel inclined to interpret the minister's praise of the emperor as irony had better not serve under an emperor.

## 32. *How Is Your Health?*

According to Buddhist legendary folklore, Nichimenbutsu is the Buddha of the longest life term, whereas Getsumenbutsu is the Buddha of the shortest life term. However, it would be better not to attach too much meaning to the mentioning of these two Buddhas. Baso's answer suggests the transient nature of human life; or the mentioning of these two Buddhas may simply be a traditional prayer of the sick.

### ANSWER

The answer of the first school implies that life is short-lived and nobody, not even Buddhas, can predict when one's term of life will be over. The master's quote suggests that one should not be carried away by bereavement when faced with the natural phenomenon of death. In the second school, the pupil's answer to the same quote simply suggests the pupil's position should his master die. The third answer ("Oh, the pain! The pain!") does not appear in the Japanese edition, but it is used with certain masters. This simple expression of the actual situation of a sick person in agony seems to me the best response to the koan. The answer was not told to me by any of the people mentioned in connection with the translation and notation of this book.

## 33. The Gate!

Suigan's "See if my eyebrows are still here" is based upon the popular saying that if one preaches too much Buddhism one's eyebrows will fall off. Hofuku, Chōkei, and Ummon were fellow pupils of Suigan. We may thus assume that this exchange of words did indeed take place. The meaning of these three masters' sayings is somewhat unclear. However, if we insist on interpreting them we may perhaps read them as:

HOFUKU: "Indeed, I am afraid you have talked too much."
CHŌKEI: "You are worried too much."
UMMON: [Don't come with these tricks] "Shut up!"

### ANSWER

In both schools the pupil's answer to Chōkei's phrase and the accompanying quotes are a simple response to "growing." The answer to Hofuku's saying is no more than its repetition. The pupil's answer (second school) concerning "Suigan's feeling" suggests that Suigan is sure there is nothing wrong with him (for if he felt he had talked too much he would not have apologized for it). However, this answer may also be interpreted as suggesting Suigan's fear that in talking too much he has spoiled things.

The most important part is the answer to Ummon's "The gate!" In both schools, the pupil's quotes to Ummon's saying suggest that Ummon's way of rebuking Suigan is the perfect response to the situation. The answers of roaring "GAAATE!" and slapping the master (first school), as well as the longer phrase on "gate" (second school), all suggest: "From here on, not a single step further!" These "gate" answers, in implying that there is a natural limit to the use of words, have a similar effect to the "Mu——" answer of the koan on "mu" (see notes to the koan on "mu," Inzan School, pp. 223–224).

## 34. Unforgivable

Whether the historical Daruma (Bodhidharma—founder of Zen) should be "forgiven" or not is not the problem. What is put into question here is Zen. In fact, there is not much difference between "knowing" and "understanding." Both terms refer to thought and speech based upon abstract concepts. In as far as we cannot do without concepts, we should be "forgiven." But from the Zen point of view, our dependence upon them is "unforgivable."

ANSWER

The last quote suggests that "knowledge" and "understanding" are actually the same (just like a "good" courtier and a "faithful" one). The koan may thus be interpreted as "that we know is forgivable, that we know is unforgivable." In his "acceptance" of "knowledge" ("that's okay") the pupil implies that we cannot do without it. In his rejection of "knowledge" ("that's bad") he implies that there is nothing we can do with it. The quote on "cleverness" and "foolishness" indicates the Zen approach to the problem of "knowledge." It implies that it may be easy to be "clever" (to know), but it is difficult to be "foolish" (to not know).

## 35. *How Do You Say It?*

Kinzan lays a trap for Tokusan. He suggests that Tokusan's masters said "it" (their Zen) in a certain way, and he asks Tokusan to show him his own way of saying "it." Tokusan is not taken in. He refuses to define his Zen, and instead requires Kinzan to say "it." Whatever Kinzan may have intended to say, he deserves to be hit, for the problem here is not Zen but the "saying" of Zen. Gantō understands Tokusan's teaching but Kinzan, who is taken in by the insult of having been beaten, fails to understand.

ANSWER

The master lays the same trap of "say Zen" for the pupil. The pupil's answer suggests that by now he is only too familiar with this kind of trap-question.

## 36. *Discuss Buddhist Law*

In his story, Nansen implies that discussing Buddhist law is absolutely superfluous. It is not clear why Jōshū suggests that Nansen himself deserves a beating. He may have meant that the argument against arguments is itself a superfluous argument. Another possible interpretation of Jōshū's saying may be: "If it is so easy to solve all problems by beating, why don't we beat you too?"

The answers of both schools suggest the moral of Nansen's story. A discussion on Buddhist doctrine (or any other futile discussion) is likened to wandering thoughts at night (first school) and to irritating pain (second school), whereas the drastic "cutting off" of the discussion is likened to deep sleep and to relief from pain. The first quote may imply that, after all, Nansen too is guilty of futile discussion. The second quote suggests a state of evenness of mind in which all arguments pro and con have been eliminated.

## 37. *Simultaneous Doubt and Enlightenment*

In his statement on "simultaneous doubt and enlightenment," Nan-in suggests that it is not enough to know the interrelation between the pupil's question and the master's answer at the moment of enlightenment "as a thing in itself" (i.e., to know it in a theoretical way). By "not holding onto the mold" he implies that the correct "working" of "simultaneous doubt and enlightenment" should not be an overly conscious process. The monk who keeps on speculating about "simultaneous doubt and enlightenment" proves that he is too conscious of the matter, upon which Nan-in hits him. Still taken in by his problem, the monk searches for an answer at Ummon's place. A monk at Ummon's place understands and suggests that Nan-in's hitting *is* the "working" of "simultaneous doubt and enlightenment" ("Nan-in broke his stick"); at this the effect of Nan-in's stick is actualized and the monk is enlightened. In "At that time I was walking by the light of a lamp" the monk suggests that, before his realization, he was in need of an external aid to "see," whereas now he is free to see by himself.

In the first two answers, the pupil suggests that there should not be too much reliance on the master. As against "the application of simultaneous doubt and enlightenment" the pupil suggests that things take their natural course, and that one should not be too conscious of what one is doing.

## 38. *Don't You Believe Me Now?*

This koan is best understood if we do not overburden it with too many suggestions. In Zen, a witty mind is highly appreciated, provided the wit is not of a too speculative kind. If you want to convince people that a dog is a cat, just call "Hey, cat" and the "cat" will respond to the call.

The answers simply praise Chinsō's cleverness.

## 39. I Never Said a Word . . .

In "I never said a word about Zen," Kassan implies that he has never "preached" Zen. In reproving Kassan for his statement, the monk may have meant to suggest that the argument "I never argue" is also an argument. It is also possible to understand the monk's reproof of Kassan as implying that if Kassan "had never said a word" he has done nothing to teach the people. Of course, Kassan did not mean he had never taught Zen, only that he had never "spoken" Zen. In any case, by throwing Kassan off his seat, the monk implies that Kassan is not fit to be a teacher of the people. Kassan, who feels he does not deserve such a terrible verdict, challenges the monk to a duel. The monk, who has neither sufficient reason to kill Kassan nor enough wit to overcome the dilemma of having to die if he does not kill Kassan, is forced to sneak away.

### ANSWER
In his answer, the pupil implies that no matter whether the monk is right in reproving Kassan or not, he would have done better had he not been taken in by Kassan's "pit-show."

## 40. Where in the World Are They?

Toku-un, in his philosophical saying, suggests that there are no distinctions of time and place in the "true" (enlightened) mind. In view of Toku-un's "philosophy," there is really no problem in Engo's question ("Where in the world are Toku-un and Zenzai?"). If all existence is included in "a simple thought," Toku-un and Zenzai could meet anywhere or nowhere and still be together. However, Engo's question is a trap. The pupil is not supposed to force "Buddhist philosophy" upon reality. In Zen, "deliverance" from the limitations of "time–space" does not mean to transcend time and space, but to eliminate "time–space" as a conceptual, abstract problem.

In his answer, the pupil suggests that in the common sphere of reality (what other sphere is there?) people simply *do* meet each other. Isn't he, in fact, meeting his master right now?

## 41.   *A Bottle Is a Bottle*

Hyakujō's question is a trap. A bottle, of course, can only be called "bottle." The head monk is well aware of this, but only in theory. In his answer ("You cannot call it a wooden log") he suggests that "a bottle is a bottle," but his answer is still speculative. In making a statement on the obvious, the head monk takes an attitude that is too self-conscious. Isan, by simply kicking the bottle over, suggests "action" (as against "words"). It is not enough to "speak" common sense. Only through the natural and immediate response to the situation does ("enlightened") common sense reveal itself.

The quote suggests the natural movement of things. The head monk's answer does not fit the mood of the quote, whereas Isan's action does.

## 42.   *A Silver Bowl Filled with Snow*

Daiba (Āryadeva) was the disciple of the philosopher Nāgārjuna (end of the second century A.D.), the originator of the Sunyata ("void") school of Buddhist thought. The term "Daiba sect" refers to one of the branches of the Sunyata School (a more common name of Chinese origin for this sect is "Sanron sect"). Zen, in its doctrinal aspect, is greatly influenced by Nāgārjuna's philosophy, whose essence is the rejection of the affirmative–negative mode of reasoning and the identification of samsara with nirvana (or "the world as it is" with "enlightenment"). The problem of this koan, however, is not the doctrine of the Daiba sect in itself but the monk's state of mind. The monk asks Haryō to express the "teaching" in words. In his answer, Haryō suggests that however "true" a doctrine may be, if it is viewed only in its verbal sphere it is of no use. Words ("snow"), even if put in the most perfect form ("silver bowl"), are bound to melt away.

In the answers of both schools, the pupil expresses his refusal to be taken in by doctrines (or mere forms). The quote suggests that the moment you open your mouth (to argue "truth") you betray yourself.

## 43. *Every Coral Branch Supports the Moon*

The monk's question on the "sharpest of all swords" suggests that he is searching for the one supreme "truth" or "enlightenment" that rules over all things. Haryō's saying implies that all things are one, and the one is all things. There is thus no need for any specific "truth."

### ANSWER
By pretending to break the "sword" and throw it away (first school), the pupil implies that he is not taken in by any specific "truth." The pupil's answer in the second school implies that all ways are "the way" provided one does the right thing at the right moment. The quotes attached to this answer complete it, suggesting harmony with the natural state of things.

## 44. *An Open-eyed Man Falls into the Well*

The monk asking for "the Way" is one-track minded. He assumes that there is a method of clearly distinguishing between the "right" way and the "wrong" way in matters of enlightenment. Haryō's answer implies that by being conscious ("open-eyed") to "the way," one misses it ("falling into the well").

### ANSWER
In his answer the pupil takes the monk's place and suggests his understanding of Haryō's warning.

## 45. *In Relation to One*

Ummon's "in relation to one" has the connotation of "monism," but such an outspoken philosophical statement would not be Zen-like. Zen scholars in Japan found it difficult to interpret Ummon's phrase, yet the answer makes its meaning quite clear.

In his answer the pupil suggests that "in relation to one" means to respond to the situation ("one by one") as it presents itself.

## 46. *In Opposition to One*

Buddha's real teaching is "in relation to one" (see Part Three, koan 45). Therefore, in "opposition to one" suggests "not Buddha's real teaching" or simply "not real" (or non-existent). What is "not right before the eyes" is in the abstract or the transcendental. But be it a "happening" or a "thing," it is all right here in front of us. Those who seek for the "truth" or "enlightenment" in the world beyond will not find it.

Instead of explaining the "meaning" of "in opposition to one" (or "not right before the eyes") the pupil, through the two quotes, suggests the human world and the world of nature (as it is "right before the eyes") with its loves and hates, flower blossoms, and chirping of birds. In his answer to "What is the transcendental?" ("A thing or a happening not right before the eyes"), the pupil simply repeats the question. Responding thus, he in a way disarms his master.

## 47. *Are You Alive?*

This koan deals with the relation between pupil and master (same theme as koan 37, see note on p. 274). If we change the metaphorical phrasing into everyday language we would get something like the following dialogue:

MONK: "I am looking for enlightenment. Will you teach me?"

MASTER: "Do you have enough energy (or will) of your own?"

MONK: "If I did not, I would not come here."

Kyōshō seems to be satisfied with the monk's attitude.

The answer suggests the reciprocal "working" of the pupil (the chick's "chirp") and the master (the hen's "peck").

## 48. The One-Piece Tower

The emperor seems to confuse Zen with the lectures he has been given by his Zen master. Regarding Zen as "teaching," he is concerned about his progress should his master die. Etchū says that when he dies the emperor should build a "one-piece tower." Every tower is, in fact, a combination of many "pieces." Taken in by the illusion that his enlightenment depends upon his Zen master, the emperor conceives himself as formed from several "pieces" stuck together. What Etchū suggests in his answer is that if the emperor understands that enlightenment is *self*-realization, he will become a "one-piece tower." Whether Etchū is alive or dead is nothing for the emperor to be concerned with. By "tower," the emperor seems to have understood a memorial tower for Etchū. Asking for the form of the "tower," he is actually asking for the form of his ("enlightened") self. In his silence, Etchū suggests that the emperor should restore his mind to where it originally is. The emperor, however, does not understand that the "tower" Etchū wants him to build is, besides being "formless," not Etchū's but solely his own.

ANSWER

*As against, "To ask the master for the form of the tower."*

The pupil's answer suggests that the form of the tower is that of oneself.

*As against, "Etchū remained silent."*

Through the quote the pupil suggests that Etchū's silence refers to the natural state of things. Everything is in its perfect state, not one thing trespasses on the other.

*As against, "South of Shō, north of Tan."*

There seem to be no such places, but even if there were, one is not supposed to be concerned with that. Wherever one happens to be is one's perfect place. Thus through "here is the shelf, here is the door," the pupil points to "right here, now!" Setchō's comment to the above quote may perhaps suggest "You have to do it yourself."

*As against, "Within it overflows with gold."*

The pupil suggests that he is not concerned with any marvelous sphere ("overflowing with gold") elsewhere, but only with where he happens to be and what he happens to see right in front of him. Setchō's comment to the quote may perhaps suggest "confusion" or "over-exaggeration."

As against, "*Under a shadeless tree rests a ferryboat.*"

As against the fiction of the "shadeless tree," the pupil by sitting down suggests that his own "working" is the commonplace action of the real world. Setchō's comment on the quote may perhaps suggest "no movement."

As against, "*There is an emerald palace that holds no Buddhist priest of fame.*"

This quote and the pupil's answer suggest that it is up to everyone to build his own "tower." The emperor (in his palace) is the emperor, whereas the Buddhist priest is the Buddhist priest. To combine the two would make a "double-piece tower." The emperor should know his own mind. Setchō rightly comments that by this statement Tangen "brought it right in front of the [emperor's] eyes."


## 49. No Meaning

Suibi and Rinzai rightly hit Ryūge for his question on the "meaning of Zen." Surprisingly enough Ryūge is neither dumbfounded nor "enlightened" by the "meaning" of Zen (as is the case in most koans of the same pattern), but categorically asserts that there *is* no meaning to Zen. Through Ryūge, Zen turns itself into an object of irony.

### ANSWER

The pupil's suggestion (in the answer and in the attached quote) that throughout his Zen study he hasn't "gained" a bit is quite all right as far as Zen is concerned. Through such irony, Zen compliments itself.


## 50. It Is Somewhat a Pity

The meaning of this koan is not quite clear. In a somewhat forced interpretation it may be said that Hofuku, by mentioning the proper name of the mountain, is taken in by "u" ("existence" or "the world of things"). In "It is all right but it is somewhat a pity," Chōkei may be expressing his sorrow for Hofuku's state of mind, or (as Setchō suggests in his first comment) his sorrow for having taken Hofuku along with him. Setchō's second comment is unclear, whereas Kyōshō's comment suggests that if it were not for Chōkei, the situation would have been much worse.

*As against, "That is the peak of Mt. Myōhō."*

The pupil represents Hofuku's state of mind and suggests that Hofuku is exaggerating in his response to the landscape.

*As against, "It is all right, but it is somewhat a pity."*

In his answer, the pupil takes the position of Chōkei and suggests that it is no use dwelling upon a situation when it is time to move on. The attached quote on the parting of the soldier from his beloved general may refer to Hofuku's state of mind regarding the landscape.

## 51. A Few Here, a Few There

Mujaku seems to think that the state of the "teaching of Buddha" depends upon the number of monks and their degree of discipline (as to the monastic law). Being too conscious of the difference between "monk" and "layman," he is taken in by distinctions (between "south" and "north," "many" and "few"). Monju's answer ("The people and saints live together. Dragons and snakes mingle"), rather than indicating the state of Buddhism in the "south," suggests his own state of mind. Thus, whereas the Zen master Mujaku, in attaching great importance to the monastic order, takes a Hinayanic view of Buddhism, Monju represents the viewpoint of Zen. In his answer ("a few here, a few there") to the question on the number of monks, Monju suggests "it is all the same."

ANSWER

The quote given as an answer and the following attached quotes all suggest that no matter how hard you try to distinguish between one thing and another, ultimately all things are interrelated. Be it "front" or "back," "head" or "tail," you cannot consider the one without the other. Mujaku is looking for Buddhism in a particular place and with a particular group of people, but what is the use of hiding your "head" while exposing your "rear"? Head and bottom, monk and layman, each is where it is supposed to be. In the horse market there are only horses.

## 52. Where Is the Mind?

Similar to Part Two, koan 133. With the past no more, the future not yet, and the present no more than the borderline between past and future, how can anything "be"? The pupil is not supposed to provide an answer to this "philosophical trap" (who can?), but to disregard it. If we deny "existence" because we cannot rationally define it in terms of "time," what are we going to do with ourselves and the world around us?

ANSWER

In the first school, the answer and the quote suggest that things are perfectly all right where they are, the way they are. In the second school, by slapping his master and refusing to comment on "no existence," the pupil simply rejects the problem of "existence" as a trap. In the third school, as in the first school, the pupil points to "the world as it is." In reference to "Where is the mind?" the answers of the first and third schools suggest that the "mind" is right in the time–place situation one is in (in reference to the "mind-of-the-moment," see Part Two, koan 51, note on p. 235). The answer of the second school suggests that we had better not speculate about this matter.

## 53.  A Speck of Dust

This koan is hard to understand. A possible, although somewhat forced, interpretation might regard Fuketsu's saying as dealing with "life" ("being") and "death" ("nothing"). This interpretation is also suggested in Setchō's comment. Whether a nation prospers or perishes certainly makes a great difference. In the same way, it is no less important for each individual whether he exists or not. Yet ultimately it does not really matter; no more than whether a speck of dust is raised ("u") or not ("mu"). Fuketsu may be suggesting that one should hold to both attitudes equally.

ANSWER

The poem on the two territories whose boundaries meet at the river, may suggest the relation between "u" and "mu."

## 54.  Gya!

## 55.  Nyan

In the older sources, these are combined into one koan. Here they are brought forth as two separate koans, apparently because each part was considered to deserve a separate answer. When Nansen holds up the cat, ready to cut it into two, he aims at driving the monks to their wits' end. Yet the monks, who are too conscious of the *master*, are taken in by speculation on the "meaning" of the situation and miss the point. What was it that Jōshū realized and the monks did not? Jōshū knew the *cat*. By putting his sandals on his head, Jōshū suggests turning things upside down. In his answer, the "human" turns into a "cat," the cat escapes Nansen, and the problem is solved. We may assume that had Jōshū been present, he would have snatched the cat away from Nansen. As for Nansen, no matter how important it is that monks be enlightened, he seems to be overdoing his Zen if he has to bother cats with it.

ANSWER

In speculating over the difference between life and death, philosophers are in danger of missing the point. The pupil's answers simply suggest the difference between the cat dying and the cat living.

## 56. *Come and Eat Your Rice*

There is nothing wrong with Kingyū feeding his pupils rice. It seems, however, that he is somewhat overly enthusiastic in trying to feed them his teaching.

ANSWER

In the first answer ("I'm full"), the pupil implies that he is in no need of Kingyū's teaching. The second answer, as against Setchō's comment ("The rice pot's empty"), suggests that Kingyū has nothing to feed his pupils with, and those who are tempted to respond to his noisy summons will return with an empty stomach. As against Chōkei's saying, the pupil recites a prayer which is usually said *after* meals, thus suggesting, as in the first answer, that he is already "full."

## 57. *Playing Ball on Rapid Water*

The Buddhist doctrine on the "person" views the psycho-physical organism as a complex interactive system of six senses—the five physical senses and the "mind" (or "thought") sense. The point of such an analysis is to do away with the concept of "self" (as a continuous "substance" above and beyond the incessant stream of personal events). Jōshū's answer implies that just as one cannot "play ball on rapid water" (there being no solid ground), there is no substratum ("self") uniting the flow of the personal events. Tōsu says the same thing in a direct way.

### ANSWER

In imitating a baby, the pupil does nothing that can be interpreted as a refutation of the traditional "no-self" Buddhist doctrine. Yet his naive response to "baby" suggests the immediate, non-speculative Zen approach to reality.

## 58. Playing with Mud

In "What should one do to shoot the deer among deer?" the monk questions Yakusan as to his insight into the enlightenment of his pupils. By "Watch out for my arrow," Yakusan simply suggests "watch me" or "watch my working." However, in letting himself fall, the monk implies that it is *he* who is "the deer among deer." Being too self-satisfied ("he plays with mud") the monk has overplayed his game ("he knows no limits").

Setchō's comment implies that there was nothing wrong with the monk's first question (provided it was simply intended to ask for Yakusan's power of insight), yet with his second pose he doomed himself as a "useless corpse."

### ANSWER

In his first answer (to "watch out for my arrow"), the pupil takes the position of the master. By "letting himself fall," he seems to be responding naively to the phrase, whereas in his last answer ("instead of the monk") he seems to assert himeslf by "shooting" his master.

## 59. The Sturdy Body of Truth

By "the sturdy body of truth" the monk asks for the permanent "essence" of things. In Buddhist philosophy, the "truth" or "essence" of existence is identified with "mu" ("nothingness"), or "kū" ("void"). The Sunyata ("void") school of Buddhist thought identifies "kū" or "mu" (the "essenceless essence" of things) with "u" ("existence" or "the world as it is"). In Zen this abstract philosophical principle is made actual and concrete in the "here–now" moment of satori (see Part Two, koans 37–39, notes on p. 234). Through the description of natural scenery, Tairyū suggests that "truth" is right where the physical body is.

ANSWER

In the first answer the pupil identifies his (enlightened) self with mountain flowers and a brook. He thus implies that he is making no distinctions between the material world and its "truth." The rest of the dialogue is centered around "rot and decay." If the "essence" (or "truth") of the world is the same as its "physical body," it is bound to rot and decay along with the myriad of things. The pupil's answers suggest that he is not overly concerned with the transient nature of existence. When things pass away, they are simply gone. What is the use of clinging to one state of nature ("life") while refusing to admit another ("death")?

## 60. Put Together

The "putting together" of a famous master with a pole suggests that every and all things are interrelated. It is no use regarding one thing as important and labeling the other as valueless. Ummon's saying on clouds and rain expresses the idea that all things become equally interrelated by turning the common sense "cause–effect" relations upside down. For the same theme see Part Two, koans 57 and 58 (notes on p. 236).

ANSWER

The answer and the first quote suggest the interrelation of all things in everyday life. In the second quote on the three schools of Taoism, Confucianism, and Buddhism, the same concept is applied to the "realm of ideas."

## 61. "Say Nothing" and Nothing Said

Monju only *says* one should be silent. Yuima *is* silent.

## 62.  Which Is Your Self?

The koan suggests the theme of "subject" (the "internal") and "object" (the "external"). In taking medicine we certainly do use an external object to cure ourselves. However, should we regard "the world" as the medicine for "existential disease, we miss the point of being alive.

ANSWER

The answer "TURRNIP" to the question "Which is your self?" may be regarded (as the author implies in his comment) as the rejection of an unanswerable question through a nonsensical statement. At the same time, however, it may be an extremely concrete form of suggesting "non-distinction" between "self" and "other" (or "self" and "the whole earth"). The quotes express the same theme through the mood of harmony between man and nature.

## 63.  Blind, Deaf, Dumb

Gensha's saying on the blind, deaf, and mute may be a suggestion that in grasping the "essence" of things, "kū" ("void") or "mu" ("nothingness"), there is no real need of the senses. However, Ummon's treatment of Gensha's saying suggests that we would do best to disregard the problem (of the "non-sensual" realm). As we actually *do* see, hear, and speak, why should we be concerned with the unseen, unheard, and unspoken in an overly conscious way?

ANSWER

In his answers, the pupil combines Gensha's words and Ummon's common sense Zen view into one phrase. The impact of this combination results in making Ummon's view the more acceptable. However, this does not necessarily mean that from the Zen point of view the combination of the two views entails contradiction. The attached quotes support Ummon's view through the description of the natural state of things in the world of the senses (colors, sounds, voices).

## 64.  Sound

The koan need not be commented upon. It should be noted however that through the artificial imitation of Kyōgen's "enlightenment-situation" the answer misses the point (see Part Two, koan 62, note on p. 236).

## 65.  *What Do You Understand by This?*

The simile of the cart is employed in some of the oldest Buddhist texts to illustrate the idea that things are without substance. True, if you take away all the parts of a cart, there is no cart any more; if you eliminate, one by one, all the physical and mental elements, there is no "person." But aren't there carts and people right here around us?

ANSWER

The pupil's answer suggests a non-speculative attitude. A cart is a cart; isn't he pushing one up the slope?

## 66.  *Not Keeping Silent, Not Using Words*

"Not using words" does not necessarily mean "keeping silent." All it means is not using words *wrongly* (see also Part Two, koan 73, note on p. 237).

ANSWER

The man on the road "understands the way" (i.e., he is enlightened), he simply does not know the way to where he is going. In explaining the way to him there is of course no misuse of words.

## 67.  *Taking a Bath*

Same theme as Part Three, koan 64, on Kyōgen's enlightenment upon hearing a piece of brick hit the bamboo. This koan has its merit in suggesting that the "taking a bath" situation is as good for the attainment of enlightenment, as any other situation. The answer, like the answer to koan 64, is superfluous for the same reason (see note 64, pp. 286–287).

## 68.  *Without Cold, Without Heat*

This koan repeats the theme of Part Two, koan 51 (see note on p. 235).

## 69. *What Do You Have in Mind?*

In Zen, the circle is sometimes used to symbolize "mu," but it is best to regard Nansen's drawing of a circle as no more than a practical joke. Kisū and Mayoku seem to be taken in by the circle's "meaning" and interpret it as a place to sit in or as an object of worship.

### ANSWER

The pupil's answer suggests a more naive attitude to the circle. It may be assumed that this answer would have satisfied Nansen.

## 70. *Don't Fancy*

No comment necessary.

## 71. *Buddha's Master*

The theme of non-distinction between "holy" and "mundane." It is to be expected that the "non-enlightened" pupil would tend to regard the Buddhas as realities of a "higher" sphere. By suggesting that the Buddhas are slaves of the common man, Hōen intends to shock the pupil into an evenness of mind.

## 72. *Swallow a River?!*

Hōkoji is looking for that which "transcends existence." It is, of course, impossible to satisfactorily answer this kind of search. Instead, Baso poses an impossible demand to Hōkoji ("swallow the waters of the river"). Hōkoji's poem suggests his realization that beyond existence there is "nothing."

### ANSWER

The answer plays on the theme of "swallow." By simply "swallowing" his tea, the pupil stresses the natural as against the metaphysical.

## 73. *Thought of the Moment*

This phrase, given an abstract philosophical interpretation, may be viewed as an expression of the "monistic" thought of the Kegon School; it is not Zen-like to put the idea of the "self-holding-the-infinite-dimensions-of-the-time-space-within-itself" into words. The quote is therefore responded to through a Zen attitude of mind.

ANSWER

As against the first part of the quote the pupil suggests "unity," not with the "boundless world" as a whole, but with each situation as it presents itself in the natural course of events. As against the second part of the quote, the pupil suggests that "the-thought-of-the-moment-which-holds-the-happenings-of-past-and-present" is not anything beyond the commonplace; it is the human thought of hate, desire, love, or pain wherever and whenever it occurs. The two popular sayings at the end suggest that the "infinite dimensions" of the "thought of the moment" are its immediacy and thoroughness.

## 74. *Where Is My Rhino?*

The attendant cannot answer Enkan's paradoxical saying. The later masters—Tōsu, Sekisō, Shifuku, Hofuku—attempt to answer instead. Setchō comments on their answers. According to my translation, it is a fan with a drawing of a rhino on it. The Chinese phrase describing the fan can also be understood as referring to a fan made from a rhino's horn. However, this would not change the meaning of Enkan's saying. What Enkan is asking for is the "substance" of the fan. Namely, as the phenomenal fan "is broken," he wants the "fanness" of it—its "immutable essence."

Tōsu's saying implies that all there is are the things as they appear and change in the phenomenal world. Thus Enkan can get no more than the "broken" rhino. To this Setchō suggests that things are all right the way they are even though "imperfect" (i.e., changing, substanceless). It is no use distinguishing between a phenomenon and its essence.

Sekisō's saying implies that once the "essence" is endowed with form (in "giving" it to Enkan), it cannot be said to be the "essence" anymore. Setchō comments ("But the rhino is still there") that Sekisō is too concerned with the "perfection" of the rhino: perfect or not, a rhino is there.

In writing the word (character) "rhino," Shifuku suggests that what is unchangeable in the rhino is no more than the word (or concept) "rhino." Setchō's comment ("Why didn't you bring it out before?") may imply that even the word (or concept) is nothing substantial (i.e., beyond time–space limitations), for it comes into being only through the occasion of its employment.

Hofuku suggests that the problem lies in Enkan's searching for "essence." Enkan appears to be no more than an old man in his dotage. In his last saying, Setchō ironically concludes the argument expressing "sorrow" that "all efforts [to find the 'essence'] are in vain."

ANSWER

As against, *"Give me back my rhino."*

The pupil's answer implies that the "essence" Enkan is looking for is gone with the fan.

As against, *"I want imperfect head and horn."*

If all there is is only the "imperfect" aspect of things, then the "essence" of things is their appearance. By the example of a commonplace object ("a piece of silk for sixty-five cents") the pupil suggests that one thing is as good as the other.

As against, *"Why didn't you bring it out before?"*

The pupil suggests that nothing *is* before it appears. By their very nature, things are there when they are, and are not there when they are not.

As against, *"All efforts are in vain."*

Setchō's saying is best taken as ironical. The pupil's response ("weeping") may be said to be largely exaggerated. The attached quote, however, is an excellent piece of irony on the futile search for "essence."

## 75. *Ōbaku's Stick*

When Rinzai became a Zen master, his Zen came to be known as "stick-Zen," for he never missed the opportunity to beat pupils and masters alike. This koan on his experience as a novice makes it quite clear that Rinzai's own enlightenment was the "working" of the stick. We may take this koan at face value if we keep in mind: (1) that beating on the right occasion is the master's way of enlightening the pupil, and the pupil's way of demonstrating his enlightenment to the master; and (2) that curses often mean praise.

Kyōzan, in his saying on the tiger, means that once enlightened, Rinzai is in full control of the situation. That is, in "riding the tiger's head and holding onto the tiger's tail," Kyōzan suggests that from now on Rinzai can handle both Ōbaku and Daigu.

In his answer, the pupil praises Ōbaku's "stick-Zen." The quote suggests the master's favor toward the pupil.

## 76. The Three Sentences of Master Rinzai

In the sources (*Rinzairoku* and *Kattōshū*) this koan is connected to koan 19, also entitled, "The Three Sentences of Master Rinzai" (p. 126). As explained in the note to koan 19 (p. 259), Rinzai deals with the "working" of the master. This koan may refer to the "working" of things in general. It implies that the "working" (or function) of things has many aspects, that it is subtle and to be judged in accordance with the situation.

### ANSWER

In the answer, the fan is used as a concrete symbol to demonstrate the variety of functions of one thing.

## 77. On an Isolated Peak; At the Crossroads

Rinzai's saying suggests that one should not be taken in by extremes. The fact that Yuima meditated in an isolated place and that Fudaishi was involved in worldly affairs should not be taken to mean that Yuima lost contact with the world or that Fudaishi was so involved with the world that he could not possibly be enlightened. Both the way of Yuima and that of Fudaishi are perfectly all right as long as we do not misconceive of them by forming too rigid a distinction between "detachment" and "involvement." One may be on a peak of an isolated mountain while still being involved with the world; one may be at the crossroads yet still not "seeing" what is in front of one's eyes. It does not really matter *where* one is, but *how* one is.

### ANSWER

The first answer refers to the Arhat "isolation" (or "detachment") way of religious practice with a touch of criticism, whereas the second answer refers to the Bodhisattva "involvement" state in a favorable mood. The combined answer of the second school seems to suggest the "involvement" state ("the old man, old-man-like; the old woman, old-woman-like"), but it may also be interpreted as meaning that all ways (both at the "mountain" and at the "river") are perfect as long as they fit in with the nature of the situation.

## 78. Why Can't the Tail Go Through?

This striking paradox seems to imply that "enlightenment" is not to be measured by common logic. Once enlightened, one is in danger of deceiving oneself that one is absolutely and completely "through." Yet although one may be "through" where it is difficult and painstaking to pass, it is at the easiest, most taken-for-granted place where one fails.

ANSWER

The pupil identifies the "cow" with his own (enlightened) "self." He implies that his "self" is not (in view of the "mu" aspect) to be conceived in terms of personal history (birthdate and birthplace); his "form" is the actual form of the situation as it presents itself. The novice being a male, the cow too is a "male cow." The pupil also suggests that his "working" lies in his relation with his master. Yet when asked, "Why can't the tail go through?" (why is enlightenment not perfect), he identifies the "cow" with his master, suggesting that as far as (the imperfection of) enlightenment is concerned, masters fare no better than pupils.

The answers of the second school do not differ much in meaning. It seems, however, that the pupil is getting somewhat too "cowish."

## 79. What Is Jōshū?

The Chinese cities of ancient times had gates in all four directions. Jōshū, faced with the unanswerable question concerning the essence of his "self," suggests through the gate simile that one may enter (Jōshū) from wherever one wishes. In view of "mu," it is perhaps permissible to interpret Jōshū's simile as a suggestion that Jōshū has no "self" (this is also what the answer to the koan seems to suggest). However, this does not result in saying that there is no Jōshū.

## 80.  A Shell Holding Moonlight

Chimon's metaphor on the "essence" and "working" of the "supreme wisdom" refer to "kū" or "mu" ("void" or "nothingness"—the essenceless essence of things). Moonlight is (according to this simile) nothing in itself. Yet through its reflection on the shell, it becomes an inseparable "aspect" of the shell. In the same way, "kū" cannot be conceived as a substance in itself but only through its "reflection" in things. The same simile is employed to explain the "working" (or function) of "kū."

In China and Japan, the form on the moon's face is not a man (as in some Western cultures) but a rabbit. Thus, the "working" of "kū" (its active aspect) in things is compared to the moonlit shell bearing the child of the rabbit in the moon. As far as the simile is concerned, whether the moon shines upon the shell or not, it does not change the shell in itself (provided of course we accept the assumption inherent in the simile that light is no-thing in itself). But we would overstretch the simile if we interpreted it as suggesting that the "supreme wisdom" (or "kū") is of a fictitious nature.

ANSWER

In his answer, the pupil points at himself as the "essence of the supreme wisdom" (or enlightenment) and identifies his activity with its "working."

## 81.  It Is Your Hearts That Move

The statement, "It is your hearts that move" is not to be interpreted as "philosophical idealism." Enō does not mean to suggest that the banner, the wind, and everything else is "mind-stuff." The "heart moves" because the monks indulge in futile argument. As the answer to the koan suggests, the solution to the monks' problem is simply, "a banner fluttering in the wind is a banner fluttering in the wind."

## 82.  The Immovable Cloak

The historical background of this koan centers around the division of Zen into the northern and the southern sects during the seventh century A.D. Zen chronicles written on the process that led to the split report various dramatic events which assert the superiority of Enō (638–713) over his rival and fellow novice Jinshū (606?–706), the founder of the northern sect. The purpose of this legend is apparently to assert Enō as the legitimate successor of his master, Gunin (602–674). It is less clear what its function as a koan is supposed to be. The pupil's stereotyped repetition of the central phrase only strengthens the impression that the story has no "koan effect."

## 83. *What the Old Woman Meant*

The old woman's "Go straight ahead" and her "This one too is no different from the others" sound very suggestive. The monk is taken in by the "meaning" of the old woman's words.

ANSWER

The first answer ("the strong one beneath the porch") is unclear, whereas the answer of the second school (repetition of the old woman's words) and that of the third school (imitation of Jōshū's "going") are clear in themselves but they do not aid much in understanding the situation. The last answer ("with certain masters") is not in the Japanese edition of the book, but I have added it into the text because it seems to be the best one. This answer implies that what Jōshū understood is extemely simple. It is so simple that neither the Chinese monk (of the koan) nor the Japanese masters (who composed the first three answers to the koan) understood it. Jōshū understood that there was "a wrinkled-faced old woman" who had said what she had said; that's all there was and is to it.

## 84. *The Tortoise Is a Turtle*

In "What is the lamp in the room?" the monk asks for the standard of absolute certainty (or "truth"). Kōrinon in his answer suggests there is no such thing.

ANSWER

The first answer suggests that a name does not indicate the nature of a person (or any other thing), whereas the second answer ridicules the distinctions people try to create through names. Whatever you *call* a straw mat, it is after all simply what it is. The quote on the "stains on the lapels" may have meant to suggest the uncertainty concerning the real nature of things.

## 85. Cut!

In asking the monk from the western capital, "Can you still get a sword?" Gantō means, "Is there Zen in the western capital?" (or which comes to equally mean, "are you enlightened?"). When the monk answers that he "can get a sword," he stretches the simile of the sword too far, for Zen (or "enlightenment") is nothing you can get hold of. In his "cut-show," Gantō ridicules the monk's "sword" conception of Zen. Seppō, by beating the monk, proves that he understands what Gantō found lacking in the monk.

### ANSWER
In his first answer, the pupil suggests that, unlike the monk, he is not taken in by Gantō's trap. The second answer and the answer "according to another school" suggest that Zen is not like a sword which one may "get."

## 86. When the Sail Is Hoisted

"When the sail is not yet hoisted" refers to the state of mind before "enlightenment"; "when the sail is hoisted" refers to the enlightened state of mind. The same dialogue is repeated twice but the meaning is the same. When striving for it, "enlightenment" is conceived as something supermundane beyond the boundaries of common logic; yet, being enlightened, things are simply what they are.

### ANSWER
The first answer seems to suggest a ship standing still. In such a state, the ship does not fulfill its function of sailing, for there is no movement. The second answer echoes the mood of "the donkey eating grass" and "the river flowing northward" by suggesting the natural course of things, only this time the pupil refers to his own situation.

## 87. Why Don't People In Know about Out?

Kempō's saying on the "self" is too doctrinaire. Ummon, dissatisfied with such an approach, suggests that rather than speculating on Buddhist doctrine it would be better to known more about the world as it is ("outside of the hermitage"). Kempō laughs his consent at this and praises Ummon. Ummon agrees he deserves the praise and thus in an indirect way praises Kempō for his understanding.

### ANSWER

The pupil's response to Kempō's saying ("scornful laugh") may be interpreted as, "[Being enlightened] I know better," but it is best taken as a suggestion that the saying is too doctrinaire. If we read the answer in the first meaning, the rest of the dialogue on Kempō's saying may suggest the difficult way one has to pass "before enlightenment." However, viewed as a criticism of Kempō's saying, it seems to suggest, "Beware, there is a trap in Kempō's words."

The pupil's response to Ummon's "outside of the hermitage" suggests that it is indeed necessary to know what is going on in the world, yet ("he slams the door shut") a monk should not forget that a monastery is a monastery. In his response to the "holy body" (of "truth") the pupil refuses to be taken in by metaphysics and simply refers to his physical body.

In the answers of the two other schools the pupil provides a doctrinaire interpretation to "three kinds of diseases" and "two kinds of light." Thus he seems to miss the point of Ummon's criticism.

## 88. Where Is the Old Man Going?

By "Tokusan does not know the last sentence," Gantō is laying a metaphysical trap for both Tokusan and Seppō. Actually there was nothing wrong in Tokusan's coming to the dining hall before mealtime. The old man was simply hungry.

### ANSWER

The pupil suggests that "Tokusan's returning to his room" is simply Tokusan returning to his room. In reporting the affair to Gantō, Seppō apparently did not intend to imply that the old master was lacking in "knowledge." Therefore, the pupil ("instead of Seppō") rebukes Gantō for his far-fetched criticism of Tokusan and suggests that the idea of the "last sentence" (ultimate truth) is no more than useless talk. It is not quite clear what Gantō in his whisper "revealed" to Tokusan. But it is a fair guess that he told Tokusan that his remark on the "last sentence" was no more than a trap. In the last section, the pupil ridicules Gantō's "prophecy" concerning the life term of Tokusan. Tokusan may indeed have died after three years, but people's life term is not something that can be predicted.

## 89.   Yet I Should Not Be Rash

In view of "mu," what is the use of "acting with proper dignity and ceremony"; but in view of "u," why should one not do what one is expected to do? As Setchō suggests ("He has got it!"), Tokusan understands both "mu" and "u" and is not taken in by either. When Tokusan calls out "Master!" Isan reaches for his stick to hit Tokusan if he says a word too much. Tokusan responds with "Katsu" and thus, in an instant, the two seem to be on common ground. Later Isan praises Tokusan, to which Setchō comments that there is no need to overburden the obvious with so many words ("to add frost on snow").

#### ANSWER
In the first two quotes ("bitter to the root" and "sweet clear through"), the pupil suggests Tokusan's thorough understanding of "mu" and "u." "Bitter" and "sweet" should not be taken in an evaluative sense. The last quote seems to suggest an agreement with Setchō that there is no use in saying the obvious.

## 90.   Every Day Is a Good Day

Ummon asks for the nature of the enlightened state of mind, and answers, "Every day is a good day." As the answers to the koan suggest, however, one ought to be aware of a double trap. Taken in by the distinction between "before enlightenment," "after enlightenment," and "the moment of enlightenment," one is deluded to believe that one's "enlightened" view may change things, but the world is just what it is. Taken in by "good" in opposition to "bad," one is deluded to believe that through "enlightenment" one may relieve oneself from suffering and death. "Every day is a good day" means that having attained "evenness" of mind, "every day is as good as the other."

## 91.  *Without Caring, Go Straight*

This koan deals with the theme of solitary practice as against organized monastic religion. The "goton" sound of the stick (first answer) suggests that the solution of this dilemma is in the moment of enlightenment. Like the people of olden times (before the formation of organized religion) one should not rely too much on "others" (i.e., masters) for guidance of "the way." But as suggested in the answers, through solitary practice ("dropping your bottom steadfast into the evenness of the plane of enlightenment") it is impossible to "lead the masses to salvation." Thus, with an independent spirit and without abhorring the vicissitudes of fate, be a *monk*.

## 92.  *Seven*

"The six things" refer to the six senses (the five physical senses and the mind sense). According to Buddhist doctrine the "person" (i.e., the psycho-physical organism) is formed through the functional interaction of the six senses (on the "six senses," see Part Three, koan 57, note on pp. 283–284). Ummon's statement of the "true self not holding six things" should not be interpreted as there being a "self" above and beyond the six senses. Ummon only suggests that one should not be taken in by the "six-sense doctrine."

ANSWER

By counting to seven, the pupil simply suggests that he is not taken in by "six" (nor by "seven"). "To say it in reference to the other," means to say it (the "self") from the objective point of view. As the "six" belongs to the "subject," the objective is not bound by "six." The pupil thus simply describes various things according to their conventional numerical definition as they appear in the objective world.

## 93.  I Have a Lot of Things to Do

In his fish-and-net question, Sanshō asks Seppō to explain to him the "subtle working" of the enlightened mind. But in viewing the enlightened person as "fish" and enlightenment as a "net," Sanshō splits into two what is in fact one. By asking Sanshō to bring forth the "net," Seppō ridicules the inappropriate simile. Sanshō, who does not understand the irony of Seppō's answer, is still conceited with his "clever" question, at which Seppō hints that he would appreciate it if Sanshō took his leave.

ANSWER

The answer suggests that the "working" of the enlightened mind is nothing mysterious. It consists of doing the right thing at the right moment.

## 94.  Rice in a Bowl, Water in a Bucket

The monk, in his philosophical Kegon-styled question, asks for the "mysterious essence" of the smallest particle. He is apparently deluding himself into thinking that through such "knowledge" he will understand the world. But one does not have to be an expert in molecular physics to know that things are what they are. Ummon's saying is of the same logical pattern as the answer the monk is expecting (in $x$ is $y$), yet it deals with the commonplace objects of the ordinary world.

## 95.  I Have a Headache Today

What the monk is actually asking of Baso is to say "the meaning of Zen" without words. He seems to have missed the point of Baso's answer ("I am tired today") and poses the same unanswerable question to Chizō and Ekai, who likewise reject him. Baso's remark on Chizō and Ekai implies "be it white or black, it is the same head." In this he praises the two, suggesting that they have behaved as a Zen-like Zen master is supposed to behave. If the reader is not taken in by a derogatory interpretation of "shit dropper" and "bed wetter," he will understand that the pupil's answer means exactly the same as Baso's.

## 96. *"All Over"; "Throughout"*

The many eyes and hands of Kannon Buddha symbolize Kannon's all-encompassing compassion. Ungan's question as to the "meaning" of the many eyes and hands is intended to test if Dōgo is taken in by esotericism. Through the description of a commonplace situation, Dōgo avoids the trap, implying (as the pupil's answer to Dōgo's phrase suggests) that "a hand is a hand." When Ungan declares that he understands the meaning of Dōgo's answer, Dōgo in his turn plays a practical joke on Ungan. Ungan's phrase (using the word "throughout") of course means exactly the same thing. However, once such a difference is pointed out, it is not easy to be simple enough to disregard it.

## 97. *Why Is That Thing Not You?*

This koan is hard to understand. As the last phrase suggests, its general meaning is that the functions of seeing and knowing are an integral part of the subject. The subject can thus "see" (or know) things only as they appear from the subject's point of view. As the quote attached to the answer suggests, our world is to a large extent a reflection of our moods and feelings. However, an overly Idealistic interpretation that the world is "mind-stuff" would be reading too much into the text.

## 98. *Go and Have Some Tea*

Buddhists often use the argument that the Buddha revealed his "real" doctrine only to the initiated, whereas to the laymen he preached in accordance with their understanding (in Japanese—"hōben"). Chōkei rejects this "double language" argument, also suggesting that the often-used argument of Buddha (or Zen) having "no language" (i.e., is not to be transmitted through words) is wrong. Naturally enough, Hofuku asks for the "one language" of Buddha. In his paradoxical answer that the deaf can hear, Chōkei seems to suggest something of the sort of a "no-language-language" (or "non-conceptual language"). Chōkei may be right but he says it in a too roundabout way. Hofuku in turn gives a more direct answer ("Go and have some tea") through the actual usage of the language of the common world.

It seems that the pupil, instead of repeating Chōkei's phrase, would do better if he took up Hofuku's pattern of stating the commonplace. However, the attached quotes, in describing the world of nature and man in everyday situations, echo Hofuku's way of saying it.

## 99.   *Made a Fool Of*

The quote from the Diamond Sutra interprets the karmic state of adversity as caused by past sins, yet at the same time holding within itself the factor of redemption and deliverance.

### ANSWER
As a point of doctrine, the statement of the Diamond Sutra is not rejected. However, the sutra's wording suggests an overly conscious attitude toward the karmic causality of one's present state. The pupil's answers and the attached quotes suggest an immediate response to the situation without questioning the causes or caring for the consequences of one's deeds.

## 100.   *"Wrong!"*

It is not clear whether Tenpyō includes himself among those who "do not understand the teaching of Buddha"; in any case, his statement is too categorical. If he does not include himself among those who do not understand, he is conceited with pride; if he does, he is conceited with humbleness. Saiin gives Tenpyō a thorough shakeup. Looking up when called by his name, Tenpyō is "wrong." Moving two or three steps—Tenpyō is "wrong." Tenpyō in admitting he was wrong—is "wrong" again. Thus Saiin drives Tenpyō out of Tenpyō. Setchō adds a blow of his own, saying that what Tenpyō thought about his being wrong is "wrong," whereas the pupil in his answer to the koan concludes that if Setchō thinks he is right in his "wrong," he is "wrong." This koan is a good lesson for those who think there is something they can teach others. However, we should not forget that in their imperfectness all are quite perfect the way they are.

## 101. Tread on the Head of Buddha

The meaning of Etchū's two sayings is made clear through the answer to the koan. To say that one is Buddha is perfectly all right. It would be wrong, however, to conclude that just because one is Buddha one is "pure." The right conclusion should be that one's "bowels being filled with piss and shit"—Buddha is "dirty."

## 102. The Body Emits Autumn Wind

The monk is concerned about the decline and decay of things. Ummon suggests that decay is a natural process no less than birth and growth. If one accepts spring and summer, one has to accept autumn too. The answer to the koan suggests that though it is part of human nature to long for the past times of youth and vigor, the flow of time–space takes its natural course. It is a futile daydream to imagine the time–space situation of the past in the present.

## 103. The Mind as It Is

No comment necessary.

## 104. No Mind, No Buddha

Baso's two sayings mean exactly the same thing. The enlightened "mind of the moment" may be termed "mind" because of its consciousness of events, but it is "no mind" in as far as it does not dwell on anything beyond the bare fact of the moment. (For the same theme see Part Two, koan 51, note on p. 235; and Part Three, koan 73, note on pp. 288–289.)

## 105. One

The phrases of the koan suggest the philosophical concept of "one" (according to the Kegon School), in which everything contains the whole. As against this metaphysical "one," the pupil simply responds with the "one" of everyday language. The answer also suggests to "cut out" philosophical speculation and have a cup of tea.

## 106. *Take Care!*

Kanzan's saying, if interpreted according to Buddhist doctrine, suggests that one should at any moment be aware of the karmic consequences of one's deeds. In the answers, however, this "warning" is interpreted as a trap. The pupil suggests that "deliverance" from karma is not a matter of being "pure" from the worldly defilements (being "naked") but of a total immersion into the karmic process moment by moment as it presents itself. For the same theme see Part Three, koan 90, note on pp. 297–298.

## 107. *What Will You Do after Three or Four Shouts?*

The shout ("Katsu") is good if it comes at the right moment—then it sweeps away everything and leaves nothing behind (or takes away nothing and leaves everything as it is). But if it is employed only as a means to draw attention to oneself, it does not differ from a dog's bark. Bokushū hits the monk simply to silence him. The answer to the koan and the author's interpretation of the answer as showing the "simultaneous working of the stick and the shout" seem to miss the point. This koan is better regarded as Zen self-irony. (For a real example of the "simultaneous working of the stick and the shout" see Part Three, koan 89, note on p. 297.)

## 108. *Non-Attachment*

Rinzai's lecture is of the nature of a Zen sermon preached by the master on certain fixed dates to all the novices. The answer to the koan consists of the pupil demonstrating his understanding of the sermon in more concrete terms.

## 109. *Calamity! Calamity!*

Note that the monk poses his question just as Rinzai is going to use "words" (in his lecture). In "to be under the threat of the blade," the monk suggests a situation where, driven into the corner, one is at the end of one's wit. Rinzai's "Calamity! Calamity!" and the answers to the koan imply an immediate, spontaneous response to the situation. The quotes attached to the answer echo the mood of "calamity," yet the "simpleton" who remains indifferent to the catastrophic events suggests evenness of mind.

## 110.  *Use the Air as Paper*

This koan is the same in pattern and theme as koan 109, Part Two (see note on pp. 240–241). Only the first answer ("the wily old fox") seems to be a suitable response to the master's "metaphysical trap."

## 111.  *What Is Your Feeling at This Moment?*

As the answers to the koan suggest, the hermit fails for two reasons: (1) he does not see through the trap the old woman set for him; (2) he does not have enough "warmth" in his heart to see the girl in her own situation. The koan would be more difficult to answer had the girl been attracted to the hermit, seeking his love of her own will. It must not be automatically assumed that a Zen monk must reject a woman seeking his love. Zen has altered the traditional Buddhist monastic prohibition. For example, the "Zen law" says that one may drink wine but one should not be "drunk" (i.e., taken in) by it. The same I suppose may be true for sexual relations. Nowadays in Japan, Zen priests and even Zen masters are allowed to marry.

## 112.  *Of a Different Color*

All humans are subjected to the natural course of life ("the snow covers a thousand hills"); why should the "enlightened" one be different ("why is only the one peak not white")? Sōzan admits the "difference" yet at the same time terms it "the absurdity of absurdities."

ANSWER

The answers of both schools suggest the natural course of life. In the first school the "peak" is likened to the head. When reaching the "age of white hair," every head ("enlightened" or not) turns white. In the first answer of the second school, the "peak" (head) is "not white," not because of some supernatural quality but simply because one shakes the snowflakes from the hair. The second answer suggests that when it is cold, everybody is cold. Only the popular saying suggests the uniqueness of the "one" ("one branch looks especially green"), but this too is within the natural framework of causality ("the monkey jumping"). The point of the koan is in admitting the uniqueness of the enlightened, yet at the same time equating it with all the rest.

### 113. *Beard*

According to tradition, Bodhidharma *had* a beard. The point of Wakuan's paradoxical question is the relation between "is" ("u") and "is not" ("mu"). If the pupil answers directly to the question (for example, "That is false, Bodhidharma had a beard"), he is taken in by the "u–mu" mode of reasoning. In view of "u," Bodhidharma *had* a beard; whereas in view of "mu," it is ultimately wrong to state that $x$ is $y$. Therefore, what is the use of making categorical statements? In all the answers to the koan, the pupil solves this dilemma through the naive response to "beard"— when unshaved there "is" a beard, when shaved there is "no" beard. That's all there is to it.

A more speculative approach to this koan may interpret Wakuan's saying as a suggestion that Bodhidharma is totally "purified" from the karmic process, and the pupil's answers as the rejection of the idea that through "enlightenment" one is unaffected by natural causality.

### 114. *It Is Here*

Kenpō's and Ummon's sayings suggest the rejection of the other-worldly approach to '"enlightenment." The question "where is enlightenment?" should not be answered in the first place (the pupil slapping his master), but if answered—anything is as good as another. In this "Buddha-world" there are no two things that are not related to each other ("strike the carp of the eastern sea and rain will come down"); you may draw a line in the air or throw up your fan—there is enlightenment.

### 115. *Is There? Is There?*

As a historical fact, there might have been a good reason for Jōshū to reject one master's fist and accept the other's. Jōshū's phrase on the second master's fist suggests thoroughness. However, all *we* know about it is simply that Jōshū did not stay in the first place and wanted to stay in the second. If one is taken in by the "difference" between the two fists, one is in a trap. The answer to the koan is a stereotyped repetition of the last phrase, but the quotes suggest that although there might be slight differences, things are ultimately the same; it is no use choosing too much.

## 116. *Where Do You Come From?*

Hōgen's and Enmei's criticism of Tokusan seems to suggest that his warning the pupils not to ask questions lest they be hit was in place, yet his explaining to the monk of Shinra the "working" of his stick was superfluous. Setchō disagrees with Hōgen's and Enmei's criticism of Tokusan. His comment seems to suggest that Tokusan knew what the monk was in need of and handled the situation in a perfect manner. The answers to the koan suggest a naive approach to the "working" of the stick; whether in beating or being beaten, it is no good speculating too much about the matter. If one is too conscious of one's "stick," one had better throw it away (last answer).

## 117. *One Got It, One Missed It*

Same theme as Part Three, koan 115 (note on pp. 305–306). Whatever Hōgen might have seen, *we* should not be taken in by the difference between the two monks. The answer to the koan is a simple, non-speculative response to Hōgen's saying.

## 118. *Yes*

As the first answer suggests, the attendant has done Etchū "wrong" in not responding attendantlike. This does not mean that the attendant's response was not humble enough. The attendant-monk does Etchū "wrong" not because he serves Etchū badly, but because he has not realized Etchū's Zen of "when called as an attendant, answer as an attendant." The pupil's answer in the second school seems to demonstrate the "attendantlike" reply.

119. *Three Pounds of Flax*

The theme and the pattern of this koan are the same as in koan 15, Part Three (note on p. 256).

120. *Even Up Till Now*

As the answer to the koan suggests, the "deep meaning" of Zen is simply to realize that things are just what they are. To say it in an extreme form—*Zen has no "meaning."* For the same theme, see koan 49, Part Three (note on p. 280).

Another possible, though less Zen-like interpretation of the koan, would be to regard the saying on Bibashi Buddha as a suggestion that no matter how hard or how long one practices, one never reaches a state of absolute perfection. Under such an interpretation, the answer may suggest the various phases of "the way."

121. *One Finger*

The koan can be viewed as a version of the koan on the "one hand." The answers to the koan appear in the same working as in the discourse on the "one hand" koan.

122. *It Is Important That the World Be in Peace*

The koan as a whole stresses the worldly as against the transcendental. In his saying on the legend of Buddha's birth, Ummon suggests the principle of "self-realization" (in Japanese, "jiriki") as against "divine-salvation" ("tariki"). Rōyakaku's comment adds to Ummon's view the Bodhisattva ideal of self-sacrifice. As the second answer and the attached quote suggest, "the world in peace" is a state in which all things take their natural course.

123. *Mother and Father*

The legend on Prince Nata implies the idea of self-sacrifice and filial piety. The first answer, through the imitation of the pilgrim, seems to suggest selflessness. The second answer ("with certain masters"), which is not in the Japanese edition, suggests the simple and natural way of fulfilling one's filial duties.

### 124. *The Eastern Mountain Walks on Water*

If the question concerning "the place of origin of Buddha" refers to the historical Buddha, it is irrelevant and unimportant. If the monk refers to Buddhahood, his question is a metaphysical trap. Through his nonsensical answer, Ummon ridicules the monk and rejects the question in both senses.

The first reply answers the monk's question in suggesting the the living Buddha right here, now. In the second, the pupil seems to identify himself with the "mountain walking on water," perhaps implying that the origin of Buddha is in oneself.

### 125. *Youngsters Like You Never Know of That*

This koan should be taken at face value. For a change, the Zen master is simply a teacher in the good sense of the term. If one takes this koan lightly, one has perhaps become too "enlightened."

### 126. *The Guy Understands This Time*

A possible interpretation of this koan could be the suggestion that the same words carry a different weight depending on whether they are said before "enlightenment" or after "enlightenment." It would be better, however, to regard the suggestion that there is a difference between Kassan's two sayings as a trap. Read thus, the koan is similar in pattern and meaning to koan 115, Part Three (note on pp. 305–306) and to koan 117, Part Three (note on p. 306). The answers to the koan suggest that the "formless" and the "blemish-free" is the world *as it is*.

### 127. *How Can We Go Through Without Interfering?*

The monk asks an important and penetrating question to which Fuketsu answers directly in a serious and delicate way. It would thus be best to concentrate on the koan itself and disregard the somewhat clumsy "answers" to it.

## 128. Peach Blossoms

Reiun's moment of enlightenment recalls Fuketsu's saying in the previous koan (127). Isan, Reiun's master, affirms Reiun's enlightenment, whereas the comments of Gensha, Ummon, and Daisen suggest criticism. Their criticism seems to refer to the mood of self-confidence in Reiun's poem and implies a warning not to be too preoccupied with any specific enlightenment experience.

## 129. I Have Nothing to Hide from You

Maidō, through the quote from Confucius, suggests that in "enlightenment" there is nothing mysterious; it is the bare moment as it is—don't we smell the fragrance of flowers right here, now? Through his question on "after death," Maidō sweeps away metaphysical delusions and awakens Sankoku's mind to the actual moment of the present. The pupil in his answer to the koan, disregards the "metaphysical" meeting (after death) and simply responds to "meeting."

## 130. Bamboo Shoots Sprout Sideways under a Rock

Kidō's "bamboo shoots will sprout sideways under a rock and flowers will grow down on an overhanging cliff" suggests the natural harmony between Nansen and the monk. Unrestricted, absolutely free, Nansen and the monk are like-minded. Kidō's poem implies that in the hustle and bustle of everyday life, people are acting in perfect concert with each other. The quote-answers to the koan refer to Nansen's longing after the monk.

## 131. Not Enter Nirvana, Not Fall into Hell

Whereas the old school (Hinayana) created a dichotomy between the "unconditioned" state of nirvana and the "conditioned" events of the samsaric world, Mahayana thought, and especially the Zen school, assumes the "unity of samsara and nirvana." According to the latter view, once the barrier of conceptual thought has been removed, the unity of samsara and nirvana is realized; there is no longer any distinction between impure and mundane, and the pure and holy. One does not "leave" the samsaric world for it has lost its samsaric nature. The answers of both schools suggest elimination of all such distinctions. Void of differentiations of category and value, the world is just what it is. Whether you call it "heaven" or "hell," it is the same Buddha-world with its thieves, roosters, farmers, dogs, artisans, nightingales, merchants, dragonflies, winters and springs, everything in its perfect condition.

## 132. *High Rank, Low Rank*

The theme of this koan is similar to that of koan 131 (see previous note). Monju's inability to arouse the woman from her contemplation may be interpreted as irony towards the "transcendental." As the answers to the koan suggest, Monju dwells in the "higher spheres" above and beyond the "trivialities" of the natural realm of cause and effect. Although the "high-ranked" Monju and the "low-ranked" Mōmyō are "the same" in being "enlightened," it is after all Mōmyō and not Monju whose enlightenment is of real "working."

## 133. *The Oak Tree in the Front Garden*

The "oak tree in the front garden" may have been the object Jōshū happened to see when asked about the "meaning of Zen." A similar pattern of answer we find in Part Three, koan 15 (note on p. 256) and koan 119 (note on p. 307). The monk suggests that Jōshū is taken in by his object of sight; Jōshū denies this and his disciple echoes Jōshū's denial, saying that Jōshū "had never said anything about an oak tree." If Jōshū insisted on "oak tree" beyond the "oak tree situation," the monk would be right in accusing him of being taken in by "u"; yet Jōshū's answer was simply *that* moment's situation. At another time, in another place, it might be a "pen" (right now in my hand), "the rice bowl," or any other "here-now."

The answers to the koan are in part a simple response to "oak tree"; however, the first three quotes (first school) and the answer, as against the "root [or origin] of the oak tree," echo "mu."

## 134. *That Is Still Not Enough*

The same theme as koan 34, Part Three (see note on pp. 272–273), and koan 49, Part Three (see note on p. 280). The answer to the koan is best taken as ironical.

## 135. *Give, Grab*

As implied in the last answer to the koan, Basho's saying refers to "thoroughness." It may, however, also suggest the attitude of total acceptance of the state of affairs as it is.

## 136. *The Three Sentences of Master Bussho*

The answers to the koan point to the trap in each of Bussho's sentences. The first sentence suggests the distinction between "heaven" and "hell." The answer rejects the notion that in the "Buddha-world" there is an "upward way" and a "downward way." There is only the straight one. If one does what one is supposed to do, one is right on "the way." The comments on Niso and Gensha in the second sentence are unclear (that might also be the reason why they are not referred to in the answer to the koan). The denial of a historical fact ("Daruma did not come to China") sounds "clever" (viewed "mu") but one should "take care" not to be taken in by such paradoxes; after all, Daruma *did* go to China. The third sentence on the "void" may tempt one to conceive of "enlightenment" as something transcendental. As against this metaphysical trap the pupil suggests the Zen conception of "enlightenment" as being "right now, right here."

## 137. *Which One Is Real?*

This koan contains the "body-spirit metaphysical trap." Hōen is asking which is the "real" aspect of human existence. Against this search for the "real," the answer to the koan points to the actual states as they reveal themselves in human life. The "real" is not to be found in any abstract concept ("body" or "spirit") but in the bare events of existence. This naked reality may be termed both "samsara" and "nirvana" (or "body" and "spirit"), or neither "samsara" nor "nirvana"—names do not change things.

## 138. *Only There Is a Word that Is Not Very Proper*

The moment-situation of Eimei's enlightenment echoes Kyō-gen's enlightenment upon hearing a piece of brick hit the bamboo (Part Three, koan 64, note on pp. 286–287), and Reiun's enlighten-ment upon seeing the peach blossoms (Part Three, koan 128, note on p. 309). Kidō's critical comment seems to follow the same pat-tern as the criticism on Reiun's enlightenment. In Eimei's experi-ence, it is not so much "a *word* that is not proper" but Eimei himself. Yet why should one be perfectly proper?

In his answer to the koan, the pupil points at his master as "not proper" (or "not perfect"). There is nothing wrong with the master's nose. The Japanese, when indicating themselves or others, always point with the finger at the nose. The answer of pointing at the master as "imperfect" seems better than the unnecessary humbleness of pointing at oneself.

## 139. *Functions Like Theft*

As the answers to the koan suggest, Kanzan's saying should be interpreted as a praise of the thoroughness and nimble effectiveness of Jōshū's "oak tree" answer (see Part Three, koan 133, note on p. 310).

## 140. *The Four Shouts of Master Rinzai*

For "Katsu," see note to koan 11, pp. 252–253. The first three "Katsus" suggest the various moods of the "shout situation," whereas the last—"a shout that does not function as a shout"—is the most natural and spontaneous of all. The pupil's first answer implies that he is not taken in by the distinction between the vari-ous "Katsus," whereas the second answer suggests the thoroughness of the "no-shout-shout."

## 141. *First, Second, Third*

This koan is a trap intended to test if the pupil is taken in by the distinctions in degrees of "truth" (or "enlightenment"). The answer suggests that there is no such distinction as "first truth" and "second truth"; a beautiful woman may *appear* somewhat different in this or that situation but ultimately she is just what she is. In the same way, "truth" (or "enlightenment") may have various functions but it does not have two faces.

## 142. Host and Guest

Mayoku asks Rinzai for the "absolute truth" ("the eye proper"), at which Rinzai throws the same question back at Mayoku and urges him to answer quickly. Mayoku asserts himself through action and Rinzai swiftly responds through action. Through this exchange, the problem of "truth" (or "essence") may not have been solved but the relation (or "working") of the two as "host" (subject) and "guest" (object) is made clear. On "host–guest" and the meaning of the koan's answer, see Part Three, koan 11 (note on pp. 252–253) and koan 19 (note on p. 259).

## 143. The Dragon Bitten by a Snake

Butsugen's saying symbolically implies that the "perfect dragon" (i.e., enlightened monk) should not by its nature be affected by worldly causes ("the snake's bite"). Ungo does not fall into the trap and suggests that being enlightened does not exclude one from the order of nature. It is a mistaken concept of "enlightenment" to conceive of it as deliverance from suffering and pain.

## 144. Zen

No comment needed, not even this.

# Sources to the Koans of Part Three

Note that the titles of the koans in this book are those of the translator. The abbreviations of the sources are as follows:

| | | | |
|---|---|---|---|
| *Kattōshū* | = KT | *Hekiganroku* | = HG |
| *Mumonkan* | = MK | *Rinzairoku* | = RR |

| | | |
|---|---|---|
| 1. KT, MK (5) | 33. HG (8) | 63. HG (88) |
| 2. KT | 34. KT | 64. KT |
| 3. KT, MK (16) | 35. KT | 65. MK (8) |
| 4. HG (5) | 36. KT | 66. MK (36), KT |
| 5. KT | 37. KT | 67. HG (78) |
| 6. HG (42) | 38. KT | 68. HG (43) |
| 7. ——— | 39. KT | 69. HG (69) |
| 8. HG (46) | 40. KT | 70. KT |
| 9. KT, MK (47) | 41. MK (40) | 71. KT, MK (45) |
| 10. KT | 42. HG (13) | 72. KT |
| 11. RR, KT | 43. HG (100) | 73. KT |
| 12. RR, KT | 44. KT | 74. HG (91) |
| 13. HG (39) | 45. HG (14) | 75. KT, RR |
| 14. HG (29) | 46. HG (15) | 76. KT, RR |
| 15. HG (45) | 47. HG (16) | 77. KT, RR |
| 16. HG (1) | 48. HG (18) | 78. KT, MK (38) |
| 17. HG (2) | 49. HG (20) | 79. HG (9) |
| 18. RR, KT | 50. HG (23) | 80. HG (90) |
| 19. RR, KT | 51. HG (35) | 81. KT, MK (29) |
| 20. HG (21) | 52. HG (37) | 82. KT, MK (23) |
| 21. HG (44) | 53. HG (61) | 83. MK (31) |
| 22. HG (11) | 54. HG (63), | 84. KT |
| 23. KT |     MK (14) | 85. HG (66) |
| 24. KT | 55. HG (64), | 86. KT |
| 25. HG (38) |     MK (14) | 87. KT |
| 26. HG (40) | 56. HG (74) | 88. KT, MK (13) |
| 27. KT, MK (2) | 57. HG (80) | 89. HG (4) |
| 28. KT | 58. HG (81) | 90. HG (6) |
| 29. KT | 59. HG (82) | 91. HG (25) |
| 30. KT, MK (42) | 60. HG (83) | 92. HG (47) |
| 31. KT | 61. HG (84) | 93. HG (49) |
| 32. HG (3) | 62. HG (87) | 94. HG (50) |

| | | | | | |
|---|---|---|---|---|---|
| 95. | HG (73) | 113. | KT, MK (4) | 129. | KT |
| 96. | HG (89) | 114. | MK (48) | 130. | KT |
| 97. | HG (94) | 115. | KT, MK (11) | 131. | KT |
| 98. | HG (95) | 116. | KT | 132. | MK (42) |
| 99. | HG (97) | 117. | MK (26) | 133. | KT, MK (37) |
| 100. | HG (98) | 118. | MK (17) | 134. | KT |
| 101. | HG (99) | 119. | HG (12), | 135. | KT, MK (44) |
| 102. | HG (27) | | MK (18) | 136. | KT |
| 103. | MK (30), KT | 120. | KT | 137. | KT, MK (35) |
| 104. | MK (33) | 121. | HG (19), | 138. | KT |
| 105. | RR | | MK (3) | 139. | KT |
| 106. | KT | 122. | KT | 140. | KT, RR |
| 107. | HG (10) | 123. | KT | 141. | KT, RR |
| 108. | RR | 124. | KT | 142. | RR |
| 109. | RR | 125. | KT | 143. | KT |
| 110. | KT | 126. | KT | 144. | KT |
| 111. | KT | 127. | MK (24) | | |
| 112. | KT | 128. | KT | | |

# BIBLIOGRAPHY

# BY BEN-AMI SCHARFSTEIN

A full bibliography on Zen Buddhism would be impracticably large. I have therefore concentrated on the scholarly books that have so extended our knowledge of Zen in recent years. Except for the translations of Nagarjuna and the accounts of the influence of Zen on Japanese culture, the books cited in the bibliography have all been used in the preparation of my introduction (see pp. 5–37). I have made a particular point of including books that I have quoted or paraphrased extensively. Not all the books listed here are of the highest scholarly standards, but I think they all make a genuine addition to our knowledge of Zen. I should particularly like to mention Holmes Welch's *The Practice of Chinese Buddhism*, which gives a full and honest report on the life of Zen monks in China, and from which I have drawn long quotations. I have listed a number of German and French books which were helpful to me, as well as the articles of which I have made direct use.

There is no ideal way to provide background knowledge, but I have tried to suggest a reasonable minimum. The bibliography also includes the books I have drawn on for the sake of the comparisons with Zen. Page numbers have been added only in the few cases in which my information or my quotations seem to me both important for my text and difficult to locate without exact references. The books are arranged by categories and, under each of these, by dates of publication. The category called Comparisons is an exception in that the books are arranged in the alphabetical order of their authors' names.

## 1. Mysticism

Scharfstein, B.-A. *Mystical Experience*. Indianapolis/New York: Bobbs-Merrill; and London: Blackwell, 1973.

Staal, F. *Exploring Mysticism*. Harmondsworth: Penguin Books, 1975.

## 2. History of Buddhism

Lamotte, E. *Histoire du Bouddhisme Indien*. Louvain: Publications Universitaires/Insitut Orientaliste, 1958, pp. 685 86 (on the origin of the debate between exponents of gradual and sudden enlightenment).

Conze, E. *Buddhist Thought in India*. London: Allen & Unwin, 1962.

Robinson, R. H. *The Buddhist Religion: A Historical Introduction*. Belmont, California: Dickenson Publishing Co., 1970.

## 3. Sutras (Scriptures)

Suzuki, D. T. *The Lankavatara Sutra*. London: Routledge, 1932.

Conze, E. *Buddhist Wisdom Books*. London: Allen & Unwin, 1958.

Hakeda, Y. S. *The Awakening of Faith, Attributed to Aśvaghosha*. New York: Columbia University Press, 1967.

Yampolsky, P. B. *The Platform Sutra of the Sixth Patriarch*. New York: Columbia University Press, 1967.

Conze, E. *The Large Sutra on Perfect Wisdom*. Berkeley: University of California Press, 1975. The first part was published by Luzac, in 1961, under the same title.

## 4. Taoism

### a. History

Fung Yu-lan. *A History of Chinese Philosophy*. Princeton: Princeton University Press, Vol. 1, 1952; Vol. 2, 1953.

———. *A Short History of Chinese Philosophy*. New York: Macmillan, 1964, esp. chaps. 19, 20.

b. Texts

Lau, D. C. *Lao Tzu, Tao Te Ching*. Harmondsworth: Penguin Books, 1963.

Chan, Wing-tsit. *A Source Book in Chinese Philosophy*. Princeton: Princeton University Press, 1963, esp. p. 186.

Watson, B. *The Complete Works of Chuang-tzu*. New York/London: Columbia University Press, 1968, esp. pp. 35, 39.

Graham, A. C. "Chuang-tzu's Essay on Seeing Things as Equal," in *History of Religions*, Vol. 9, Nos. 2–3, November and February 1969–70. A careful discussion and translation of the second chapter of Chuang-tzu, from which all but one of my Chuang-tzu quotations come. A single quotation from this chapter is taken from Chan's *Source Book*, and another, from the first chapter, from Watson's translation.

## 5. *Madhyamika Philosophy* (of Emptiness)

a. History and Exposition

Murti, T. R. V. *The Central Philosophy of Buddhism*. London: Allen & Unwin, 1955.

Chang, G. C. C. *The Buddhist Teaching of Totality*. University Park, Pa.: Pennsylvania State University Press, 1971.

b. Translations

Stcherbatsky, T. *The Conception of Buddhist Nirvana*. Reprint. The Hague: Mouton, 1965.

Ramanan, K. Venkata. *Nagarjuna's Philosophy as Presented in the Maha-Prajnaparamita-S'astra*. Rutland, Vt. Tokyo: Tuttle Press, for the Harvard-Yenching Institute. Paraphrase with explanation.

Streng, F. *Emptiness: A Study in Religious Meaning*. Nashville/New York: Abingdon Press, 1967.

Inada, K. K. *Nagarjuna: A Translation of his Mulamadhyamikakarika*. Tokyo: The Hokuseido Press, 1970.

## 6. *Transfer of Madhyamika to China*

Robinson, R. H. *Early Madhyamika in India and China*. Madison, Wis.: University of Wisconsin Press, 1967.

7. *Chinese Buddhism*

a. History

Wright, A. F. *Buddhism in Chinese History*. Stanford: Stanford University Press, 1959.

Ch'en, K. S. *Buddhism in China*. Princeton: Princeton University Press, 1964.

de Bary, W. T. "Individualism and Humanitarianism in Late Ming Thought." In *Self and Society in Ming Thought*, edited by W. T. de Bary. New York: Columbia University Press, 1970.

Hurvitz, L. "Chu-hung's One Mind of Pure Land and Ch'an Buddhism." In *Self and Society*.

Okada, T. "Wang Chi and the Rise of Existentialism." In *Self and Society*.

Ch'en, K. S. *The Chinese Transformation of Buddhism*. Princeton: Princeton University Press, 1973.

Chung-yuan Chang, "'The Essential Source of Identity' in Wang Lung-ch'i's Philosophy." *Philosophy East and West* 23 (January/April, 1973).

Okada, T. "The Chu Hsi and Wang Yang-ming Schools at the End of the Ming and Tokugawa Periods," in *Philosophy East and West* 23 (January/April, 1973).

b. Translations

de Bary, W. T. *Sources of Chinese Tradition*. New York: Columbia University Press, 1960.

8. *History of Japanese Religion*

Anesaki, M. *History of Japanese Religion*. London: Kegan Paul, 1930.

9. *History of Zen*

Dumoulin, H. *A History of Zen Buddhism*. London: Faber & Faber, 1963.

10. *History and Nature of Koan Meditation*

Suzuki, D. T. *Essays in Zen Buddhism. Second Series*. London: Rider & Co., 1953.

Miura, I. and Sasaki, R. F. *Zen Dust: The History of the Koan and Koan Study in Rinzai (Lin-chi) Zen* (parts 1, 2, 3 originally published under the title *The Zen Koan*). New York: Harcourt, Brace & World, 1966.

## 11. *Translations of Zen Classics*

de Bary, W. T., ed. *Sources of Japanese Tradition*. New York: Columbia University Press, 1958.

Blofield, J. *The Zen Teaching of Huang Po*. New York: Grove Press, 1959.

Gundert, W. *Bi-yän-lu: Meister Yüan-wu's Niederschrift von der Smaragdenen Felswand*. Munich: Hanser, 1960.

Luk, C. *Ch'an and Zen Teaching*. Series 2. London: Rider, 1961.

Blofield, J. *The Zen Teaching of Hui Hai*. London: Rider. 1962.

Blyth, R. H. *Mumonkan*. Zen and Zen Classics, Vol. 4. Tokyo: Hokuseido Press, 1966.

Chang, Chung-yuan. *Original Teachings of Ch'an Buddhism, Selected from The Transmission of the Lamp*. New York: Pantheon Books, 1969.

Sasaki, R. F., Iriya, Y., and Fraser, D. S. *The Recorded Sayings of Layman P'ang*. New York/Tokyo: Weatherhill, 1971.

Yampolsky, P. B. *The Zen Master Hakuin: Selected Writings*. New York: Columbia University Press, 1971.

Demiéville, P. *Entretiens de Lin-tsi*. Paris: Fayard, 1972.

Masunaga, R. *A Primer of Soto Zen: A Translation of Dogen's Shobogenzo Zuimonki*. London: Routledge & Kegan Paul, 1972.

## 12. *Life of Zen Monks*

a. In China

Welch, H. *The Practice of Chinese Buddhism, 1900–1950*. Cambridge, Mass.: Harvard University Press, 1967, esp. pp. 55, 62–71, 80–88.

b. In Japan

Kuzunishi, S. and Sato, K. *Zen Life*. New York/Tokyo/Kyoto: Weatherhill/Tankosha, 1972.

Shibata, M. *Dans les monastères Zen au Japon*. Paris: Hachette, 1972.

## 13. *Influence of Zen on Japanese Culture*

### a. General

de Bary, W. T., ed. *Sources of Japanese Tradition.* New York: Columbia University Press, 1958.

Suzuki, D. T. *Zen and Japanese Culture.* Princeton: Princeton University Press, 1959. See chapters on Zen and Confucianism, Samurai, Swordsmanship, Haiku, and the Art of Tea.

### b. The Tea Cult

Hayashiya, T., Nakamura, M., and Hayashiya, S. *Japanese Arts and Tea Ceremony.* New York/Tokyo: Weatherhill/Heibonsha, 1974.

### c. Gardens

Hayakawa, M. *The Garden Art of Japan.* New York/Tokyo: Weatherhill/Heibonsha, 1973.

### d. Painting

Fontein, J. and Hickman, M. L. *Zen Painting and Calligraphy.* Boston: Museum of Fine Arts, 1970.

Awakawa, Y. *Zen Painting.* Tokyo: Kodansha, 1970.

Suzuki, D. T. *Sengai the Zen Master.* London: Faber & Faber, 1971.

Tanaka, I. *Japanese Ink Painting: Shubun to Sesshu.* Rev. ed. New York/Tokyo: Weatherhill/Heibonsha, 1974.

Matsushita, T. *Ink Painting.* New York/Tokyo: Weatherhill/Shibundo, 1974.

## 14. *Comparisons*

Alexandre, P. "Riddles." In *Dictionary of Black African Civilization,* edited by G. Balandier and J. Maquet. New York: Leon Amiel, 1974.

Bambrough, R. "How to Read Wittgenstein," in *Understanding Wittgenstein,* Royal Institute of Philosophy Lectures, Vol. 7, 1972–1973. London: Macmillan, 1974, esp. pp. 121–25.

Bascom, W. "African Dilemma Tales: An Introduction." In *African Folklore,* edited by R. A. Dorson. New York: Doubleday/Anchor, 1972, p. 150.

Boswell, James. *Life of Johnson*. London: Oxford University Press, 1953, p. 333.

Bowler, B. *The Word as Image*. London: Studio Vista, 1970.

Brouwer, L. E. J. *Collected Works*. Vol. 1: Philosophy and Foundations of Mathematics, edited by A. Heyting. Amsterdam/Oxford: North-Holland Publishing Co., 1975, p. 108.

Feldman, S. *African Myths and Tales*. New York: Dell, 1963, pp. 201–202.

Freud, Sigmund, "Analysis Terminable and Interminable." In *The Complete Psychological Works of Sigmund Freud*, ed. J. Strachey, Vol. 23 (London: Hogarth Press, 1955).

Moore, G. E. *Philosophical Papers*. London: Allen & Unwin, 1959, pp. 145–46.

Watts, H., ed. *Three Painter-Poets: Arp, Schwitters, Klee, Selected Poems*. Harmondsworth: Penguin Books, 1974.

Wisdom, J. *Philosophy and Psycho-Analysis*. Oxford: Blackwell, 1953, p. 37.

15. *Zen Logic*

Cheng, Chung-ying, "On Zen (Ch'an) Language and Zen Paradoxes." In *Journal of Chinese Philosophy* 1 (1973): 77–102.